Robert Edward Myhill Peach

Historic Houses in Bath

Vol. 2

Robert Edward Myhill Peach

Historic Houses in Bath
Vol. 2

ISBN/EAN: 9783337152345

Printed in Europe, USA, Canada, Australia, Japan

Cover: Foto ©Andreas Hilbeck / pixelio.de

More available books at **www.hansebooks.com**

PERSPECTIVE VIEW OF THE OLD MANOR HOUSE, CLAVERTON.

HISTORIC HOUSES IN BATH

And their Associations.

DEDICATED, WITH GREAT RESPECT, BY PERMISSION,

TO

HIS GRACE THE DUKE OF BUCKINGHAM AND CHANDOS,

G.C.S.I., C.I.E., &c.

BY

R. E. PEACH.

I I .

LONDON: SIMPKIN, MARSHALL, & Co., STATIONERS' HALL COURT.
BATH: R. E. PEACH, 8, BRIDGE STREET.

1884.

DEDICATION.

To his Grace the Duke of Buckingham and Chandos, G.C.S.I., C.I.E., &c.

Sir,—

I have the honour to dedicate this, the Second Series of " HISTORIC HOUSES IN BATH AND THEIR ASSOCIATIONS," to your Grace. It seems to me an appropriate recognition of those services which your Grace's Ancestor rendered to Bath. The Duke of Chandos was amongst the first to encourage the enterprise of Wood, to whose genius modern Bath owes its grandeur, and not a little of its material prosperity. And I may here remind your Grace that in the year 1728, your Ancestor employed the same Mr. Wood to re-build the Hospital of St. John upon the site of the old one, erected in Queen Elizabeth's reign, and that that charity, which was, shortly before that time, by the judgment of Sir John Trevor, revived, and placed upon a satisfactory footing, is at the present day, one of the best administered institutions in this city. Much is due to the Duke of Chandos also for his generous co-operation with the same eminent architect and citizen, Wood, in rendering the river Avon navigable between this city and the neighbouring city of Bristol.

If I might offer another reason for this Dedication, it is the profound respect I feel for the memory of another, but nearer relation of your Grace—the late Lady Anna Gore-Langton. I might plead simply the personal kindness, which for many years I received at her hands, but I would put it on higher grounds,—the fact indeed that in her was renewed the desire of her distinguished Ancestor, to promote on all occasions the true interests of the city to which she was so much attached.

I have the honour to be,

Sir,

Your Grace's obedient Servant,

R. E. PEACH.

PREFACE.

"THE ETERNAL LANDSCAPE OF THE PAST."

WHEN the author of "HISTORIC HOUSES AND THEIR ASSOCIATIONS," *undertook the task, he thought it might have been comprehended in one volume. On proceeding with the work, it soon became obvious that this could not be accomplished. The materials grew under his hands, and he was tempted to treat the subjects with rather more fulness than he at first contemplated.*

This being so, and the subjects remaining to be dealt with being not only very numerous, but very interesting and important, the author felt that he had no option in the matter. Instead of publishing the Second Series in parts, as he did the former series, the author deemed it more satisfactory to produce the volume in a complete form at once. The second Series, though it terminates his work for the present, leaves much undone, and if at some future time a further Publication should seem to have a chance of success, the author will be glad to renew his labours; but for the present he must "rest and be thankful."

The historical pictures sought to be presented in these Volumes, even for what they ostensibly profess to be, are, the author is painfully aware, far from perfect; they are, from the nature of the case, unavoidably fragmentary, but he trusts that the reader may, to some extent, realize the characteristics of those personal associations and events in the traditions of Bath, which may be searched for in vain, in the ordinary historical records and annals.

The author has incurred—too justly incurred—the imputation of having made numerous errors in the former series. If it will afford any gratification to that class of critics who indulge in general charges of inaccuracy, without specifying its nature and extent, the author, by anticipation, is willing to admit that in the present series they may VIEW HIM WITH A CRITIC'S EYE, *but he prefers the criticism by which he and the public can profit—the helpful criticism, based upon knowledge, not ignorance.*

To those friends who have rendered him their valuable aid in the acquisition of facts—facts so very difficult sometimes to get at—he offers his sincere thanks. To Mr. J. N. Willan, Mr. Russell, the Rev. F. J. Poynton, Mrs. Henley Jervis, Mr. B. H. Watts, and Mr. Willcox, he is under the strongest obligations. On all occasions they have rendered him good service, "service sweat¹ for duty, not for meed." He wishes also to acknowledge the courteous assistance of Mr. C. T. Bleeck, the able editor of the "Bath Chronicle."

¹ *sweet.*

HISTORIC HOUSES IN BATH
And their Associations.

BATHWICK, continued.—The author is permitted to continue the "Remembrances" of Lady Jervis, which, so far as they relate to Bath, are brought to a conclusion.

"**M. de Luppé** told me (1856) that he was at the battle of Leipsic, serving in that campaign under Napoleon I., whom he described as always riding '*ventre à terre*' the swiftest horses. From his plain attire he was often taken for the servant, and his generals for the Emperor. His 'better star,' Josephine, '*belle sevère, avec les traits romains*,' was kind and excellent. Joseph, the ex-King, had nearly become my tenant at Rochetts, after I had quitted, but I forget why the negotiation failed. In the dining-room he must have beheld a fine bust of his imperial brother, which had been presented to Earl St. Vincent by Captain Tower.

When the war in Spain first broke out, a M. de la Cocardière, who was a prisoner on his parole at Bath, predicted ' *Ce sera la perte de Bonaparte.*' This M. de la Cocardière being a most elegant dancer was a great favourite with the young ladies, and *Cotillons* used to be danced at the Upper Assembly Rooms on Thursday evenings, previous to the introduction of Quadrilles. Two *Cotillons* were danced and then succeeded Country Dances, the whole ceasing at 11 o'clock. This reminds me of the **DUKE OF CLARENCE,**[1] afterwards William IV., whom I saw there one evening, not very long after the death of the Princess Charlotte, the Queen being then drinking the Bath Waters. Her Majesty

---

[1] The house in which the Duke resided, 103, Sydney Place, has been already referred to in "Royal Visits." It was the former residence of Sir Gerard Noel, Bart. Sir Gerard's mother was the last representative of the Noels, Earls of Gainsborough ; she married Gerard-Anne Edwards, Esq., of Welham Grove, co. Essex, and Tixover, Rutland, and her only son, Col. Edwards, having assumed the family name of Noel, succeeded to his father-in-law's (Lord Barham) baronetcy. Sir Gerard married Diana, only daughter of Lord Barham, who was First Lord of the Admiralty in 1805, when Nelson won the Battle of Trafalgar. This lady inherited not only the estates of her father, but also the Barony, which on her death, in 1823, devolved upon Sir Gerard's eldest son, upon whom ultimately also was conferred the ancient honours of his family—the Earldom of Gainsborough. (See also Claverton Lodge.)

occupied a large house in **Sydney Place.** She daily passed in a sedan-chair to the Pump Room, and graciously as well as gracefully acknowledged the obeisances of those who assembled to behold her. She made various visits to old and faithful adherents, one of whom was a lady of very small fortune who lived on Bathwick Hill.[1] The royal visit being unexpected, she had no refreshment in the house but tea, and this was stored away in a closet, to reach which it would be necessary to pass Her Majesty. In her dilemma the Lady-in-Waiting was consulted, who named it to the Queen ; she kindly and considerately received the apology, and ere long bestowed an acceptable and well-selected token of regard on her hostess. Her Majesty did not receive in equally good part the offering of some rich dishes from **Mr. Parish,**[2] the Hamburgh merchant, which had been prepared by his German cook. Among her excursions the Queen called on Lady Isabella King, at Bailbrook House, where she had established a community of ladies of slender means, of whom she was the head. The widow of Bishop Harper, *née* Heathcote, was presented to Her Majesty, who was so much pleased with her manners as to appoint her as governess to the Misses Fitz-Clarence,[3] a post which she long held, both beloved and respected. On my observing to Mr. Livingstone that the accommodation was insufficient in Sydney Place for the royal attendants, he replied that from experience he had remarked that no persons were worse lodged than those who belonged to a Court ; this was in 1817. Mr. Livingstone had carried a musket at the Battle of Culloden, having ever been faithfully devoted to the Stuarts. He was fully appreciated by George III., who consulted him much about the Duke of Cambridge, and I rather think employed him on some private mission concerning H.R.H. He travelled a good deal, and was a great favourite in the foreign courts. He told me that William, Duke of Cumberland, had been very desirous to know Home, the author of ' Douglas,' of uncouth manners ; Mr. Livingstone introduced him to the Prince, and in his conversation he talked of 'the *stoup* of a bottle.' One day Mr. Livingstone received from a quarter unknown a print of Charles Edward, and under it was written, ' We have marched many a mile since we two have borne arms together.'

[1] The name cannot be ascertained.

[2] An eccentric old gentleman who lived at **40, PULTENEY STREET.** His gastronomic feats were wonderful, and his digestive organs superlatively fine. When he was not eating he was smoking. In appearance he was singularly strange. His favourite resort was the Sydney Gardens. In the warm weather he usually appeared with a long pipe, in his shirt sleeves, sitting in one of the alcoves, or wandering about, in a slouched, broad-brimmed, straw hat. Nevertheless, he was kind, generous, and on occasion showed much public spirit.

[3] A little more than three years before, namely, on January 17, 1814, the mother of these ladies, Mrs. Jordan, played *Lady Teazle* at the Bath Theatre, with immense applause.

To return to Queen Charlotte ; she was unpopular, and the real worth of her character was little understood. She was an affectionate wife and mother, and she suffered intensely before the fatal malady of the King, her husband, had not openly declared itself. She had been brought up in the strictest etiquette of a German court, and the commencement of her married life was extremely dull, till its routine was happily varied by the birth of the Prince of Wales. On him she doted, and to the blindness of maternal love may be ascribed the enmity to his unfortunate wife, and which might also have over-shadowed her feelings towards the Princess Charlotte, though I must add that · she was greatly affected by her untimely death. While incurring the charge of parsimony, so great was the extent of Her Majesty's acts of charity and benevolence, that her Privy Purse, Col. Disbrowe, declared that the quarterly payments of her allowance were generally anticipated. The presents which she made to her ladies were handsome and well selected. She had been highly educated, and read, I believe, a good deal.

In the spring of 1820 I went to visit some old friends who had taken for a few weeks Woolbrook House, at Sidmouth,[1] where the **Duke of Kent** had breathed his last in the preceding January. We were, of course, very desirous to obtain every particular relative to that afflicting event. H.R.H. had walked in snow and rain, and returned to the house with his boots completely saturated. Instead of immediately changing them, he remained playing with his infant daughter, her present Gracious Majesty. This imprudence was attended with · cold and fever, which, alas ! soon terminated fatally.

General Floyd had a pretty cottage near Sidmouth, and at the time I was staying at Woolbrook ; the late Sir Robert Peel was then paying his addresses to his beautiful daughter. I know not if it was she of whom as an infant I heard that the mother was pretty, not over wise, and much younger than her husband. One morning, in India, when the General was exercising some troops, she was playing with the baby, when she suddenly threw it into the General's arms, and ran off. Before he could dispose of his burden, the regiment defiled past him !

Once (I think 1813) when H.R.H. the Duke of Clarence was seeking a bride among the .large fortunes of England, we found on reaching Rochetts the whole house in commotion, in consequence of H.R.H. having arrived there to commission Earl St. Vincent with a tender embassy to Miss Tylney Long,[2] who

---

[1] The house belonged to General Baynes, father of Colonel Baynes, an old Bath resident, who died a few years ago in Gay Street,

[2] She married Mr. Wellesley Pole, afterwards Earl of Mornington.

then resided at Wanstead, but she proved inexorable. A *jeu d'esprit* of the time I recollect :—

> To win a great Heiress a Royal Duke tried,
> Received as a Prince, but his offer denied.
> ' Return to your mistress,' the lady replied,
> ' And do not forsake her to make me your Bride.
> For sooner than wed you or one of the whole,
> My person and fortune I'll hang on a pole.'

When H.R.H. was in Bath, in the autumn of 1817, he sat to Jagger, the miniature painter, who one morning was a good deal *posed* by the interrogation— ' Why are my portraits always painted so thick about the chops ? ' ' Because painters sometimes see differently,' was the reply. The Duchess of Clarence, as when afterwards she ended as Queen Dowager, was excellence and amiability itself. When she was at Plymouth, at the period of Lord Northesk being the Port Admiral, she expressed to my aunt much regret for the Duke's infractions of the Sabbath in journies, receptions, etc., and she promised her to exert her influence for its better observance.

The Duke of Sussex came to Rochetts with the Dowager Marchioness of Downshire and her daughter.

My first recollections of Bath were going thither from Clifton, when Laura Place and Pulteney Street were covered with a deep snow. My sister and I were taken to No. 8, Argyle Street, where our Grandmother Ricketts then lodged. We wore black petticoats under our white frocks, in mourning for our grandfather. When we afterwards returned to Bath, I was taken in the arms of the footman (James Dacle) to the Great Pump Room. I well remember it, as we came in sight of it from Wade's Passage, and being struck with the Greek inscription over the entrance, supposing that ΥΔΩΡ must mean Pump.

Union Passage, vulgarly called Cock Lane, was the sole communication between the upper and lower town, the Bear Inn yard occupying the site of the present Union Street. Borough Walls was inconveniently narrow and crowded. A flood had carried away part of the Old Bridge at the bottom of Bridge Street, and for some time there was a temporary wooden bridge till the present building was constructed. Foot passengers either passed through the market, or by Boat-stall lane, in proceeding from Bathwick to the lower town, and it was a service of danger from the cattle being brought there on market days to be slaughtered, and the skins of the victims were cast out in disgusting heaps. All the precincts of the Abbey, Orange Grove, and the Parades were paved, while shops were crowded round, and some built on to the former, Wade's Passage being in the space between the Market Place and the Church. Quiet Street, the south side of which was occupied by trees, to which abundance of rooks were wont to resort, did not certainly merit its appellation.

Mount Beacon was a bare crag, with here and there sheep-paths. A ferry opposite Walcot Parade is now Cleveland Bridge, and a farm-house where we used to resort for new milk and curds and whey was situated at the bottom of Bathwick Street. An iron-foundry stood near the then church. Gardens occupied Henrietta Park, and a narrow and steep footway connected it with Henrietta Street. In the centre of Laura Place was a wooden watch-box. Johnstone Street, which only contained one or two houses, was terminated by a path conducting to a large mill by the river, and traversing Pinch's Timber Yard, on the site of the famous Spring Gardens. On the opposite side of the river was Monks' Mill[1] and weir, the river bathing the foot of a most unsightly slaughterhouse. Heavy rain or snow caused frequent inundations, and the fields, now called the Dolemeads, were under water to a wide extent. I remember a very high flood, 1807, the effect of a sudden thaw ; several houses were washed away, and my sister and I watched the furniture floating down the river. The water ascended half way up the cellar stairs of our grandmother's house, No. 8, Argyle Street, and left so much mud when it subsided that a man was employed to cleanse it. During this process he discovered that the main beam which supported the house was cracked across, and it had sunk some inches before my grandmother was informed, when she ordered an immediate repair. So late as the autumn of 1822, when coming from Chippenham to Bath, Mr. O. Markham and myself encountered one of these sudden inundations at the bottom of the hill at Batheaston, when the water entered our carriage. In the summer of 1864 a terrific thunderstorm tore down several trees which grew on Beechen Cliff, leaving for many years an unsightly chasm.

Mrs. Jefferys, a sister of John Wilkes, often passed in a sedan-chair, the interior of which had rich decorations, grey and white. She was said to be very like her brother, and she was certainly a frightful old woman. **Dr. Parry** drove about in a blue chariot. He then lived at **Summerhill,**[2] and open meadows extended from thence to Winifred House."

FROM LADY JERVIS'S COMMONPLACE BOOK.

"July 31, 1833.—To Ashcombe, to call on Mrs. Gunning. Mr. Gunning

---

[1] Burnt down January 2nd, 1884.

[2] Now the residence of R. S. Blaine, Esq., who has, however, now enlarged it, and the grounds of which he has greatly improved.

("Counsellor Gunning")[1] walked back with me.   He says that he is of the same family as the famous beauties.[2]   Bishop Gunning,[3] who composed the prayer,

[1] The Rev. Peter Gunning, D.D., was Rector of Farmborough. He married the sister of the Rev. Dr. Randolph. Of this marriage there were three sons, the eldest of whom was John, commonly called Counsellor Gunning (as above stated), whose town-house was 3, Vane Street ; the next was Peter, who was for many years Rector of Newton St. Loe and Bathwick. This gentleman married Sarah, eldest daughter of Archdeacon Phillott (Rector of Bath) and his wife, Lady Frances Phillott. Counsellor Gunning died Sept., 1843, and the Rev. Peter Gunning died 1840.

[2] Maria and Elizabeth Gunning, whom Mrs. Montague styled "those goddesses," were the daughters of John Gunning, of Castle Coote, in Ireland, by Bridget, daughter of the sixth Lord Mayo. Maria, the elder, was born in 1733, and Elizabeth in 1734. The eldest married the Earl of Coventry, March 5, 1752, and the younger, James, sixth Duke of Hamilton, February 14, 1752, and afterwards Col. Campbell, who became Duke of Argyll. These two ladies were superlatively beautiful and superlatively foolish. Horace Walpole describes their marriages with his usual pungency, and they afforded him no little scope for the exercise of his ill-natured wit.

     "The event that has made most noise since my last, is the extempore wedding of the youngest of the two Gunnings, who have made so vehement a noise. Lord Coventry, a grave young lord, of the remains of the patriot breed, has long dangled after the eldest, virtuously, with regard to her honour, not very honourably with regard to his own credit. About six weeks ago, Duke Hamilton, the very reverse of the Earl, hot, debauched, extravagant, and equally damaged in his fortune and person, fell in love with the youngest at the masquerade, and determined to marry her in the spring. About a fortnight since, at an immense assembly at my Lord Chesterfield's, made to show the house, which is really most magnificent, Duke Hamilton made violent love at one end of the room, while he was playing at pharaoh at the other end ; that is, he saw neither the bank nor his own cards, which were of three hundred pounds each : he soon lost a thousand. I own I was so little a professor in love, that I thought all this parade looked ill for the poor girl ; and could not conceive, if he was so much engaged with his mistress as to disregard such sums, why he played at all. However, two nights afterwards, being left alone with her, while her mother and sister were at Bedford House, he found himself so impatient, that he sent for a parson. The doctor refused to perform the ceremony without license or ring ; the Duke swore he would send for the Archbishop ; at last they were married with the ring of the bed-curtain, at half-an-hour after twelve at night, at Mayfair Chapel. The Scotch are enraged ; the women mad that so much beauty has had its effect ; and, what is more silly, my Lord Coventry declares that now he will marry the other, which he did three weeks later."

     Never did beauties—who had little but rank and beauty—create such a sensation ; they were talked of everywhere. A shoemaker at Worcester got two guineas and a-half by showing the shoe he was making for the Countess, at a penny a head. Walpole says, "Her genius is not equal to her beauty ; she every day says some new *sproposito*. She had taken a turn of vast fondness for her lord. Lord Downe met them at Calais, and offered her a tent bed, for fear of bugs in the inns. 'Oh,' said she, 'I had rather be bit to death than be one night from my dear Cov. !'"

     On one occasion George III. was talking to her on the dulness of the town, and regretting, for her sake, that there had been no masquerades during the year. "As for sights," said the inconsiderate beauty, "she was quite satisfied with them ; there was only one she was eager to see, and that was a Coronation !" On another occasion, as again related by Walpole, she was "at a great supper t'other night at Lord Hertford's. If Lady Coventry was not the best-humoured creature in the world I should have made her angry. She said in a very vulgar accent, if she drank any more she should be *Muchi-buss !* 'Lord,' said Lady Mary Coke, 'what is that ?' 'Oh,' I said, 'it is only Irish for sentimental.'" Lady Coventry died October 1, 1760, her death having been occasioned by the quantity of paint she put on her cheeks, which, checking perspiration, caused the disorder of which she died.

     The Duke of Hamilton died in 1758, and his widow married in the following year Col. Campbell, who succeeded his relative as fifth Duke of Argyll. She was the mother of George, seventh Duke of Hamilton, and Douglas, eighth Duke of Hamilton ; and by her second husband of George William, sixth Duke, and of John Douglas Edward Henry, seventh Duke of Argyll. She was, therefore, the wife of two, and the mother of four dukes. The duchess died December 20, 1790.

[3] Dr. Peter Gunning, Bishop of Ely. The Bishop was never married ; born at Hoo, Kent, 11th January, 1613 ; Bishop of Chichester 1669 ; translated to Ely 1674 ; died 6th July, 1684 ; buried in Ely Cathedral. His great-grandfather was John Gennynge, of Turney's Court, in the parish of Cold Ashton, Co. Gloucester, and of Northstoke and Swainswick, Co. Somerset ; died 1562. The cele-

' For all sorts and conditions of men,' was of the same family. Many letters of his were extant in the life of Mr. Gunning's grandfather, but they were destroyed by one of those vexatious fatalities which often attend antique documents. Mr. Gunning's grandmother was a Miss Leman, of Lyme, in Dorsetshire, and was a beautiful little woman. Her eldest son lived at *Turney's Court*, near Tadwick, and afterwards in the house which I now inhabit." [1]

CLAVERTON LODGE.—This villa, situated on the southern slope of Bathwick Hill, was built by the **Hon. Capt. Frederick Noel, R.N.,** [2] fifth son of Sir Gerard Noel and Lady Barham, his wife. About 1827, Capt. Noel married Mary, eldest daughter of William Woodley, Esq., and dying in 1833 was buried in Claverton Churchyard. Mrs. Noel married secondly General Sir T. Hawker, K.C.H., and died in 1867. Claverton Lodge is now the residence of Mr. and Mrs. Ashworth-Hallett. In 1837 the late **REV. FRANCIS KILVERT,** a Bath " worthy," of whom many now living will have the liveliest remembrance, became the owner. He resided here until his death, which occurred September 16, 1863. The character and career of Mr. Kilvert have been delineated in the volume of his *Remains*, by the graceful pen of his accomplished friend, the REV. W. L. NICHOLS.[3] It is too little known, both on account of its intrinsic merits as a composition, and of the admirable man who is the subject of it. No one was better qualified to do justice to the peculiar merits of Mr. Kilvert than Mr. Nichols ; and he has, perhaps, by reason of the special resemblance he bears in

brated beauties descended from Richard Gunning, who settled in Ireland 1604 ; brother to the Bishop's father. Swainswick and Turney's Court Gunnings descend from the eldest son of John Gennynge and Mary his wife, daughter of William Doddington, Esq.

            [1] The house in Swainswick.

   [2] One of the ancestors of the Noels was Sir Andrew Noel, Knight. of Dalby, in the county of Leicester. who was a person of great note in the time of Elizabeth, living in such magnificence as to vie with noblemen of the largest fortunes. Fuller, in his *Worthies of England*, said that this Andrew "for person, parentage, grace, gesture, valour, and many other excellent parts (amongst which skill in music), was of the first rank in the court." He was knighted by Queen Elizabeth, and became a favourite, but the expenses in which he was involved obliged him to sell his seat and manor of Dalby. Her majesty is said to have made the following distich upon his name :—
                " The word of denial and a letter of fifty,
                Is that gentleman's name who will never be thrifty."
He was thrice sheriff of the county of Rutland, and member of that shire in several parliaments during the reign of Queen Elizabeth. Sir Andrew married Mable, sixth daughter of Sir James Harington, Knight, and sister and heir of John, Lord Harington, of Exton (still the property and one of the seats of the family of Noel).

   [3] The Rev. W. L. Nichols came to St. James's on the 1st February, 1834, and resigned it 31st March, 1839. The church was nearly deserted when he came, and he left it with a large congregation, nearly every pew being let. He left it from want of sympathy with much of Archdeacon Law's pro-

many respects to his late friend, succeeded in giving, by a few simple, but masterly touches, the very man himself. Mr. Kilvert was born in Bath in 1793, and was the eldest of seven sons, of six of whom, after the death of their father, he became the guardian. Mr. Kilvert was one of that band of Bathonians who received their education at the Grammar School, under Mr. Morgan. George Norman, De Quincey, Sir Sidney Smith, and many others, deemed it an honour to have been flogged by that famous schoolmaster. They carried something away besides this remembrance; they were well taught, and they had imbibed a knowledge of themselves, and their responsibilities; they were self-reliant men, who, whatever they did, did with a will. Amongst these Grammar School pupils there were more brilliant boys, but not one who developed so many lovable qualities in after life as Francis Kilvert. His own love of Bath he seemed to have imbibed with his mother's milk, and no writer on modern Bath has done more to render its bibliographical and biographical history interesting and valuable. It was the author's privilege to have known him from the year 1845 until his death, and one of the most agreeable recollections in connection with him is that with regard to the frequent conversations between him and the Rev. Edward Mangin. Both were at their best, and the latter seemed to have an unusual pleasure in the society of Mr. Kilvert. The complete mastery of his subject, the low but exquisite tones of his voice, and the quiet yet dignified deference he paid to his older friend, were singularly charming. Amongst the many friends with whom Mangin conversed, not one, except perhaps Mr. Mortimer Harris,[1] ever brought out the vigorous mental and conversational power of Mangin with such striking effect as Mr. Kilvert. He and Mr. Harris were of the few to whom he said when parting, "Sir, I am pleased to have seen you."

ceedings, but with no unfriendly feelings on either side. The Bath Rectory had been sold to the Simeon Trustees, and Walcot was " bought and sold " several times afterwards, and finally fell into the hands of the same parties. The Trinity Church was offered to Mr. Nichols by Mr. Woodham, but only with the intention of selling it to better advantage. Mr. Nichols only held it for twelve months, Mr. Elwin, afterwards editor of the Quarterly, and joint editor of Pope's Works since, being his assistant. Mr. Nichols has since resided at Woodland House, near Nother Stowey, in a beautiful district, of which he has printed, for private circulation amongst his friends, a descriptive volume, entitled, " The Quantocks and their Associations." Bath : 1873.

Mr. Nichols says—"I left Trinity and soon after left Bath. One of the happiest periods of my life succeeded. I was offered the incumbency of a district church near Ottery, Devon. Here I had the society of Bishop Coleridge, Sir John Coleridge, and his son, the present Chief Justice, and that of the kind and good Mr. Justice Patteson, at Feniton Court. A year or two afterwards I succeeded to a living in my father's gift in Devon, and resided on it for five years. On my father's death, and my own failing health, I resigned the living, and succeeded to his property. I have before me the letters of the Bishop of Exeter, expressing his regret at my determination, and one from Archdeacon Froude, whose Rural Dean I was, conveying to me his own regrets, and those of my clerical brethren."

[1] Mr. Mortimer Harris, formerly connected with the Great Western Railway, and at present manager of the London, Dover, and Chatham line. Mr. H. is a first-rate classic and an admirable scholar. After a conversation with Mangin and Kilvert, he would say, with sparkling eye and quiet energy, "Ah! they are something like men."

This same quiet power characterized Kilvert's preaching. The choice of words and the sequence of ideas were remarkable in themselves, but it was the fulness of his knowledge and the simple illustrations which gave such interest and power to his discourses. In private life he commanded respect and won the love and esteem of all classes. It may be truly said of him, what was said by Richard Warner of another famous Bath worthy, Dr. Maclaine :—" He was wise, without austerity ; deeply learned without arrogance ; sincerely pious without ostentation ; of refined wit, untinctured with severity ; of polished manners, unsophisticated by affectation ; of warm benevolence and lively sensibility, but cool in judgment, and unbending in principle " . . . and he confuted by his life and his genial association with his fellows, Soame Jenyns's paradox, that "the religion of Christ cannot go hand in hand with secular business and rational enjoyments." There was one conspicuous feature in his character which Mr. Nichols notes with especial emphasis—it is a remarkable characteristic of his own—" the invariable practice of discouraging, either by his rebuke or by his expressive silence, that spirit of malicious detraction which is the bane of social intercourse." It is to Mr. Kilvert's industry and care that so much has been preserved to us relating to Ralph Allen, Graves, and " Pope, in his Connection with the West of England in General and Bath in Particular." It is to be regretted that in the " Remains," in which these Essays are reprinted, together with his collected Poems, the Essay on Philip Thicknesse should have been omitted.[1][1] Mr. Kilvert, it has been said, was educated at the Grammar School, and before taking his degree he became one of the masters. After taking his degree at Oxford, he was admitted deacon in 1816, and was appointed to the curacy of Claverton, a " place already classic ground." The "residence, for fifty years, of its clever but eccentric rector," Graves, "a haunt of the poet Shenstone," "the place in which lies the body of Ralph Allen," was likely to be a favourite resort of Mr. Kilvert, with his calm, contemplative, and poetic mood. All the famous men whose names are associated with Claverton and Prior Park—Warburton, Hurd, Fielding, and the others to whom reference has been made—have been the subjects of his graceful and able pen. He edited an edition of Warburton's " Literary Remains," and wrote the Life of Bishop Hurd, to whom he bore a relationship. After his connection with Claverton ceased, he for some time took no regular duty, but was engaged

[1] This and the other essays were read before the Bath Literary Club, of which Mr. Kilvert was a member from its formation until his death. In the essay on Allen, Mr. Kilvert has made a few mistakes, and has repeated a few others made by other writers in reference to Fielding, which the author has endeavoured to correct in the notice of Fielding.

[1] It should be mentioned that his Essay on the Batheaston Vase, delivered on the 2nd of June, 1858, at the Royal Literary Institution, is also omitted, but the substance will be given in the article on Lady Miller and the Batheaston Vase.

in private tuition. In 1827, he published a volume of Sermons, preached at Christ Church. In 1836 he was appointed Evening Lecturer at S. Mary's, Bathwick; and in 1837 he published a selection from his sermons preached there. In the same year he entered upon Claverton Lodge, "to which he transferred his private pupils, sons of gentlemen of birth and fortune." A small volume of sermons, preached at various times to his pupils, which he printed privately, are models of what such addresses should be—simple but suggestive, earnest, and such as are especially calculated to arrest the attention of youth and to interest them. "In the years 1848—50, Mr. Kilvert sent from the press a little work, in two small volumes, entitled *Pinacothecæ Historicæ Specimen*, the amusement of the few intervals of hard-earned leisure he could snatch from his professional duties. It was an attempt to delineate, under the form of Latin inscriptions, the characters of the most remarkable personages he met with in his reading. The result was a very interesting, though somewhat miscellaneous portrait-gallery of the worthies of all times and nations."[1]

If an esteemed acquaintance or friend passed away, Mr. Kilvert not unfrequently contributed a graceful notice of him to *The Bath Chronicle*. These occasional and brief biographies he called his "black work." No man of the present century has been so thoroughly a "Bath worthy" as Mr. Kilvert. He loved it with all his heart. Its memories, its history, its associations, were cherished by him. As is evident, they formed the theme, and, to a great extent, the study of his intellectual life; but withal they never tended to diminish his sympathies, nor to cramp the vigour of his mind. Those pupils whom he trained in youth, and who for the most part entered public life and attained to eminence, fully recognized his careful training, and how much they owed to his firm and gentle discipline.

59, PULTENEY STREET.—This house in Pulteney Street was, in all probability, intended by **SIR W. JOHNSTONE PULTENEY** as a residence for himself. On the death of General Harry Pulteney, the property, as has been already stated, devolved upon the Scotch representative of the Pulteney family, the wife of William Johnstone, of Westerhall, who assumed the arms and name of Pulteney, and ultimately succeeded to the baronetcy on the death of his elder brother. Sir William showed much interest in the property, and actively promoted the building upon the estate. He obtained an Act of Parliament to build the bridge to connect the "upper" with the "lower town." The house, which is about the centre of the south side, has an imposing frontage, and

[1] "Kilvert's Remains in Verse and Prose."

upon the entablature of the pediment are sculptured the Pulteney Arms. Lady Pulteney died before the street was completed, and Sir William never occupied the mansion. Sir William married, secondly, in 1804, Margaret, daughter of Sir William Stirling, Bart., and widow of Andrew Stewart, of Castlemill, and died the following year.[1] During the present century, the house has been occupied by numerous persons. In 1844, and for a few years after, it was the residence of **SIR EDWARD THOMASSON**, a Birmingham manufacturer, who was knighted by George IV. for his ingenious productions. Sir Edward wrote his own Memoirs in Brummagem-English, and with true Brummagem vanity. After Sir Edward's death, **LORD and LADY WILLIAM POWLETT**, who, on Lord William's accession to the property, had for a time resided at **98, Sydney Place,** purchased the house, and made it their occasional residence until the death of the former. On the death of Henry, second Duke of Cleveland of the present creation, Lord William succeeded as third Duke, and died in 1869. The next occupant of this house was **BISHOP THIRLWALL.** After a life of intellectual activity, in 1874, this distinguished prelate, like the still greater Bishop Butler, came here to die. It might have been hoped that, with perfect rest, a few more years of life would have been vouchsafed to him, but it was not to be. He was physically worn out; happily, his intellect, his bright and cheerful disposition, and his kindly nature, survived everything, and within a few days of his death, he was as cheerful and his mind as unclouded as ever. A few friends only were admitted to his house, and he was too feeble to take more than occasional exercise in Pulteney Street, or a short drive in the country. He died in 1875. After his death, his library was sold by auction in 1877. It was not quite the sort of library which most bibliophiles might have expected to see. It was manifest the bishop did not buy many books. The collection was large, but of a very miscellaneous character, and the larger portion presentation books from the authors, few of which were cut. The collection of foreign books on Philology, Divinity, and the Classics was very considerable, but not one in fifty was cut, and throughout the whole library there was scarcely an annotation to be found. The pamphlets, nearly every one of which bore the autograph of the author, were purchased for Trinity College, Cambridge. It was an honour to Bath to have seen the last of a man who for

---

[1] It has been already stated that the only daughter of Sir William Johnstone Pulteney succeeded to the enormous property of the Pulteneys, and that she was created Baroness, then Countess of Bath. She married Sir James Murray, who took the name of Pulteney. On her death in 1808, she bequeathed the whole of her personalty, amounting to nearly £1,000,000, to Mrs. Fawcett, daughter of Sir Richard Sutton, Bart., and wife of John Fawcett, Esq., of Northerwood Park, Hampshire. Mrs. Fawcett was the divorced wife of Dean Markham, of York, by whom she had a large family. Lady Bath was a credulous, weak-minded woman, and yielded to the influence of this lady, it appears, in all things. By her second marriage with Mr. Fawcett, who assumed the name of Pulteney, Mrs. Fawcett had two sons, one of whom was the father or grandfather of the Rev. Mr. Pulteney, Rector of Ashley, Northamptonshire.

half a century had been regarded as one of the most learned, fearless, and honest, in an age when men bid high for popular applause and the favour of the minister of the day.

LOUIS XVIII.—In the year 1813 there was a good deal of excitement in the city generally. It was a year of distress, but it was also a year of triumph and elation. There were meetings to relieve the distress ; meetings to keep alive the military spirit, greatly stimulated by the victories of Wellington. But when this feeling had been developed to the highest pitch of enthusiasm, a change of military policy was announced by the Government ; the militia was organized and extended, and with the exception of the Rifle Company, under Capt. Randolph, the *Volunteer corp* was disbanded. Capt. Randolph's Company made an offer of their services without any expense to the Government. In the month of August, Louis XVIII., with his *suite*, visited Bath and remained for a short period. The King, under the title of **Count de Lille**, occupied **72, PULTENEY STREET**; his *suite*, or a portion of it, **34, PULTENEY STREET.** The citizens, with their usual hospitality and courtesy, received the illustrious but proscribed prince with great warmth. After a brief visit, the Royal party left, and the King made a short valedictory address to the citizens (who had met to wish him God-speed) from the drawing-room windows.

It was at the close of this year that the necessity for additional church accommodation in the parish became irresistible. The **EARL OF DARLINGTON** (afterwards Duke of Cleveland) gave the site, and the preliminary measures were adopted for building a new church. It would serve no good purpose to give the history of the building, nor of the unhappy results which followed. Certainly, the methods adopted, at the time, were such as alone appeared practicable. No one could be selected for especial blame, but it is equally clear that no one could claim any credit. Trouble began at once, and after the original promoters, for the most part, had disappeared, a legacy of trouble was left to their successors, which continued until 1870. The building itself was not finished until 1821. Originally, not a good specimen even of the late Perpendicular style, its interior was odious. Those alone who knew it fifteen years ago can tell the extent of the change which has since then been effected. There is a legacy, however, which yet remains, and which reflects neither honour nor credit upon the parish. Pew-rents are rendered legal still (though certainly inexpedient), because there remain a few pews unredeemed by the Rector and Trustees of the Church.

CHARLES X.—After the Revolution of 1830, the unfortunate monarch sought refuge in England. On August 3, 1830, the King, accompanied by his suite, left Rambouillet. The Duke D'Angoulême and the Duchess de Berri, with her two children, were of the party. The Duchess, strange to say, wore man's attire, namely, a dark frock coat, trowsers, and boots. Her two children stood by her side, and now and then she would take the hand of the Duke de Bordeaux or touch his cheek. The party reached Cherbourg and embarked for England. On the 17th they arrived at Spithead. After some days the Royal party sailed for Cowes, Isle of Wight. On the 26th of August the King and a large suite landed at Poole. For a short period the King resided at Lulworth Castle, and in the latter end of November he and his family arrived at Holyrood Palace.

In 1831, the King, accompanied by the **DUCHESS DE BERRI**, who was afflicted with severe rheumatism, arrived in Bath, and occupied the house in which **WILLIAM PITT** [1] had resided thirty years before. Her son, the **DUC DE BORDEAUX**, better known as the **COMTE DE CHAMBORD**, remained at Holyrood. The young Prince, in the account given of him at the time at Cowes, is described as a beautiful boy, dressed in blue cloth jacket and cap and broad

---

[1] [The author is indebted to the Rev. E. W. L. Davies for the following note, relating to **W. PITT**, in 1805, when he visited the Earl of Harrowby, who was living at that time in the Duke of Northumberland's mansion, 11, Laura Place.]

" In the summer of 1860, a great treat was in store for me : I had been promised a view of no less than seven of Gainsborough's grand pictures, two of them perhaps the finest he ever painted ; namely, 'The Return from the Harvest Field,' and ' The Bradford Parish Clerk.' They were at Shockerwick, where Mr. John Wiltshire, the owner of these treasures, kindly acted as showman on the occasion. We were standing together, looking at the famous portrait of Quin, the comedian, when Mr. Wiltshire turned to me and said, 'A very remarkable incident occurred to me once when, as a boy and in the absence of my father, I was showing that picture to a gentleman ; who, as I soon discovered, was no less a man than Mr. Pitt, the distinguished statesman, and at that time Prime Minister of England. He was looking intently at the picture through the hollow of his two hands ; when suddenly a sound caught his ear—it was that of a horse galloping furiously up the gravel road leading to the house.' 'That must be a courier,' he said eagerly, ' with news for me !' and almost immediately a man, booted and spurred, and splashed from head to foot, entered the room and handed his despatches to the Minister, still standing before the picture. Tearing them open, he became intensely agitated, and' exclaimed, ' Heavy news, indeed ! do get me some brandy' ; ' On which,' said Mr. Wiltshire, ' I rushed out, and brought in the brandy myself ; and can at this moment well remember the little water he added to the spirit, as he tossed off a tumbler-full at a gulp ; he then took another, and I believe if he had not done so, he would have fainted on the spot. The Battle of Austerlitz had been fought and won by Buonaparte. The Emperors of Russia and Austria had commanded at it, and the coalition had been mainly due to a brilliant effort of Pitt's genius, by which he hoped to crush the hydra-headed power of Napoleon. The disappointment overwhelmed him ; it was more than he could bear, and in less than two months from that date he sank under the weight of it. Austerlitz was fought on the 2nd of December, 1805, and the great statesman died on the 23rd January, 1806.''

collar, and sometimes in the crimped frill of the period. The King and the
Duchess remained some weeks, and the latter derived much benefit from the
waters.

LORD LYTTON was a visitor to Bath in his youth, in his early manhood,
and at various periods later in life. With his friend Mr. Disraeli he visited Bath
when they were both young (Series 1, p. 20), and once during the early period of
his married life. On both these occasions he found ample comfort at the *White
Hart*, at that period in its most flourishing days. The *White Hart* was only
second to *The Bear*, which it long survived, and, until eclipsed by the *York
House*, was the leading hotel in the city. It was famous under the *Pickwick*
dynasty, both as a coaching-house and as the rendezvous of all the choice spirits
of the age. A source of infinite speculation amongst the readers of Dickens has
been whether the name was or was not the origin of his immortal story. It is not
enough that Dickens had never seen the *White Hart*, nor heard of the respected
landlord until many numbers of his book were published ; the name was
singular ; hence it must have been plagiarized. If Dickens had not written the
book in which Mr. Pickwick and Sam Weller figure, it is difficult to know
what many modern historians would have found to say about Bath. As it
is, they have said a good deal that is amusing, some of it very charming, and
all of it untrue, but on that account of course not to be objected to. If Lord
Lytton had laid the scene of either of his novels in Bath, we should have
had another phase of Bath "history," and the sub-editor of every London
"daily" would have got quite enough "history" out of it to point a moral
and adorn a tale. When Lord Lytton began to feel the infirmity of advancing years and a diminution of his early vivacity, he remembered Bath. Here
he wrote, and strolled, and smoked. In 1866 he came to **9, ROYAL
CRESCENT**. From 1867 to 1872, during his occasional visits, he resided
at **STEAD'S HOTEL, 2, PULTENEY STREET**; there he wrote portions of
Kenelm Chillingly and *The Parisians*. Courteous and agreeable he was, but
being deaf he shrank from intercourse with strangers. One could never quite realize
that this dapper gentleman, with his dyed hair and whiskers, and who certainly
was not above the middle height, was the *puissant* Edward Bulwer Lytton, the
invincible *Pelham* of other days. With all his faults, or alleged faults, he was a
gentleman, kind to his inferiors, scrupulously honourable in his dealings, and
if there remained evident indications of personal vanity, he was free from all
ostentation and vulgar pride of rank. In all respects, Lord Lytton was the

reverse of his wife, who, thirty years before, had made Bath her home and tradesmen her victims.

LADY LYTTON.—About the year 1840, a handsome, over-dressed, "fat, fair, and forty" style of lady took up her abode at **7, JOHNSTONE STREET**; this was Lady Lytton. She had just then acquired a somewhat equivocal kind of notoriety by her publication of *Cheveley*, in which she lampooned her husband in a vulgar manner. Her object in coming to Bath was the tranquillity and leisure to enable her to pursue the calling for which she deemed herself eminently fitted, namely, literature. A Miss Augusta Boys acted as her secretary, and there was a great flourish of trumpets. The first thing was to proclaim Lord Lytton to be a literary impostor, and that all his better novels were the production of his wife; the next was to prove the truth of this by her intended works. She engaged a local librarian to negotiate with a London firm for the publication of her next novel; much expense was incurred, and the time arrived when her pretensions collapsed, and the debts she incurred were never paid. Beautiful once she might have been, but her beauty was no longer attractive. She had grown large, and her manner and carriage were of that defiant character that repelled, and excited curiosity and surprise rather than admiration. You looked at her and passed on with the happy reflection that your destiny was not cast with that of such a resolute-looking lady. A neighbour who lived opposite to her said she approached the door of her house in a menacing attitude, and as if she entertained an *animus* against the unoffending door-knocker. She was, in fact, a woman who neither understood what was due to her own dignity and position, nor the reticence imposed upon her by her unfortunate relations with her husband. Moreover, she got into the hands of people who flattered her vanity, and who, knowing nothing of Sir Edward, considered they held a special commission to vilify him. Her career in Bath was in every way discreditable. She lived beyond her income; she showed a vulgar loquacity; she left her tradesmen in debt, and never made an effort afterwards to pay them; and her name to those who have reason to remember her is associated with pretentious claims never fulfilled, and attempts to excite sympathy by means which excited contempt.

BENJAMIN BARKER, OAKWOOD.[1]—About two hundred yards above Claverton Lodge, on the same side, is the residence of William Dobson, Esq., **Oakwood**, built by Benjamin Barker, the Painter. The sloping grounds, the exquisite situation, and the very beautiful and extensive scenery, render this one

[1] Formerly called Smallcombe Grove.

of the most delightful places that can be imagined. Benjamin Barker, with the eye of the artist even for potential beauty, selected the site when it was covered with rough brushwood and an undergrowth of centuries of roots and dank vegetation for the house which was to be a picture-gallery and the retreat of his later years.[1] The younger brother of Thomas Barker, he was more successful, for a time, in a pecuniary sense, though he was less eminent as a painter. In many respects their styles were essentially different, so that they afford few points of comparison. Benjamin has been called the *English Poussin*, and not without reason. In his best pictures there is a charming combination of colour, harmony, and grouping. In manner he was genial, unassuming, and full of kindliness. He failed to realize the dreams of his youth. The success of his earlier career was arrested by misfortunes, and the fairy place he had designed for himself he never inhabited, or if he did it was for a brief period only. Barker was born in 1776; settled in Bath about 1807. He died at Totnes, March 2nd, 1838, aged 62. His English Scenery was published in 1843. *Thales Fielding* engraved 48 of his landscapes in aquatint.

WILLIAM WILBERFORCE.—It may, without fear of contradiction, be affirmed that amongst the many eminent personages who at various periods have made Bath their temporary or permanent place of residence, no one has ever been received with such cordial, such affectionate welcome as **WILLIAM WILBERFORCE.** All classes of citizens held him in the highest esteem, and it was in Bath he met with his most intimate political friends and fellow-philanthropists, and more fully than elsewhere enjoyed their society. He it was who was the first to welcome his beloved friend, **WILLIAM PITT,** in 1802. Wilberforce was then lodging at **36, PULTENEY STREET**, and he relates how deeply anxious he felt on account of the great statesman's health. Wilberforce seems to have been attracted to Bath by something more than considerations for his health from the use of the Bath Waters. He loved the scenery and the associations of the place. It is almost amusing to find him occasionally making excuses to justify his residence in a place in which pleasure and excitement were such prominent elements. His natural cheerfulness, his love of innocent pleasures, both intellectual and otherwise, made him tolerant and gentle in his judgment of others. What he complained of in a half-serious, half-joking manner, was the frequent interruptions by callers and the perpetual rap, rap, rap, at his front door. He said he always found more to do at Bath than anywhere else.

[1] Barker was the intimate friend of John Britton, who, in his Autobiography, says:—"At this delectable retreat, I spent many happy hours in company with some of the Bath 'worthies,' amongst whom was James Hewett, a distinguished English flower-painter, whose sister Barker married."

No doubt this arose from the fact that he was more disposed to work because Bath suited him better than any other place. His health and spirits were better, and he felt greater energy. Writing to his mother in 1797, he said, " I scarce know how it is, but there is no place in which I find more full employment for myself than at Bath." The first record of his visit to his favourite residence is in 1787, on which occasion, also in April, 1788, he stayed at the York House. He says the " use of the waters and the effect of a proper use of opium " greatly improved his health. Year after year he revisited Bath, and always with beneficial results ; in fact, it seems that without this invigorating source he could never have performed the labours of political public life, and the scarcely less arduous duties appertaining to the great philanthropical work with which his name will ever be associated. In 1791 he, in conjunction with his intimate friend, **HENRY THORNTON, M.P.**, took for a term the exquisite **VILLA AT PERRYMEAD.**[1] Wilberforce's relations with Bath and its citizens were singularly happy. His simple dignity, his benignant cheerfulness, his love of children·wherever he met them, and, above all, the careful avoidance in society of ill-timed reference to religious topics, proclaimed him to be a true-hearted man and a Christian gentleman. His affability to his inferiors was so absolutely unaffected that all classes showed him the utmost deference and respect.

In June, 1791, again with Mr. Henry Thornton, on this occasion he stayed at Perrymead. " To have grass up at my door, after the parching of my heels on the pavements of London, is not a luxury but a necessary for me. I have, therefore, leased a country house, within reach of the Pump Room, and so shall enjoy the comforts of a beautiful country residence ; whilst with the salubrious waters of King Bladud I am washing away the ' sorder ' contracted in the course of a long session." In speaking of the place he says :—" This Perrymead is situated in a country which, except in the article of water, comes not far behind Cumberland and Westmoreland themselves : close to Prior Park, and about three-quarters of a mile from the Pump Room, there old Henry Thornton and I are lodged, and are leading a rational kind of life." In 1792, 19th August, he was lodging in Bathwick. He speaks of the old and venerable pastor, who has had the living since 1745.[2]

1 The house occupied forty years ago by a well-known philanthropist, Capt. Pickering Clarke, R.N., whose name and kindly actions will not soon be forgotten. The house is now occupied by a worthy citizen—Captain Western.

2 The Rev. Peter Grigg was instituted to the Rectory of Bathwick, June 24, 1749 (not 1745).; He also held the living of Ubley, Somersetshire. Mr. Grigg died in 1804.

In 1797, after a severe attack of illness, he arrived in Bath at the close of December, and remained until February. On February 2nd he dined at the poet Anstey's with a large and miscellaneous party, and rout afterwards. On Feb. 5th he attended Laura Chapel, and heard Rev. Dr. Randolph preach, and on this day he heard of the defeat of the Austrians.

A Cambridge newspaper, edited by one Flower, charged him with hypocrisy, and stated that he always had a Prayer Book in the Pump Room, and said his prayers there.[1] In 1798 he spent the Christmas Recess in Bath, on this occasion at 2, Royal Crescent. On 6th Nov., John and David Hartley[2] dined with him. In 1800 he came to Bath in the early part of the year, and remained four months.

The following letter to Lord Muncaster will show how the interruptions of Bath life fretted him, though he could never altogether sever himself from it.

"Near Bath, Nov. 5, 1799.

"My dear Muncaster,—

"My history is this. Smarting from past experience of the incessant interruptions inseparable from a residence in Bath, from the first week of my arrival I employed myself in looking about for a villa, and my industry was quickened when it became probable that I might be able to spend the following three months at a distance from the capital; but we searched in vain for near a month. At length we have succeeded, and we are quartered in a middling house,[3] which, however, has the comfort of a tolerable garden, and above all the recommendation of withdrawing us from the circle of the Pump-room ; and by showing that we are willing to pay a price for retirement, of procuring for us a right to be quiet without offence. The Chancellor, Pepper Arden, Lord Camden, and the Archbishop of Canterbury have all been here ; the latter is still with us. . . . . . . I went last Sunday to a church where he administered the sacrament, and heard him read service inimitably. . . I thank God I am certainly better, and Mrs. Wilberforce, and Mrs. Clarke, and our little ones are as well as can be expected. . . . I have just received your letter, and knowing the keenness of your sensibility, I feel for you on the convention of Holland. I own I never much relished the expedition,

---

[1] Presumably the Cambridge editor, like the Scotch boatman, did not trouble his Maker with prayers at any time unless he wanted something.

[2] David Hartley, it will be remembered, was a Bath man ; and although his politics were not those generally held by Wilberforce, they were fast friends on all other points. Hartley, like Wilberforce, represented Hull. Of Hartley, Warner says, " Mr. Hartley engaged in public concerns in a spirit more lofty, and with views more pure, than those which influence the herd of common politicians."

[3] This was at Bathford, but what house it is difficult to say.

nor do I think that such schemes are the *forte* of our Administration. I used to blame your extravagant exaltation of the talents of our Premier. I, who yet declare it as my fixed opinion that, in many intellectual and some moral excellencies, I never knew his equal (so far as religion is not concerned), am not blind to his infirmities.' . . . . . Gisborne another book! he deserves to live in a forest. May God bless you and yours. Kind remembrances.

" Yours éver,
" W. WILBERFORCE.

" P.S.—I dare not be quite certain, but am nearly so, that you may send back your war-horse to his former peaceful pursuits, and call for the . . . . What a business that provisional cavalry ! "

In August, 1803, he left Woodhall, and on Sept. 3rd he arrived at Batheaston, where he took the **MANOR HOUSE**,' now occupied by Mr. Harper, surgeon. At this time the public dangers which beset the nation induced him to make his residence at Batheaston a season of more than usual devotion at this period. (See Life of Wilberforce, vol. 3, p. 122.) This residence was occupied by Wilberforce for a longer period than any other in Bath.

In 1821 his family were staying at **26, PULTENEY STREET**. The Easter of that year he spent in Bath. As the year advanced he moved, by Dr. Chambers's advice, again to Bath—"the worst of all places for getting my business done. There is walking between the glasses and after the glasses, and then in rolls the tide of visitors, full as regularly as that of the ocean, and like that, this human influx makes its way through and over every obstacle. . . Continual knockings while I have been writing, and at last one intruder has actually made a lodgement." "1824, Oct. . . On October 19 dined with venerable Rowland Hill."

¹ Mr. Pitt.

² " Wilberforce has bought a house near Bath," says Henry Thornton in a letter to Hannah More, Oct. 30, " which I a little lament, on the ground of the bad economy of it ; for he is a man, who, were he in Norway or Siberia, would find himself infested by company, since he would even produce a population, for the sake of his society, in the regions of the earth where it is the least. His heart also is so large that he never will be able to refrain from inviting people to his house. The quiet and solitude he looks to will, I conceive, be impossible, and the Bath house will be troubled with exactly the same heap of fellows as the Battersea Rise one." " I bless God," he tells Mr. Babington, Nov. 5, " I certainly am much improved in health since our arrival here ; and we are now on a plan of great quiet, regularity and ease. This is using the means, and I desire to use them with cheerfulness and gratitude, leaving the event to God. We have been reading, and are still engaged on, Gisborne's Moral Philosophy ; and I am quite pleased, I own, to be able to say that I think he has fully established his charge against Paley, and shown, with great effect, how little such a principle as general expediency is fit for man. If I mistake not there are some errors, and I doubt if he might not have made his charge against Paley still more manifestly valid. I am glad to find he is publishing again. While he goes on thus I will allow him to live in a forest. I found that so much use was made of my going to Jay's that I have kept away." [Nevertheless, his intimacy with Jay continued to the last.]

In 1825 Wilberforce was at the **YORK HOUSE,** and at the same time the **MARQUIS CAMDEN,** who was then Recorder of Bath, was there also. Wilberforce relates the fact that he spent a very pleasant evening with his noble friend. In 1830, Wilberforce lodged at **7, SOUTH PARADE.** His last visit was made to Bath in the autumn of 1832, on which occasion he lodged at **2, RUSSELL STREET.** He died the following year.

FREEMASONRY.—The history of Freemasonry in Bath—*i.e.*, of **Craft Masonry**—may not be without interest even to the *outer world.* With the exception of London itself, no provincial city can so distinctly trace back the annals of Masonry as Bath. It is not difficult to trace this unbroken continuity of the "working" of the order in this city. It would be less easy to show precisely when the order assumed its present form and system ; but there is no doubt that masonry has existed from time immemorial, under different aspects, though not perhaps for the purpose of attaining the same objects. Sometimes, as in its earliest and, it may be said, most occult stage, it was confined to the learned communities, between whom it constituted a universal bond of fellowship, and who locally were governed by its rules and laws. As science and learning became more general, and less subject to legal interference and repressive tyranny, this phase of masonry ceased, or, rather, by a gradual transition, it took a more practical form in connection with the monastic system. The ecclesiastical buildings were to a great extent erected under its direction. All the ceremonials were in like manner under its conduct and control. In nearly all the most important capitular bodies there existed a *masonic fraternity*, whose functions, as will be seen, (in addition to the religious and moral obligations which subsisted universally) were practical, and, if not strictly architectural, were directed to the careful and scientific supervision of the noble works committed to their care, and which now are the glory of the world. Modern Freemasonry is, no doubt, the direct offspring of the system to which reference has just been made. The difference between the two systems is that the former was speculative as well as practical ; the latter is purely ideal and speculative, yet having the grandest, the most perfect, and most universal of any organization that has ever existed in the world. It takes, like the body which preceded it, Solomon's Temple as its ideal of form, beauty, proportion, and perfection, and all its imagery and learned speculations are derived from it. The mysticism supplies ample scope for the contemplation of the student, whilst its moral teaching and practical philanthropy appeal universally to the hearts of men of all nations who value truth, honour, justice, and benevolence.[1] There is little doubt that the Monastery of Bath was the depository and guardian of learning and science from the time of John de Villula[2] down to the very period of Prior Gybbs or Holway, the last Prior, at the time of the dissolution. Now, this Prior Gybbs, or Holway, was the chief of the order, as his predecessor, Prior Birde, was before him. It cannot be supposed that the order was *created* in the time of Birde, and its existence, therefore, may be assumed at least as early as John de Villula. In the 28th year of the reign of Henry the Eighth, Pryor Gybbs granted for life the reversion of the subordinate office of master of all the works of the convent, "commonly called Freemasonry," to John Multon, freemason, in reward for his former diligence and faithful service, together with an annual salary of forty shillings.[3] Edward Leycester, Multon's predecessor in the office, is mentioned in the same grant (see Warner's Appendix, LVIII).

It is remarkable that the Monastery of Bath has been associated with men not merely of singularly holy lives, but of distinguished genius. William of Malmesbury, who wrote the Life of John de Villula, says that in the reigns of Rufus and Henry I. he collected about him a society of religious associates, who were eminently distinguished for their learning. Amongst these was the Monk, **ADELARD**, a name which deserves most especial notice.

"Adelard having acquired what could be learned at home, visited Spain, Egypt, and Arabia. He made himself master of the language of Arabia, and

[1] The following returns for one year would justify the existence of Freemasonry, and this justification is all that is needed, even if it were admitted that it is the only practical result of the existence of the order :—

"MASONIC BENEVOLENCE IN 1883.—The three Masonic Charitable Institutions, which are supported by the voluntary contributions of the craft, during the year just closed realised a total income of £55,994 14s. 3d. Of this sum the Boys' School received £24,895 7s. 1d., the Benevolent Institution £18,449 6s., and the Girls' School £12,650 1s. 2d. The largest total attained previous to 1883 was in 1880, when the sum amounted to £49,763. The Boys' School, which is now at the head of the list, is boarding, housing, clothing, and educating 221 boys ; the Benevolent Institution, the second on the list, is granting annuities of £40 each to 172 men and £32 each to 167 widows ; and the Girls' School houses, boards, clothes, and educates 239 girls between the ages of 7 and 16. The boys leave their school at 15. During the year, £8,675 has been granted to 334 cases of distress from the Fund of Benevolence, which is composed of 4s. a year, taken from every London Mason's subscription to his lodge, and 2s. a year from every country Mason's subscription."

This return, it must be understood, is independent of the local action of Provincial Grand Lodges, Private Lodges, and private members. One striking peculiarity in connection with these Schools is that, whilst the children are well taught, they never feel humiliated by a sense of dependence. The masters and mistresses stand to the children under their care in *loco parentis*, and the supervision is perfect. The children after leaving the schools are watched with solicitude and encouraged with judgment until they "begin the world."

[2] Temp. William Rufus, 1088.

[3] Britton's Bath Abbey Church, page 52.

learned what the Arabian professors could teach him. He brought from those countries treatises in natural philosophy; he is, in fact, the main link by which western science is connected with that of the east. But he brought home a more precious volume than any of the writings of the Arabian philosophers. This is no less than the Elements of Euclid, not in its original form indeed, but in an Arabic translation, from which Adelard made a Latin version that continued to be used all over Europe till some centuries after the Greek original was discovered. He wrote on the Abacus and the Astrolabe, which were the first attempts at making the skill of the mechanic minister to the views of the philosopher; on the causes of natural compositions, in which it may be supposed that some of the principles of chemical affinities are to be found; and seventy-six problems in natural philosophy, which Leland, no incompetent judge, pronounces to be highly valuable. An account of his travels was once to be read in a manuscript preserved in the library of Corpus Christi College, in Oxford. We must join with Dr. Wallis in the regret which he expresses in the preface to his Algebra, that some wicked hand has torn away the precious leaves.

"Such a man as this must have given a character to society at Bath. He could not but diffuse around him a spirit of inquiry and research; and he who could unlock the secrets of Arabian philosophy, then known to few, must one supposes, have attracted hither a multitude of inquirers eager to sit at his feet. We are not informed on whom the rich treasures of his knowledge were more peculiarly poured forth; but later in the same century, Prior Walter is celebrated for his science as well as for his piety.

"In the next century there was one Reginald of Bath, a physician, who may be presumed to have been eminent, as he was sent by King Henry III. to attend a Queen of Scotland at Edinburgh. Contemporary with him was Henry of Bath, a lawyer, who is described by Pits as *legum terræ peritissimus*; and to about the same period is to be referred a William of Bath, a divine, some of whose homilies were collected, and the volume was still in existence in the time of Leland." [1]

The old monastery—that is, the predecessor of the monastic house or priory—pulled down in 1755, which stood upon a part of the same site, extending, in fact, further southward, was crowded with literary treasures. Leland saw the library, which contained gifts from King Athelstan, Translations from the Arabic, Poems of the middle ages, Roman classics, works on Chemistry, Alchemy, and Physic. Amongst these Arabic works, it is more than

---

[1] Hunter on the "Connection of Bath with the Literature and Science of England."

probable that there were allegorical treatises on Freemasonry, which even then was practised by the Arabian tribes, amongst whom Adelard had lived, and from whom he would have acquired a knowledge of the symbolic and mystic science. With the insignificant exceptions alluded to by Mr. Hunter, and the Red Book,[1] which is a collection of miscellaneous old treatises on Surgery, Poetry, History,[2] etc., all the treasures have disappeared and no trace of them discovered.

Whatever the precise nature might have been of Freemasonry as practised in Birde's time, it could not have originated with him, and, conjectural though it be, there is every reason to believe that, from what is known of the famous monk, Adelard, and his association with the learned Orientals of his time, it owes its origin in Bath to him.

The peculiar square head and corner emblems,[3] of the Abbey east window, are irresistible evidences of its masonic origin. The glazing, the gift of Bellot, was a clear indication of masonic arrangement, and yet in Bellot's time we have no record of the existence, working, and fellowship of any masonic fraternity.

It may be asserted that Masonry, in its present recognized form, began in Bath in 1723. Preserved and cherished for centuries, as it undoubtedly was by tradition and oral usage, it assumed its more cognate and practical shape at that time. The purposes it had accomplished previously in its less realistic form were no longer possible in an age of advancement and more general utility. The good in the order was to be developed by adapting it to the exigencies of the times and the enlarged needs of humanity. A brief sketch of the order from 1723 to 1736, by Mr. Hughan, a very distinguished member of the fraternity, the author has been permitted to avail himself of :—

"Read at the meeting of the Royal Cumberland Lodge, No. 41, held at the Masonic Hall, on Thursday, Jan. 6th, 1881.

"The fact of the 'Constitutions of the Freemasons' of 1738, containing no reference to a Lodge at Bath before that of 1733 (present No. 41) seems to have led many to suppose that this Lodge was the *first* warranted for the city. There was, however, an earlier one chartered during the latter part of 1723 or 1724. There is an engraved list of 1723 preserved, unique, but all the Lodges therein are for the London district and neighbourhood. If any list of Lodges was issued for 1724, no copy is known at the present time, but of 1725 two copies are now extant. In both of the latter date is to be found a Lodge at the

[1] In the Longleat Library.

[2] Its "contents" are given in the Appendix to the Third Report, Historical Commissioners, p. 182.

[3] When the reparations of the church took place, in 1834, these corners were filled in, to make the window Perpendicular in form ; but Sir G. Scott restored the original shape of the window. The paragraph refers obviously to the period before the present window was inserted.

'Queen's Head, Bath,' and as it was the first warrant ever issued by the Grand Lodge of England for any part of the country, Bath is entitled to the distinction of being considered the PREMIER MASONIC PROVINCIAL CITY OF ENGLAND. At and before that year, the Grand Lodge had warranted about fifty lodges, but none for a country district, and when the Lodges were known by their numbers, several had lapsed, so that the Lodge at Bath in the numeration of 1729 was numbered 28 instead of 30.

"It was one of the most distinguished Lodges, as respects the membership, of any ever warranted before or since 1724. When it ceased to exist is uncertain, but certainly not before 1736. Mr. Robert Freke Gould, S.G.D. of England, and author of 'The Four Old Lodges,' &c., has made diligent researches on this point in the records of the Grand Lodge, and considers it was about the year 1737. It was left out of the engraved lists of 1738-9. On March 2nd, 1732, the Grand Lodge Archives contain a notice of payment of *one guinea* from the Lodge for 'charity.' Mr. Gould thinks that it was constituted in 1723. However, to be within the mark, the year 1724 may be accepted, the Grand Master of England being then the Earl of Dalkeith or the Duke of Richmond. There *was not another Grand Lodge in England at this period*, and indeed that in London was the *first* of its kind. There was, however, an old Lodge at York, meeting in 1724, but *not* as a Grand Lodge until 1725. It was never antagonistic to the Grand Lodge of England (London), and was known as the ' *Grand Lodge of all England, held in the City of York.*' Some years later it issued warrants for Lodges, but never *for any part of the West of England*, and mainly confined its operations to Yorkshire. There was another Grand Lodge, which sprang out of a secession from the regular Grand Lodge (or ' Moderns,') and was known as the ' Ancients '—' York Masons,' or ' Athol Masons.' This body, however, never did any work that is known until 1750, and after that many Lodges in England were started, such as at Bristol in 1753; all, however, long after No. 28, Bath, was formed, and years after the present No. 41 was warranted. Save, then, any independent old Lodges, not meeting by warrants from the Grand Lodge of England (and those being all north of the City of Bath, or east thereof), Bath was the first city which had a regular Masonic Lodge out of the London district, and was the first ever *warranted in the country* by the Grand Lodge.

"This Lodge assembled to about 1736, and as the present No. 41 was constituted in 1733, by the same Grand Lodge, it is quite clear, as the latter has regularly met as a Lodge ever since, that Freemasonry has existed in the City of Bath from the year 1724 *continuously* to the present time; which is more than can be said for any other city or town in the country.

" Mr. Gould has traced a list of members of No. 28, Bath, from 1725, with additions to 1729. Unfortunately he cannot find any later list in the returns of Lodges to the Grand Lodge, or doubtless we should find several Brethren who belonged to No. 28, and started the present No. 41 in the year 1732. Only one, so far, has been discovered, namely, Bro. St. John Smith (or Smyth), who is mentioned in the early records of ' The Royal Cumberland Lodge.'

" In the return of the No. 28 Lodge to the Grand Lodge, A.D. 1725, His Grace the Duke of St. Albans was Master, and the Rev. George Vezey and Erasmus Earl, Esq., Wardens. The list of Members, from **1725 to 1729**, comprises the following Brethren :—

'Queen's Head, Bath.

(Copied from the Register, 19th October, 1880.)

His Grace the Duke of St. Albans, Master.

Rev. Mr. George Vesey, Erasmus Earl, Esq., Wardens.

Dr. Edward Harington[1]; Thomas Selfe; James Leake;[2] Charles Stone; Milse Smith; Lord Viscount Cobham;[3] John, Lord Hervey ;[4] Richd. Nash, Esq.; Thomas Mee, Esq.; Geo. Dashwood, Esq.; Thomas Gore, Esq.; Knox Ward, Esq.; William Bristow, Esq.; Hugh Barker, Esq.; William Chamber, Esq.; Colonel Robert Reading; Rev. Mr. John Boswell; Thomas Thailes, Esq.; Samuel Pye, Esq.; John Granoe, Esq.; St. John Smith, Esq.; Samuel Bush, Esq.; Wm. Barwell, Esq.; Edward Cookey, Esq.; Sir John Buckworth; Fra. Bave, Esq.; Rev. Mr. Markhall; Mr. Thomas Short; Mr. Thomas Clark; Charles Broome, Esq.; Wriothesley, Duke of Bedford; William Aglionby, Esq.; Francis Lewis, Esq.; George Henry, Earl of Lichfield; William, Earl Craven; Sir Humphry Morroux, Bart.; Sir Robert Walker, Bart.; James Harrett, Esq.;

[1] Descended from Sir John Harington. Dr. E. H. was the uncle of Dr. Henry Harington.

[2] The Bookseller, brother-in-law of Richardson the Novelist.

[3] Richard Grenville, of Wotton, born on the 23rd of March, 1767, married in 1710 Hester, second daughter of Sir Richard Temple, of Stowe. Her brother was created Viscount Cobham on the 23rd May, 1718, and is the Viscount Cobham referred to above. This Viscount Cobham died unmarried, and the Lady Hester Temple was created, after the death of her elder sister, Countess Temple, with limitation to the heirs male of her body, on the 18th of October, 1749. She was the mother of the first Earl Temple and six other sons and one daughter, who was the Lady Hester Grenville, afterwards the wife of the famous Earl of Chatham. Her grandson, the second Earl, was created Marquis of Buckingham. His elder son, who assumed the name of Bridges Chandos, was, on the 4th Feb., 1822, created Earl Temple of Stowe, Marquis of Chandos, and Duke of Buckingham. He was the grandfather of the present Duke of Buckingham and the late Lady Anna Gore-Langton, whose son the present Stephen Gore-Langton, Esq., M.P., of Newton Park, through his mother, is heir-presumptive to the Earldom of Temple of Stowe, under the special remainder of the creation of tho Earldom of Temple of 1822.

[4] John, Lord Hervey, was the eldest son of the first Earl of Bristol. He was called up to the House of Peers, June, 1733, as Baron Hervey of Ickworth, but dying before his father he never succeeded to the Earldom. Lord Hervey married "sweet Molly Lepell," and was the father of George William, 2nd Earl of Bristol, and Augustus John, 3rd Earl. This was the "Captain Hervey," who was the first husband of the Duchess of Kingston. Lord Hervey was a frequent visitor to Bath.

Richard Hare Chester, Esq. ; and the Earl of Darnley, who was also a *Grand officer* of England.[1]"

In 1767, a gentleman who was a Grand Officer of England was a frequent visitor of the Lodge, and who so long as he lived exhibited a lively interest in its proceedings. This was **Mr. DUNKERLY.** He became an honorary member, and his portrait was presented to the Lodge. This gentleman was an officer of militia. He possessed a small fortune, which he used liberally in the promotion of benevolent objects. Warner relates how much he loved children, and nothing pleased him so much as to join in the children's parties in St. James's parish. Dunkerly was an illegitimate son of George II., and bore a striking resemblance to that monarch's grandson, George III. As soon as his parentage and history became known to his Royal nephew, the King provided for him in the most kindly and considerate manner, frequently invited him to Court, and treated him with most friendly and affectionate regard. It is not a little interesting to know that in simplicity of character, kindness of disposition, and private virtues, he was the counterpart of the King, and was beloved and respected accordingly. The King, moreover, provided Dunkerly with apartments in Hampton Court Palace.

The Lodge now known as "THE ROYAL CUMBERLAND LODGE, No. 41," is, beyond all doubt, the immediate successor, without any breach of continuity, of the Lodge first established in Bath. The Warrant is dated April 20, 1733, and the proceedings have been conducted from that time until now. Sir Christopher Wren had been Grand Master of England, but he took more interest in real than speculative masonry, and in 1714 he gave place to Anthony Sayer, who, retiring in 1719, was succeeded by Dr. Desaguliers. In 1723, the Duke of Wharton[2] was elected Grand Master and *Dr. Desaguliers*[3] became his Deputy. The latter was a constant visitor to the Lodge during his frequent residences in Bath. Before the Lodge received the Warrant, one meeting was held at *The Bear,* and

[1] John Bligh, eldest son of Thomas Bligh, of Rathmore, co. Meath, M.P. for Athboy, who died at Bath on 28th Aug., 1710. John Bligh, also M.P. for Athboy, married in 1713 Theodosia, Baroness Clifton in her own right. He himself was successively created Baron Clifton, Viscount and Earl of Darnley, in the Peerage of Ireland. He died at Epsom on 28th September, 1728 ; ancestor in the fifth generation of Lord Clifton, himself a mason, who has made a long residence in Bath, during 1883—4. Edward, the second Earl of Darnley, was elected Grand Master of England in the year 1737.

[2] It is remarkable that Col. Kemeys-Tynte, who was Provincial Grand Master of the Province of Somerset for many years, until his death in 1860, inherited the Duke's estates in this county, and, through his mother, claimed the minor title of the barony of Wharton. The claim was admitted as proved. The Duke was attainted in 1728, but although the attainder did not permanently affect the minor titles, it was in the way of Col. Kemeys-Tynte's assumption of the barony, and is still in the way of his heirs.

[3] Dr. Desaguliers was a French Huguenot, and he, with James Anderson, a Scotch Presbyterian, was one of the most zealous organizers of the *craft.*

the next regularly-constituted Lodge, under the new Warrant, signed by Lord Montague, was also held there. After a time, the Lodge held its meetings at the *Shakspeare and Greyhound Tavern* (afterwards called the *Greyhound* simply), and it is very curious, in going through the books and muniments of the Lodge, to observe how many names of famous citizens figure as W.M.'s or otherwise in the proceedings :—The Attwoods, Masterses, Cottells, Chapmans, Phillotts, Sprys, Boyces, Wests, Gearys, Keanes, down to recent times, in fact.[1]

Towards the close of the century, other Lodges sprang up :—" The Shakspeare," " The Royal York Lodge of Perpetual Friendship." In 1785, there was an amalgamation between *The Lodge* and *The Royal Cumberland Lodge,* No. 458, a Lodge of which little or no record exists, except that it was so named in honour of the Duke of that name. *The Lodge,* whose number was 39, adopted the more distinctive title by which it has ever since been known. *The Royal Sussex Lodge* was warranted in 1756, and although for some years it ceased to work, its Warrant was preserved, and in 1854 it resumed its active career, and is at this time one of the most flourishing Lodges in the Province. *The Lodge of Honour,* No. 379, which obtained its Warrant in 1825, if not so successful as its sister Lodges, may fairly claim its share of usefulness in the past. The late Dr. Falconer said, partly in earnest and partly in jest—he being a member of it—" We make men for exportation." And there was much truth in the remark. ·

In 1819, another step in the order was effected. Up to that period, the masonic bodies had held their meetings in hotels—historic hotels, truly. But as these hotels changed in character, their adaptation to masonic purposes became more than questionable, and inasmuch as the members had increased, it was deemed desirable that a hall should be built, sufficiently capacious and dignified to accommodate the whole fraternity. In 1817, the foundation-stone was laid by the Duke of Sussex, and in 1819[3] the Lodge was consecrated by the same illus-

[1] In 1758, a Mr. Ferry was Master of the Lodge. This gentleman was the lessee of the Villa in Bathwick. His sister married Mr. Thomas Flower, of Melksham, who was the grandfather of **Mr. BRUGES FLOWER,** of Bath, an eminent botanist. Ferry died about 1783. In May of that year, his effects were sold by auction by a Mr. Plura. The priced catalogue is quite a curiosity in its way.

[2] The Hall built in York Street ; now the Friends' Meeting House.

[3] The following lines formed a part of the Newsmen's Address for 1820 ; they were from the pen of the Rev. Richard Warner, who was a member of the *craft* :—

Miss Prim—	*Bridget Soberside—*
"Of dear Freemasons who of late	" Fye, fye, Miss Prim ! you're much to blame,
Met, their new hall to dedicate ;	To speak with praise on such a theme.
And, headed by the Royal Grand	I can't endure the wicked *craturs*—
(Bowing, and holding hat in hand),	They're nothing more than woman-haters,
March'd to the Lodge, in sober state,	For, if they loved our sex, the fellows
Their secret craft to celebrate.	Would, readily, their secret tell us.
Oh ! how I wish they would but show it !	Besides, they carry swords and trowels,
I'd give the world and all to know it !"	To thrust into each other's bowels ;

trious personage. Whether the body was too ambitious and had over-rated its resources, or whether owing to vicissitudes not foreseen and not within its control, the hall was wrested from it in about the year 1831, and the various Lodges went each its own way, until fortune again favoured a combination of the several Lodges, who now meet in a hall, once the Theatre, then the Catholic Chapel, in Orchard Street.[1]

THE EARL OF SALISBURY.—The history of Bath is honourably associated with the Cecils. The visit of Queen Elizabeth, in 1574, seems to have stimulated the generosity of many of her personal friends and courtiers, who became benefactors of the city. Thomas, Earl of Essex, paid the cost of glazing the clerestory windows on the north side of the Abbey choir; **Lord Burleigh** and his steward and friend, **Thomas Bellot** (afterwards his executor), enclosed and fitted up the choir for Divine Service. Bellot expended, moreover, £60 for repairing and glazing the great east window in masonic fashion, which remained for the most part until it was replaced by the present noble window in 18 . He also gave £200 towards finishing the south transept. Britton says the church was then re-consecrated, but this is very doubtful.   Bellot built and endowed the hospital known after his name, and he seems to have been the esteemed friend and adviser of Lord Burleigh's two distinguished sons, the first Earl of Exeter and the younger, the Earl of Salisbury. The visit of the latter to Bath is not only interesting, but one of the most touching narratives on record. An account of it will be found in the Rev. Francis Peck's *Desiderata Curiosa*, vol. I., pages 206-7-8. Peck, who was born in Stamford, grew up to take an intelligent interest in the town and especially in the Cecil family, of whom he gives a most interesting account.

And in their lodge have irons hot,
To burn, or singe ; I know not what ! "

Tom Trudge—

"Lord, love your soul, my worthy dame !
You need not be in such a flame
About these honest mason brothers ;
They're harmless as our buried mothers.
The instruments you rave about,
Some upright principle point out,
Which every mason good and true,
Will steadily through life pursue.
Thus, in the trowel bright, you see
An emblem meet of industry ;
The sword speaks this intention plain—
With life he'll Church and King maintain ;
The apron shews he's always ready ;

The level marks him ever steady ;
And by the square is understood,
His views are just, his meaning good ;
That he'll from every wrong forbear,
And deal with all men on the square.
His secret, too, need not alarm,
Because it never can do harm.
It only teaches worthy ends—
To love as brothers, live as friends.
Ah ! would to heaven I could see
Such principles of unity
O'erspreading now my native land ;
And Peace and Order, hand in hand,
Marching, like masons in a band,
And sowing, wheresoe'er they went,
The seeds of virtue and content !
Were this the case, we soon should ken
A difference in our countrymen."

[1] The Royal Arch Chapters belonging to the Lodges, as well as the Christian Orders, or Orders of Chivalry, also hold their meetings in the same hall.

"Soon after this marriage the Earl's health began to fail, and in April, 1612, he sought the h ·aling waters of Bath. His journey thither must have been wearisome. His chaplain, Mr. John Bowles, who afterwards became Dean of Salisbury and Bishop of Rochester, has left us the touching record of his latter days. Those who may like to read it will find it at Peck's 'Desiderata Curiosa,' Vol. I., page 205 They went from Kensington the 28th of April, 'My lord being very wearie, fainte, and ill,' and arrived on May 3rd. 'On Fridaye, the 8th of May, my lord was exceedingly revived by the Bathe. The first thinge he did was the sacrifice wee offered to God of thanksgivinge.' But the amendment did not last; the end evidently was drawing nigh. Sir Michael Hickes, Sir Walter Cope, and Sir John Harington were at different times by his bedside, conversing on holy subjects, and concluding their meetings with prayer. 'Sir Michael Hickes took the speech that although it is just to accuse oneself yet that his Lordship was not to that degree a sinner, but that he might sooner find mercie at God's hendes than many other, yf wee consider their sinnes.' My Lord did hereupon replie, 'That he did confesse himself a great sinner. That his onelie trust was in the saveing mercies of Chryste. And that his resolution was not to commit sinne if God spared him lyfe. But that he was prepared to dye, and knewe that his sinnes, though red as scarlet, weare made as white as snowe in the bloud of Jesus Chryste.' He said to Sir Walter Cope, 'I forgive the whole worlde, Sir Walter, and I desire the whole world to forgive me.' To Sir John Harington, 'who dwells near the Bathe at Kelston, and who is sicke of a dead palsie : 'Sir John, nowe doth one cripple come to see and visit another. Death is the center to whome woe all doe move. Some diameter-wise, some circularly ; but all men must fall downe to the centre . . . . God, by His visitation, hath sweetened death to me, because He hath given me the light of His grace. And I knowe that though my sinnes were of a crimson or scarlet hue, yet they shall all be bathed in the bloud of the Lambe and shall be made whiter than snowe. I do not dispaire of life, and I do not feare death. God's will be done, I am prepared for it.'

"On the 30th of April Lord Salisbury was somewhat better, 'removed his lodgings, and was desirous to see the great Church (the Abbey) in Bathe, where ould Master Bellott, his father's steward, and one of his executors, had bestowed some money of his father's committed to his trust, and a great part likewise of his owne substance. The Church he much liked, and the liberalities of such benefactors as had brought it to see good perfection.' Adding, that he would himself bestowe some good remembrance to the finishing thereof. And because ould Master Bellott had spent all uppon charitable uses, and left nothinge for his kinsman, my lord in the Churche said, 'I give to my Servant Bellott £20 a-yeare during his natural life.'

"The Kensington Register styles Lady Clifford his sole daughter.[1] She was not his only child ; his son and successor, William Cecil, had married, two years before his sister, Catherine, youngest daughter of Thomas Howard, Earl of Suffolk. About this lady the dying man was evidently anxious : 'My daughter, Catherine, hath shee not received the Sacrament ?' Mr. Bowles replied, 'three times at my hands.' 'I am glad of it,' said he. 'Praie her uppon my blessing to be constant in true religion.

"My daughter Frances, I beseech God to blesse, and her husband (Henry Lord Clifford). And I beseeche the King to be good to my Lord of Cumberland for her sake, since he hath matched into my house. And I charge my daughter to love and honour her husband.' I replied, 'My lord, I have had often and private conference with your daughter Clifford, and though passion and affecions are sometymes violent in younge persons, yet I have found in her a good hart, reverend to God, desirous of knowledge, and readinge, and studyinge of Scriptures, and, I doubt not, but wheare religion goes before all morall and civill duty will follow after. 'I thanke God for this,' said my lord, 'and God blesse her.' . . . . To his son he said, after mutual teares, 'O my sonne, God blesse thee ! The blessings of Abraham, Isaak, and Jacob, light upon thee. My good sonne, embrace true religion, live

<hr>

[1] The Earl's only daughter to Lord Clifford.

honestlie and virtuously, loyallie to thy prince, and faithfully to thy wyfe.　Take heed, by all meau, of bloole, weather iu publiquo or private quarrell, and God will prosper thee in all thy wayes.' Soo they fell againe to weopinge, and my lord commaunded me to adinynister the Sacrameut unto him, which incontinently was performed.　And then he began to take a little rest . . . . :.' "On the 21st the sad family party started on their homeward journey.　Much must the dying mau have suffered from the rough joltings of the litter as he was slowly borne towards London. Even in delirium, which the quaint language of Mr. Bowles terms 'speaking of importinent things,' all Lord Salisbury's sayings ' Were of such thinges as tooke most impression in his myude. . . . . or repeatinge of sentouces and prayers out of the Book of Common Prnier, espuciallio this one sentence, 'And take not Thy Spirit from us.'　On Sunday, May 24th, Mr. Bowles preached at Marlborough ; after service it was plain that life was rapidly ebbing away.　All his speech was 'O Jesus ! O sweet Jesus !' and such short ejaculations as the weakness of his body did give him leave.　Soon after the happy spirit was released.　He cried, 'O Lord !' and so sinoked down, without groano, or sigh, or struggling.　At the same instant I joyned in prayer with him, that God would receive his soule and spirit . . . . And I doubt not but it was the passage of one Sabbath to another ; unto his eternal rest and quietness. ' Who shall separate us from the love of Christe, who hath prepared for us eternal life ?' "

LORD BYRON.

LORD BYRON.—In 1784, died Lady Conyers (in her own right), who was the divorced wife of the Marquis of Carmarthen.　Her second husband was that " mad Jack Byron," who was the father of the poet, Lord Byron.　The lady, it appears, caught a cold in attending a hunt before she had completed her recovery from the accouchement which gave birth to *Augusta Byron* (afterwards the *Hon. Mrs. Leigh*).　After the death of Lady Conyers, " Mad Jack " came to Bath in search of an heiress, and here, in the spring of 1785, he met with Miss Gordon, of Gight, in Aberdeenshire.　This lady was short in stature, plain in person, irascible in temper, and without any compensatory quality, except the not very large fortune of £25,000.　On the 13th of May, 1785, the wedding was cele- brated at St. Michael's Church, in the presence of Dr. and Mrs. Alexander Hay.[1] In 1802, Mrs. Byron, accompanied by her son, then a handsome boy of 16, again visited Bath.　Lady Riddle gave a great party and a masquerade at the Theatre, and the future poet appeared "in the costume of a Turkish boy, with a diamond crescent in his turban."[2][3]　He never came to Bath after.

[1] " John Byron, Esq., of the parish of St. Peter and St. Paul, in the city of Bath, a widower, and Catherine Gordon, of the parish of St. Michael, in the same city, spinster, were married in this church by license, this thirteenth day of May, in the year one thousand seven hundred and eighty-five, by me, John Chapman, Rector.　This marriage was solemnized between us—John Byron, Catherine Gordon.　In the presence of Sarah Hay, Alexander Hay."　The foregoing is taken from the Register of Marriages, by the present Rector of St. Michael's, the Rev. J. C. Burnett, M.A.

[2] " The Real Lord Byron."　By John Cordy Jeaffreson.

[3] A few years before Lady Byron's (the poet's wife) death, she contemplated settling in Bath, and was in treaty for Summerhill, now the residence of R. S. Blaine, Esq ; but it came to nothing.　She was known to the author years before in Gloucester, when she resided for a short time at " The Spa."　Years and sorrows had rendered her very wayward and difficult to please.

No. 30, MILSOM STREET.—It may be remembered that the author of *Memorable Houses* stated in his work that **WILLIAM COWPER** wrote *John Gilpin* in this house in 1782. It was shown conclusively that the poet could not have been in Bath at that period. The story, in truth, rested on no other evidence than that of mere gossip,[1] and it is now referred to merely to put on record a more permanent refutation of the story than is afforded by the newspaper controversy of 1881. Cowper was in Bath, as is well known from Southey's Life, (Vol. 1, p. 37,) when he wrote the "Lines on Finding the Heel of a Shoe" in the old Pump Room. This occurred in 1748, before Milsom Street was built. Where the poet lived there is no evidence to show, but it seems probable that his residence in Bath was of short duration.

No. 38, MILSOM STREET (Messrs. Lord's place of business) was the residence of **FIELD-MARSHAL, SIR ROBERT RICH.** Sir Robert died there in 1768.[2] He was made a Field-Marshal in 1757. His Brigadier's Commission was dated as far back as 1727, so that he must have been very aged when he died. There is no mention of his having been employed on active service. He was succeeded in the baronetcy and estates by his eldest son, General Rich, who lost an arm at Culloden; one of his daughters married George, first Lord Lyttelton (second wife). This baronetcy became extinct in 1785, and in 1791 was revived in the person of the *Rev. Charles Bostock*, who married the last baronet's only daughter, and assumed the name and arms of Rich, and in that year was created a baronet.

The building now used as **MESSRS. STUCKEY'S BANK** was the first built in the street, and no doubt at one time stood alone. The house on each side was evidently in design intended to represent a wing, and the whole seems to represent an undivided mansion of considerable size and grandeur. The three houses were built probably about the same time as Queen Square or a few years later, and in a similarly free Classical style.

There was another link connecting Lady Byron with Bath. The well-known Lord Ligonier, a former representative of Bath, had a son, at whose death the title became extinct. He married Lady Mary Henley, daughter of Lord Northington. After his death, she became Lady Wentworth, but had no children by either marriage. Lord Wentworth's sister married Mr. Milbanke, and was the mother of Lady Byron, who inherited all her uncle's property.

[1] The story is to the effect that, on a certain occasion, Sir T. Fowell Buxton went into the shop of the late Mr. Finigan, and during the process of having his hair cut, he informed Mr. Finigan that the house then occupied by him was the house in which Cowper wrote *John Gilpin.*

[2] Sir Robert Rich died in Feb., 1768. "The king, who learnt the news on coming from Richmond, would not dare tell he had written to Mr. Conway that he gave him the vacant regiment, and intended him a better—meaning the Blues, after Lord Ligonier."—*Horace Walpole.*

The north and south wings are marked with well-proportioned pediments, each of which is supported on four fluted Corinthian columns, standing on the basement-story. The central part now occupied by the Bank projects as a curved bay. The main cornice is well moulded and modillioned, and is supported over the central part on six fluted Corinthian columns matching those of the wings, and standing on a rusticated basement. Lion-headed masks break the plain frieze at intervals. Between the pedimented wings an open, balustraded, parapet crowns the front. The pediments are terminated by tazzas. The central windows of each group on the first floor and those also of the central part on the same line have well-carved friezes and cornices. The ceiling of the banking office shows some carefully-executed and well-designed plasterer's work. (See *Banks.*)

HENRY FIELDING.—The association of the name and fame of **HENRY FIELDING** with Bath is involved in some obscurity. There is scarcely a single statement made with regard to him that will bear investigation, or that is based upon any other foundation than conjecture. The most absurd and contradictory fables have been engrafted upon the local histories of Bath in connection with the famous novelist, until it has been impossible for those really interested in him, to know what to believe. And yet the story is simple enough; at any rate, with a little trouble it may be understood. It is not without interest, too, even though it fail to throw any fresh light upon the career and character of Fielding himself. The connection of Henry Fielding with Bath cannot be disassociated from that of his sister, **SARAH FIELDING**, the author of " DAVID SIMPLE " (Vols. 1 and 2, 1742; Vol. 3, 1752), "Familiar Letters between the Principal Characters in David Simple," 1747; "Xenophon's Memoribilia," translated from the original; "The Cry, a new Dramatic Fable," 3 vols., 1743; "Lives of Cleopatra and Octavia," 1 vol.; "History of Ophelia," 2 vols., 1785. The whole of these works, except the last (published ten years after her death), which was written in one of the old cottages in Bathwick Street, in which she lodged from 1757 until her death, were written in her cottage, in Church Street, Widcombe. This lady was the second daughter of General Fielding, and was a woman of singular energy, learning, and ability. It is more than probable that if she had not made Bath her residence, the name of her brother would never have been known in connection with it. She was born in 1710, and although there is nothing to show precisely when she settled in Bath, there is little doubt it was about 1739. She died in this city, 1768, and was buried in the Abbey, Bishop Hoadley having written her epitaph :—

" In this City died SARAH, second daughter of General HENRY* FIELDING,
    By his first wife, daughter of Judge Gould ;
        Whose writings will be known
    As incentives to virtue, and honour to her sex,
        When this marble shall be dust.
    She was born 1714, and died April, 1768.
    Her unaffected manners, candid mind,
    Her heart benevolent, and soul resigned,
    Were more her praise than all she knew or thought,
    Though Athens' wisdom to her sex she taught.

The Rev. *Dr. John Hoadley*, her Friend, for the honour of the Dead
and emulation of the Living, inscribes this deficient Memorial of her
virtues and accomplishments."

* General Fielding's name was EDMUND. Sarah Fielding was born 1710, NOT 1714.

There is no doubt that humble as was her home and straitened her means,
she, at various times, made the former an asylum for her brother, Henry, in his
distress and when not knowing where to flee from his creditors. That little cottage
in Church Lane, called "**WIDCOMBE LODGE**,"[1] which she occupied, was close
to the stately mansion called **WIDCOMBE HOUSE**,[2] at that time the residence of

[1] During the incumbency of the Rev. G. E. Tate in the Vicarage of Widcombe he enlarged
and greatly improved the Cottage, which was the oldest house in Church Lane. At the time it was
occupied by Sarah Fielding it stood alone, and in fact was the only one. The garden sloped down to the
borders of the garden of the "squire." The house was formerly called **YEW COTTAGE**.

[2] Widcombe House is a Palladian villa. of two storeys, situated close to the road from Widcombe
Hill to Prior Park, and said to have been designed by *Inigo Jones*.
    Prominence is given to the south front by a central Pediment, supported on each side on double,
fluted pilasters, of the Roman Ionic order. An oval window occupies the centre of the pediment,
from which clusters of well-grouped, festooned flowers and fruit hang from cornucopiæ. A deep and
boldly-moulded cornice and balustrade run round this and the west front, but only the main features
of the cornice are continued round the other two fronts. Over the pilastered angles of this south front
the cornice is broken by large shields, with scrolled surroundings.
    The chief entrance—under a well-designed door-casing, having a curved pediment—occupies
the central position of the south front. The grotesques carved on the key-stones of the windows are
characteristically good. The south front is marked by simplicity of fenestration and well-thought-out
detail. The west front is similar in its general detail, but it has been altered, about 35 years ago, by
General Clapham, by the addition of a canted bay-window, having stone balconies projecting from the
first-floor windows, and fluted Ionic pilasters across the angles, over which the main cornice breaks. A
terraced and balustraded walk completes the base of the building. The other fronts and offices have
no architectural character.
    The house is most beautifully situated, close to, and partly surrounded by, the extensive woods of
Prior Park ; a view of Ralph Allen's noble residence peeps out, to break the sky-line. The back
ground is made up of the picturesque and closely-contiguous west end of Widcombe Old Church and
tower, and the interesting farm-stead.
    The sloping lawn from the house, terminated by ornamental water, with its cascade and a belt
of shrouding trees, through which peeps of the valley of Bath can be seen, adds a great charm to this
beautiful place.
    A difference of opinion exists as to the architect of the house. It has been attributed to Inigo

the **BENNETS**,[1] whose crest still surmounts the two pedestals at the entrance gates, and whose descendants still survive in Somersetshire.   Mr. Monkland says—" A gentleman of the name of Bayly [in Fielding's time], I have ascertained, then lived at the house close to the church at Widcombe." This is certainly erroneous.   Mr. Monkland must have mistaken the name ; no person named Bayly having at any time occupied Widcombe House.   The popular impression is that Fielding was a regular resident in the house at Twerton called " Fielding Lodge," and that, being a member of a noble house, he must have been vain enough to erect his crest over the front door.   Now Fielding never remained long in Bath, either when he abode with his sister, or on the occasion when he occupied the house in question.   The crest over the door is not the Fielding crest at all.   It bears no resemblance to the Denbigh crest, either the earlier or the later one used by the Fielding family.   The Denbigh crest in the time of Henry Fielding was the Imperial Double-Headed Eagle, denoting the Imperial line from which the family is descended.[2]   For some reason, about the beginning of the present century, the family changed the crest, and it is now the bird called the *Nuthatch*, perched upon and pecking a hazel branch.   Sir B. Burke   says :—" I have traced back the Nuthatch to a remote period among the family records."   As regards Fielding's connection with Twerton, Graves, in his personal reminiscences, says :—" Mr. Fielding, also, who then lived at Twerton (in the first house on the right hand, with a *spread eagle* over the door, now inhabited by Mr. Williams, a respectable brewer)."   So that most persons, on looking for the " first house on the right hand side, with a spread eagle over the door," would be puzzled.   Since Graves wrote many houses have been built, which fill up the space between the supposed house

---

Jones, and it is worthy of his genius.   Free from the smoke of the city, it preserves the bright, pristine appearance of early youth rather than the premature decrepitude of old age, induced by exposure to the dust and dirt of the town, and hence it may be really of a somewhat earlier date than is generally supposed.

[1] Ralph Allen left a legacy to Bennet's daughter, Anne, of £100.

[2] " Our immortal Fielding is a younger branch of the house of the Earls of Denbigh, descended from Rodolph, in the ninth century, Count of Hapsburgh.   Far different have been the fortunes of the English and the German branches of the house of Hapsburgh.   The former, the Knights and Sheriffs of Leicestershire, have slowly risen to the dignity of the Peerage.   The latter, the Emperors of Germany and the Kings of Spain, have invaded the treasures of the Old, and threatened the liberties of the New World.   The successors of Charlemagne may despise their brethren of England ; but the Romance of Tom Jones, that exquisite picture of human manners, shall survive the Palace of the Escurial and the Imperial Eagle of the house of Austria."—*Gibbon.*   [With reference to this Thackeray says, " There can be no gainsaying the sentence of this great judge.   To have your name mentioned by Gibbon, is like having it written on the dome of St. Peter's.   Pilgrims from all the world admire and behold it."]

and the city boundaries. Accompanied by a friend, the author has twice carefully explored this region, and having regard to the character of the buildings, what they are and what they may have been, on the line of road indicated by Graves and confirmed by the old lines of territorial demarcation, it is clear that the cottage called "Fielding Lodge" is the veritable dwelling of Fielding, as it certainly is the house in which the brewer, Williams,[1] lived. The house itself is in a degenerate condition. There are evidences of its having been much larger and more luxurious than it is at present. At the back of the house was a large garden, and in the front extended a long row of poplars. The "Spread Eagle"[2] in Fielding's time was most probably in a perfect state ; at present the bird has lost its beak, and the right wing is broken off close to the body, and of the left very little is *left*. The history of the crest is lost in obscurity, nor is it easy to tell whose it was, nor by whom it was placed in so singular a position. It rests on an *abacus* of stone, supported by well-proportioned brackets. Fielding was by no means likely to have placed his own crest over the door, and still less likely that of some other person. There is no doubt that Fielding paid frequent visits to Bath, and that his object was to visit his sister, through whom he was introduced to Ralph Allen.

His sister, Sarah Fielding, had long been the friend of Allen, before even Prior Park was built[3] ; and it was to her, not her brother's widow, as is generally supposed, to whom he bequeathed a legacy of £100. Graves says that Allen allowed her £100 a-year in his lifetime. She was a lady not only of remarkable ability, but of singular moral worth, self-reliance, and individuality of character, and there is no doubt that she exercised considerable influence over her brother, between whom and herself a very strong bond of affection existed. Graves, it appears, never saw Fielding, but he says that he " dined there (Prior Park) more than once with Mrs. Fielding, the author of *David Simple.*" But he evidently

---

[1] This Mr. Williams established a brewery in Bath, which ultimately developed into the important "Ambury Brewery." He was the ancestor of the Williamses, who were highly-respected citizens, some of whom lived at Lyncombe House, thirty-five years ago. This Lyncombe House was formerly the Lyncombe Spa. The supply of water having ceased some sixty years ago, owing, it is supposed, to some interception of the spring, the building was converted into the present mansion. (See Wood's Bath, 2nd edit., vol. I., pp. 79—80).

[2] The figure has been frequently described as a phœnix rising out of a mural crown, and this was the author's impression on first examining it, but on a second and more careful examination its real character became manifest.

[3] Wood, who built Prior Park, and who gives the reasons why it was built, together with many minute details, gives no dates in connection with the building. Collinson says it was completed about 1743, and most modern writers repeat that years before that period, and, during his visits to Bath, Fielding was the guest of Allen at his city residence. It is a common error, and even Mr. Kilvert falls into it, to connect Prior Park so exclusively with Allen's liberality. Allen's generous, almost lavish, hospitality began years before Prior Park was built ; it was proverbial when he occupied his beautiful mansion built for him in Bath by Wood.

knew little of Fielding's personal movements in Bath. It is true, no doubt, that Fielding visited frequently at Prior Park, and previously at Allen's town-house. It is almost certain that *Tom Jones*, which was published in 1749, was being written about the period when the author lived at Twerton, but it is doubtful whether a line of it was written *there*. It is more likely that *Joseph Andrews* (published in 1742), or portions of it, were written in the Cottage in Church Street, two years before Sarah Fielding wrote, or before she published vols. 1 and 2 of *David Simple.* No dedication appeared to *Joseph Andrews.* Mr. Kilvert quotes a passage from Lawrence's *Life of Fielding* to the effect that Allen at his decease bequeathed an annuity of £100 a-year to Fielding's family. Allen's will contains no such provision. Mr. Kilvert also quotes a letter, written by Derrick (the M.C.) in 1763, and published in his collected works, in which he says, "You cannot forget that *Tom Jones* was dedicated to Ralph Allen, to whom he was a great friend." No correction is made of this error.

Tom Jones was dedicated to the *Hon. George Lyttelton, Esq.*, one of the Lords Commissioners of the Treasury :—"To you, sir, it is owing that this history was ever begun. It was by your desire that I first thought of such a composition. So many years have since passed, that you may have perhaps forgotten this circumstance ; but your desires are to me in the nature of commands, and the impression of them is never to be erased from my memory," etc.

Amelia was dedicated to *Ralph Allen, Esq. :—*" Sir,—The following book is sincerely designed to promote the cause of virtue, and to expose some of the most glaring evils, as well public as private, which at present infest the country ; though there is scarce, as I remember, a single stroke of satire aimed at any one person throughout the whole," etc.

In Mr. Kilvert's Essay on Allen, he prints in the Notes a letter from that accomplished gentleman, the late Rev. Joseph Hunter. The letter is based on certain anecdotes related to him by the late Mr. Howse, of Lyncombe Hall.[1] One of these anecdotes had reference to Fielding. The letter bears date Jan. 21, 1857, which in all probability was many years after Mr. Howse (a careful chronicler) had told the story to Mr. Hunter, whose memory, on which he seemed solely to have relied, evidently failed him, inasmuch as, though one of the most accurate of men, the letter is erroneous in almost every particular. He says, in

[1] Lyncombe Hall is said to have been the residence of King James II. for a short period after his abdication. Hence it was called King James's Palace. So goes the tradition. But whatever the fact may be, it is quite clear King James never could have lived there after his abdication. It is more probable that he might have occupied it as a kind of country house during his visit, when he was accompanied by his Queen, Mary of Modena, even though he then ostensibly occupied the Royal apartments in the Westgate. This "King James's Palace," from the middle of the last century to its close, was, with the grounds, used as a place of public entertainment.

reference to Mr. Howse, he had a good deal of Bath anecdote, " which I should
have done well to have preserved in writing, and not left to pass away with the
life of him whose memory was perhaps the only depository of it. You are now
the Bath bibliographer, and I will tell you another of his (Howse's) stories, not
supported, however, by anything in the lately published volume on the Life of
Fielding. His wife died at Twerton, and on the evening of the day a friend met
him at a party. ' I am very glad to see you, Mr. Fielding, for there was a report
in Bath that your wife died this morning.' ' It is very true,' was the reply, ' and
that is the very reason that I have come into town to join the pleasure party.' "
Now, if this story were true, it would imply that Fielding was a cold-blooded,
heartless brute ; it would also imply that every writer who has said anything
about Fielding has wholly misrepresented the nature and disposition of the man.
Without exception, one and all have agreed that, in spite of his follies, his dissi-
pation, and his vices, he loved his first wife, " *Sophia Western*,"[1] with a
tenderness and a deep passionate affection, such as few men can feel. The very
nature, the intensity, the vehemence of the man, were all concentrated in his love
for his wife. "The fortitude of mind with which he met all the other calamities
of life deserted him on this most trying occasion," says Murphy, his biographer.
The true story, or at any rate the more probable story, is this. It rests only on
oral authority, but it comes from a man who was not only careful to note all his
facts with care and to state them with great clearness, but who was better
acquainted with the literary history of that period in Bath than any man of the
present century—the late Rev. Edward Mangin. He was the editor of an edition
of Richardson's works, and a most diligent collector of every fact relating to
him and his contemporaries. The story, which he related from notes to the

---

[1] Fielding's first wife was a Miss Charlotte Cradock, of Salisbury, a lady of great worth and
equal beauty. She was the heroine, " Sophia Western," in *Tom Jones*, and the prototype of
Amelia. The popular supposition that Squire Western and his daughter had their counterparts in the
Mr. Bennet and his daughter, who occupied Widcombe House, is without any sort of foundation.
The character of *Squire Western* was a pure creation, and it is hardly possible to believe that any
gentleman, even of that day, could have been so low and brutal as Fielding depicts *Squire Western*.
If he were a type of any *gentleman* that could have been found at that period, he must have been
an exception. Bennet, at any rate, was a gentleman in habit, taste, and feeling, and even if it
were not so clearly proved that his wife, Charlotte Cradock, was the heroine in whom he delighted,
it would be necessary to seek her elsewhere than in the unassuming and unpretending Anne Bennet.
Speaking generally, it may be that the Somersetshire squire was given to sporting, and that his
habits and language occasionally were coarse ; but it is contrary to fact that he spoke in a low,
vulgar, Somersetshire vernacular, worse than that of the uneducated boor of the previous century.
The very worst and most illiterate county squire of the last century never talked as Fielding makes
Squire Western talk :—" It's well for un I could not get at un : I'd a liked un ; I'd a spoiled his
caterwauling ; I'd a taught the son of a w——e to meddle with meat for his master. He shan't
ever have a morsel of meat of mine, or a varden to buy it. If she will ha' un, one smock shall
be her portion. I'd sooner give my estate to the sinking fund, that it may be sent to Hanover to
corrupt the nation with." When Allworthy says he is sorry for it, the squire retorts in language
which is abominable in its vulgarity, and, what is more, is not the least bit like *Zummerzet*, which

writer, is this :—Mr. Mangin "took up" his residence in Bath in 1800, and he then formed an intimate acquaintance with a gentleman whose father was personally acquainted with Fielding, and who visited him in Church Street at his sister's house. Meeting him one day unexpectedly, not long after the death of Mrs. Fielding, *who died in London*, he said, ' Ah, Mr. Fielding, I am surprised to see you.' ' Yes,' said Fielding, ' having lost my wife, I have come to Bath to dissipate,' using the word *dissipate* in the obvious sense of change of scene—a change from which he would derive solace and comfort, under the care and wise direction of his excellent sister. As the other inaccuracies do not concern this narrative, they are passed over, but as they chiefly relate to the disposition of Ralph Allen's property, a copy of his Will will be given in the Appendix (1).

Much controversy has existed as to the character of Allworthy and the scenes described in *Tom Jones* and *Amelia*. Most people who are interested in Fielding seem anxious to prove or believe too much. Whilst there can be no doubt that in delineating the character of "Squire Allworthy," Fielding had in his mind the salient points in the disposition and generous nature of Allen, there is nothing to show that either in any of the rest of the characters, the scenery, or the local circumstances of the period, Fielding was describing anything that he had not created out of the depths of his own consciousness. Kilvert quoted a passage from Graves's Anecdotes, which leaves no doubt that Allen was the

remains to-day just what it was when " Tom Coryat* " wrote his *Crudities* and his paraphrase of Bladud's story, about 1608 :—

> "*Lud Hudibras*, a meazle voule, did zend his *zun* a graezing,
> Who vortuend hither for to cum, and geed his pigs zum peazun.
> Poor *Bladud*, he was manger grown ; his dad, which zum call vather,
> Zet *Bladud* pig, and pig *Bladud*, and zo they ved together,"
> Then *Bladud* did the Pigs invect, who, grunting, ran away,
> And vound whot Waters presently, which made him fresh and gay.
> *Bladud* was not zo grote a Vool, but zeeing what Pig nid doe,
> He Beath'd and Wash'd, and Rins'd, and Beath'd, from Noddle
>   down to Toe.
> *Bladud* was now (Gramercy Pig !) a delicate vine Boy,
> So whome he trudges to his Dad, to be his only Joy ;
> And then he built this gawdy Town, and sheer'd his Beard Spade-ways,
> Which Voke accounted then a Grace, though not so now a-Days.
> Thwo thowsand and vive hundred Years, and Thirty-vive to That,
> Zince *Bladud's* Zwine did looze their Greaze, which we *Moderns* cal Vat.
> About that Time, it was alzo, that *Ahob's* Zuns were hanged,
> A *Jezabel*, their Mam, (curz'd Deel !) caus'd *Naboth* be stone-hanged,
> Chee cud zay more, but cham aveared, Voke will account this Vable,
> O Invidlus ! if yee woon not me, yet chee pray believe the Table."

* Thomas Coryat, son of George Coryat, Rector of Odcumbe, in Somersetshire. He invented dinner-forks, discoursed upon all kinds of subjects, introduced, if he did not invent, umbrellas, and clearly understood "pure" Zummerzet. Chapman provided him with an epitaph, which is, it need scarcely be added, a joke. " I here present you with a Legendary Epitaph, and, for caution, would not have you tye your faith too much upon it, although (I assure you) it is *Purii-per-pale*, as our West-Country Housewives order their pudding, with Vatt and Lean ; this my countryman (to my knowledge) dyed in *East-India*, on which Peter Hatch bestowed this Epitaph—
            ' *Here lyes Tom Coryat, Odcombe's Pride,
            Who came to Surat and there he dy'd.*' "

immortal Allworthy :—" In *Joseph Andrews* that character is introduced as thus referring to the good deeds and celebrated mansion of Mr. Allen : Some gentlemen of our cloth report charitable actions done by their lords and masters ; and I have heard Squire Pope, the great poet, at my lady's table, tell stories of a man that lived at a place called Ross, and another at the Bath, one Al— Al—. I forget his name, but it is in the book of verses. This gentleman had built up a stately house, too, which the Squire likes very well. But his charity is seen further than his house, though it stands on a hill ; aye, and brings him more honour, too." Kilvert also quotes the story that Allen at his death left an *annuity* to Fielding's children of £100 a year each. He left to three of Fielding's children a legacy of £100 each. Though Fielding was a frequent guest at Prior Park, Graves never met him there. Pope, Warburton, Richardson, and others were guests at the same time. Hurd, before he became a bishop, met him once, but the frigid, cold, and dignified Hurd thought Fielding a vulgar fellow. What Fielding thought of Hurd will never be known, but it is not difficult to conceive what two such dissimilar spirits would think of each other. The gay, rollicking humour of Fielding would turn into stone a man like Hurd, and this, except so far as good breeding might restrain him, would provoke Fielding into further sallies of wit and fun.

The author does not presume to offer any opinion or criticism upon the genius and works of Fielding. He gives extracts from the writings of the ablest critics who have analysed the works of this wonderful man with more or less power. There is a certain agreement amongst them all, but they differ upon the tendency of the stories and the moral to be deduced from them. Most readers will, perhaps, attach the greatest value to the criticism of Thackeray, the very ablest novelist of these later days, and who, therefore, is best qualified to judge of the creations of a genius in many respects so similar to his own.

MR. RUSSELL LOWELL,

The United States Minister, in unveiling a memorial bust to Fielding, at Taunton, in 1883, which has been placed in the Shirehall of that town, spoke of Fielding as not only an original writer, but an originator :[1] "This is not the place or occasion for a critical estimate of Fielding. Even could one add anything of value to what has been already said by competent persons, if there were a recognised standard in criticism as in apothecaries' measures, so that by adding a grain of praise to this scale or taking away a scruple of blame from that, we could make the balance manifestly even in the eyes of all men, it might be worth while to weigh Hannibal, but when each of us stamps his own weights and warrants the impartiality of his own scales, perhaps the experiment may be wisely foregone. Let it suffice here to state generally the reasons for which we set a high value

[1] This word is the key to all fair criticism upon Fielding. Sir Joshua Reynold's said, Fielding was voted low, and, above all, was tabooed to ladies who value their reputation for propriety. *The novels of the day were wretched farragos of stilted sentimentality and high-flown commonplace.*

on this man whose bust we unveil to-day. Since we are come together not to judge but only to commemorate, perhaps it would be enough to say in justification of to-day's ceremony that Fielding was a man of genius, for it is hardly once in a century, if so often, that a whole country catches so rare and shy a specimen of the native fauna, and proportionally more seldom that a county is so lucky. But Fielding was something more even than this. It is not extravagant to say that he marks an epoch, and that we date from him the beginning of a consciously new form of literature. It was not without reason that Byron, expanding a hint given somewhere by Fielding himself, called him ' The prose Homer of human nature.' He had more than the superficial knowledge of literature which no gentleman's head should be without. He knew it as a craftsman knows the niceties and traditions of his craft. He saw that since the epic in verse ceased to be recited in the market-places, it had been an anachronism that since Milton every epic had been born as dead as the Pharaohs—more dead, if possible—as dead as the ' Columbiad ' of Joel Barlow and the ' Charlemagne ' of Lucien Bonaparte are to us. He saw that the novel of actual life was to replace it, and he set himself deliberately (after having convinced himself experimentally in Parson Adams that he could create character) to produce an epic on the lower and more neighbourly level of prose. However opinions may differ as to the other merits of ' Tom Jones,' they are unanimous as to its harmony of design and masterliness of structure. Fielding, then, was not merely, in my judgment at least, an original writer, but an originator. He has the merit, whatever it may be, of inventing the realistic novel, as it is called. I do not mean to say that there had been no stories professedly of real life before, but before Fielding it seems to me that the real life formed rather the scenic background than the substance, and that the characters are after all merely players who represent certain types rather than the living types themselves. Fielding, as a novelist, drew from nature and not from artificial life. When I read ' Gil Blas ' I do not become part of the story. I listen to an agreeable storyteller who relates and describes, and I wait to hear what is going to happen ; but in Fielding I wait to see what people are going to do and say, and I can half guess what will happen, because I knew them, and what they are, and what they are likely to do. They are no longer images, but actual beings. Nothing can persuade me, for example, that I do not know the sound of Squire Western's voice. Fielding did not, and could not, idealize, his object being exact truth ; but he realised the actual life around him as none had done before and few since. As a creator of characters that are actuated by a motive power within themselves, and that are so livingly real as to become our familiar acquaintance, he is among the greatest. Parson Adams is excellent, and has had a numerous progeny ; but I think that even he is inferior in originality, in coherence, and in the entire keeping of look, speech, motive, and action to Squire Western, who is, indeed, one of the most simple, perfect creatures of genius. If he has been less often copied than Parson Adams, may it not be because he is a more finished work of art, and therefore more difficult to copy ? I need not expatiate on the simple felicity and courteous ease of his style, the unobtrusive, gentlemanly clothing of a thought, as clear as it is often profound, or on the good nature of his satire, in which he reminds one of Chaucer, or on the subtle gravity of his irony, more delicate than that of Swift, and therefore, perhaps, even more deadly. I will only say that I think it less perfect because more obviously intentional in ' Jonathan Wild ' than in such masterpieces as the account of Captain Blifil's death, and the epitaph upon his tomb, where it seems most casual and inadvertent.

I must not forget to say a word of his dialogues, which (except where he wishes to show off his attainment in classical criticism, as in some chapters of ' Amelia ') is altogether so admirable, spirited, and characteristic that it makes us wonder at his failure as a dramatist. We may read Fielding's character clearly in his books, for it was not complex, but especially in his ' Voyage to Lisbon,' where he reveals it as artless inadvertence. He was a loving, thoughtful husband, a tender father, a good brother, a useful and sagacious magistrate. He was courageous, gentle, thoroughly conscious of his own dignity as a gentleman, and able to make that dignity respected. If we seek for a single characteristic which more than any other would sum him up, we should say that it was his absolute manliness—a manliness in its type English from top to toe. It is eminently fitting, therefore, that the reproduction of his features which I am about to unveil should be from the hand of a woman."

GEORGE ELLIOT.

" A great historian, as he insisted on calling himself, who had the happiness to be dead a hundred and twenty years ago, and so to take his place among the colossi whose huge legs our living pettiness is observed to walk under, glories in his copious remarks and digressions as the least inimitable part of his work, and especially in those initial chapters to the successive books of his history, where he seems to bring his arm-chair to the proscenium and chat with us in all the lusty ease of his fine English. But Fielding lived when the days were longer (for time, like money, is measured by our needs), when summer afternoons were spacious, and the clock ticked slowly in the winter evenings. We belated historians must not linger after his example ; and if we did so it is probable that our chat would be thin and lager, as if delivered from a camp-stool or a parrot-house. I, at least, have so much to do in unravelling certain human lots, and seeing how they are woven and interwoven, that all the light I can command must be concentrated on this particular web, and not dispersed over that tempting range of relevancies called the universe."[1]

TAINE.[2]

" One day Garrick begged him to cut down an awkward scene, and told him ' that a repulse would flurry him so much, he should not be able to do justice to the part.' ' If the scene is not a good one, let them find that out,' said Fielding ; just as was foreseen, the house made a violent uproar, and the performer tried to quell it by retiring to the green-room, where the author was supporting his spirits with a bottle of champagne. ' What is the matter, Garrick ? are they hissing me now ?' ' Yes, just the same passage that I wanted you to retrench.' ' Oh,' replied the author, ' I did not give them credit for it : they have found it out, have they ?' In this easy manner he took all mischances. He went ahead without feeling the bruises much, like a confident man, whose heart expands and whose skin is thick. When he inherited some money, he feasted, gave dinners to his neighbours, kept a pack of hounds and a lot of magnificent lackeys in yellow livery. In three years he had spent it all ; but courage remained, he finished his law studies, prepared a voluminous Digest of the Statutes at Large, in two folio volumes, which remained unpublished, became a magistrate, destroyed bands of robbers, and earned in the most insipid of labours ' the dirtiest money upon earth.' "

" Such a man was sure to dislike Richardson. He who loves expansive and liberal nature, drives from him like foes the solemnity, sadness, and pruderies of the Puritans. His first literary work was to caricature Richardson. His first hero, Joseph, is the brother of Pamela, and resists the proposals of his mistress, as Pamela does those of her master. The temptation, touching in the case of a girl, becomes comical in that of a young man, and the tragic turns into the grotesque."

[1] *Middlemarch, vol. i., chap. xv.*   [2] *Critical Essays, vol. iii.*

"Mr. Joseph Andrews, after leaving Lady Booby, is felled to the ground, left naked in a ditch, for dead ; a stage-coach came by ; a lady objects to receive a naked man inside ; and the gentlemen, 'though there were several greatcoats about the coach,' could not spare them ; the coachman, who had two greatcoats spread under him, refused to lend either, lest they should be made bloody. This is but the outset ; judge of the rest. Joseph and his friend, the good Parson Adams, give and receive a vast number of cuffs ; blows resound ; cans of pig's blood are thrown at their heads : dogs tear their clothes to pieces ; they lose their horse. Joseph is so good-looking, that he is assailed by the maid-servant, 'obliged to take her in his arms and to shut her out of the room ;' they have never any money ; they are threatened with being sent to prison. Yet they go on in a merry fashion, like their brothers in Fielding's other novels, Captain Booth and Tom Jones. These hailstorms of blows, these tavern brawls, this noise of broken warming-pans and basins flung at heads, this medley of incidents and downpouring of mishaps, combine to make the most joyous music. All these honest folk fight well, walk well, eat well, drink still better. It is a pleasure to observe these potent stomachs ; roast-beef goes down into them as to its natural place. Let us not say that these good arms practise too much on their neighbours' skins : the neighbours' hides are tough, and always heal quickly. Decidedly life is a good thing, and we will go along with Fielding, smiling by the way, with a broken head and a bellyful."

"Shall we merely laugh ? There are many things to be seen on our journey : the senti-ment of nature is a talent, like the understanding of certain rules ; and Fielding, turning his back on Richardson, opens up a domain as wide as that of his rival. What we call nature is this brood of secret passions, often malicious, generally vulgar, always blind, which tremble and fret within us, ill-covered by the cloak of decency and reason under which we try to disguise them ; we think we lead them, and they lead us ; we think our actions our own, they are theirs. They are so many, so strong, so interwoven, so ready to rise, break forth, be carried away, that their movements elude all our reasoning and our grasp. This is Fielding's domain ; his art and pleasure, like Molière's, in lifting a corner of the cloak."

"Out of such he creates his chief characters. He has none more life-like than these, more broadly sketched in bold and dashing outline, with a more wholesome colour. If sober people like Allworthy remain in a corner of his vast canvas, characters full of natural impulse, like Western, stand out with a relief and brightness, never seen since Falstaff. Western is a country squire, a good fellow in the main, but a drunkard, always in the saddle, full of oaths, ready with coarse language, blows, a sort of dull carter, hardened and excited by the brutality of the race, the wildness of a country life, by violent exercise, by abuse of coarse food and strong drink, full of English and rustic pride and prejudice, having never been disciplined by the constraint of the world, because he lives in the country ; nor by that of education, since he can hardly read ; nor of reflection, since he cannot put two ideas together ; nor of authority, because he is rich and a justice of the peace, and given up, like a noisy and creaking weathercock, to every gust of passion. When contradicted, he grows red, foams at the mouth, wishes to thrash someone. 'Doff thy clothes.' They are even obliged to stop him by main force. He hastens to go to Allworthy to complain of Tom Jones, who has dared to fall in love with his daughter. His daughter tries to reason with him ; he storms. Then she speaks of tenderness and obedience ; he leaps about the room for joy, and tears come to his eyes. Then she recommences her prayers, he grinds his teeth, clenches his fists, stamps his feet : 'I am determined upon this match, and ha him you

shall, damn me, if shat unt. Damn me, if shat unt, though dost hang thyself the next morning.'
He can find no reason ; he can only tell her to be a good girl. He contradicts himself,
defeats his own plans ; is like a blind bull, which buts to right and left, doubles on his path,
touches no one, and paws the ground. At the least sound he rushes head foremost, offensively,
not knowing why. His ideas are only starts or transports of flesh and blood. Never has the
animal so completely covered and absorbed the man. It makes him grotesque ; he is so natural
and so brute-like : he allows himself to be led, and speaks like a child. He says : ' I don't
know how 'tis, but, Allworthy, you make me do always just as you please ; and yet I have as
good an estate as you, and am in the commission of the peace just as yourself.' Nothing holds
or lasts with him ; he is impulsive in everything ; he lives but for the moment. Rancour,
interest, no passions of long continuance affect him. He embraces people whom he just before
wanted to knock down. Everything with him disappears in the fire of the momentary passion,
which floods his brain, as it were, in sudden waves, and drowns the rest."

" . . . . Harkee, Allworthy, I'll bet thee five pounds to a crown, we have a boy to-
morrow nine months. But prithee, tell me what wut ha ? Burgundy, champagne, or what ?
For, please Jupiter, we'll make a night on't."

" Pardon him for having muscles, nerves, senses, and that overflow of anger or ardour
which urges forward animals of a noble breed. But he will let himself be beaten till the blood
flows, before he betrays a poor gamekeeper. He will pardon his mortal enemy readily, from sheer
kindness, and will send him money secretly. He will be loyal to his mistress, and will be faithful
to her, spite of all offers, in the worst destitution, and without the least hope of winning her. He
will be liberal with his purse, his trouble, his sufferings, his blood ; he will not boast of it ; he will
have neither pride, vanity, affectation, nor dissimulation ; bravery and kindness will abound in
his heart, as good water in a good spring. He may be stupid like Captain Booth, a gambler
even, extravagant, unable to manage his affairs, liable one day through temptation to be unfaith-
ful to his wife ; but he will be so sincere in his repentance, his error will be so involuntary, he
will be so carefully, genuinely tender, that she will love him exceedingly, and in good truth he will
deserve it. He will be a nurse to her when she is ill, behave as a mother to her ; he will himself
see to her lying-in ; he will feel towards her the adoration of a lover, always, before all the world,
even before Miss Matthews, who seduced him. He says, ' If I had the world, I was ready to
lay it at my Amelia's feet ; and so, heaven knows, I would ten thousand worlds.' He weeps like
a child on thinking of her ; he listens to her like a little child. ' I believe I am able to recollect
much the greatest part (of what she uttered) ; for the impression is never to be effaced from my
memory.' He dressed himself ' with all the expedition imaginable, singing, whistling, hurrying,
attempting by every method to banish thought,' and galloped away, whilst his wife was asleep,
because he cannot endure her tears. In this soldier's body, under this brawler's thick breastplate,
there is a true woman's heart, which melts, which a trifle disturbs, when she whom he loves is in
question ; timid in its tenderness, inexhaustible in devotion, in trust, in self-denial, in the communication of its feelings. When a man possesses this, overlook the rest ; with all his excesses
and his follies, he is better than your well-dressed devotees."

" We tire at last of your fisticuffs and tavern bills. You flounder too readily in cowhouses,
among the ecclesiastical pigs of Parson Trulliber. We would fain see you have more regard for
the modesty of your heroines ; wayside accidents raise their tuckers too often ; and Fanny,

Sophia, Mrs. Heartfree, may continue pure, yet we cannot help remembering the assaults which have lifted their petticoats. You are so coarse yourself, that you are insensible to what is atrocious. You persuade Tom Jones falsely, yet for an instant, that Mrs. Waters, whom he has made his mistress, is his own mother, and you leave the reader during a long time buried in the shame of this supposition. And then you are obliged to become unnatural in order to depict love; you can give but constrained letters ; the transports of your Tom Jones are only the author's phrases. For want of ideas he declaims odes. You are only aware of the impetuosity of the senses, the upwelling of the blood, the effusion of tenderness, but you are unacquainted with nervous exaltation and poetic rapture. Man, such as you conceive him, is a good buffalo ; and, perhaps, he is the hero required by a people which gives itself the nickname 'John Bull.'"

THACKERAY.[1]

" As a picture of manners, the novel of 'Tom Jones' is indeed exquisite : as a work of construction quite a wonder : the by-play of wisdom ; the power of observation ; the multiplied felicitous turns and thoughts ; the varied character of the great Comic Epic ; keep the reader in a perpetual admiration and curiosity. But against Mr. Thomas Jones himself we have a right to put in a protest, and quarrel with the esteem the author evidently has for that character. Charles Lamb says finely of Jones, that a single hearty laugh from him ' clears the air '—but then it is in a certain state of the atmosphere. It might clear the air when such personages as Blifil or Lady Bellaston poison it. But I fear very much that (except until the very last scene of the story), when Mr. Jones enters Sophia's drawing-room, the pure air there is rather tainted with the young gentleman's tobacco-pipe and punch. I can't say that I think Mr. Jones a virtuous character ; I can't say but that I think Fielding's evident liking and admiration for Mr. Jones, shows that the great humourist's moral sense was blunted by his life, and that here in Art and Ethics, there is a great error. If it is right to have a hero whom we may admire, let us at least take care that he is admirable : if, as is the plan of some authors (a plan decidedly against their interests, be it said), it is propounded that there exists in life no such being, and therefore that in novels, the picture of life, there should appear no such character ; then Mr. Thomas Jones becomes an admissible person, and we examine his defects and good qualities, as we do those of Parson Thwackum, or Miss Seagrim. But a hero with a flawed reputation ; a hero spunging for a guinea ; a hero who can't pay his landlady, and is obliged to let his honour out to hire, is absurd, and his claim to heroic rank untenable. I protest against Mr. Thomas Jones holding such rank at all. I protest even against his being considered a more than ordinary young fellow, ruddy-cheeked, broad-shouldered, and fond of wine and pleasure. He would not rob a church, but that is all ; and a pretty long argument may be debated, as to which of these old types, the spendthrift, the hypo-crite, Jones and Blifil, Charles and Joseph Surface,—is the worst member of society and the most deserving of censure. The prodigal Captain Booth is a better man than his predecessor Mr. Jones, in so far as he thinks much more humbly of himself than Jones did : goes down on his knees, and owns his weakness, and cries out, ' Not for my sake, but for the sake of my pure and sweet and beautiful wife Amelia, I pray you, O critical reader, to forgive me.' That stern moralist regards him from the bench (the judge's practice out of court is not here the question), and says, ' Captain Booth, it is perfectly true that your life has been disreputable, and that on many occa-

¹ *English Humourists.*

sions you have shown yourself to be no better than a scamp—you have been tippling at the tavern, when the kindest and sweetest lady in the world has cooked your little supper of boiled mutton and awaited you all the night ; you have spoilt the little dish of boiled mutton thereby, and caused pangs and pains to Amelia's tender heart.' "

The associations of Bath with Fielding do not go beyond this. His life in London, his career on the Bench, and his voyage to Lisbon, etc., do not concern this work.[1]

Fielding, as every reader well knows, died at Lisbon. His body rests in *Os Cyprestes*, the English cemetery, near the gracefully-domed Church of the Estrella, the earthquake sparing his newly-dug grave.

No. 11, MARLBOROUGH BUILDINGS ; GEORGE MONKLAND.—A little work, in two small 8vo. vols., was written by Mr. Monkland in 1854-5, entitled "The Literature and Literati of Bath." The substance of the work had been the subject of " Papers " delivered by the author, before the Bath Literary Club, and published by the request of the members. The object was similar to that of the present work, but more limited in its scope, and varying in treatment. In Mr. Monkland's work no attempt was made to identify the residences of the eminent personages whose associations with Bath have given the city celebrity. The book is interesting, but in literary merit it will not bear comparison with the little work which preceded it, "The Connection of Bath with the Literature and Science of England," by the Rev. J. Hunter, which was published under the auspices of the same club in 1853. Mr. Monkland was by profession a soldier, and a gallant soldier too. He was present at *Buenos Ayres* [2] under the unfortunate General Whitelock, in 1807. One of his companions in arms said,

---

[1] Those who want to know all that is likely to be known of Fielding will find it in the Biographical notice by Leslie Stephen, which precedes the *edition de luxe* of his works, published in 10 volumes, 1882, and in the admirable Life, written by Austin Dobson, in the " Men of Letters Series," 1883.

[2] The strange conduct of the General on this occasion was ordering his men to enter the city filled with the enemy, who had barricaded the streets and fortified every dwelling and public building, with unloaded muskets. Two corporals marched at the head of each column, with tools to break open the doors of the barricaded houses. The doors would not yield ; the windows and roofs were crowded with the hostile population ; and a terrible fire mowed down the advancing soldiers. Trenches had been dug in the streets ; and cannon planted there swept away hundreds with grape shot. Auchmuty, in spite of these obstacles, made himself master of the Plaza de Toros, a strong post ; and another place of strength had been taken, when the action was ended at nightfall. Two thousand five hundred British had been killed and wounded, or were prisoners. General Linieres, the commander in the city, addressed a letter next morning to General Whitelock, offering to give up the prisoners, and those made in the previous year, if he would desist from further attack, and withdraw the British forces from La Plata. Monte Video was, of course, to be surrendered. Whitelock agreed to these degrading terms ; returned home with a whole skin ; ran great risk of being torn to pieces by the English popu-

speaking to the author, that he, Captain Monkland as he then was, bore himself
with much spirit and bravery. On retiring from the service he settled in Bath; and
in every good work he was always active, diligent, and persevering. Passionately
fond of the drama, he displayed his histrionic powers on the Bath boards. He was
an admirable *Sir John Franklin*, in *Money ;* and his rendering of *Sir Anthony
Absolute* was perfect ; and in similar characters no one in the amateur dramatic
representations fifty years ago " brought down the house " with more hearty
enthusiasm than Mr. Monkland. As a shrewd, sensible citizen he was ever ready
in the promotion of every valuable local institution. He was proud of being a
citizen of Bath ; and hence it was that he so thoroughly identified himself with
all that concerned the best interests of the city.[1] Mr. Monkland died on the
10th August, 1870. It may be noted here that Mr. Monkland was one of the
" great unpaid," of whom there are a great army in Bath, and to whom Bath owes
so much. The " great unpaid " are peculiar to this country. They constitute the
chief counterpoise to beaureaucracy and centralization. Bath, having so large a
proportion of independent gentlemen, owes more to the services of the " great
unpaid " than any other city or town of similar size. The work done is immense,
and the quality of the work is worthy of all praise and gratitude.

ROBERT NELSON.—Amongst the many benefactors of the city, no one
left a brighter memory, or a more useful memorial of his practical benevolence,
than Robert Nelson. The **BLUE-COAT SCHOOL**, with which his name will always
be associated, is one of the most valuable institutions in the city. The schools were
begun in the year 1711, and carried on by the interest and unwearied endeavours

---

lace, who nicknamed him General Whitefeather ; was tried by court martial, and was declared "totally unfit and unworthy to serve His Majesty in any military capacity whatever."

Captain Monkland embarked with his regiment at Portsmouth on board the *Active* (transport), in October, 1806, and took his final departure from Falmouth Nov. 12th. The expedition was under the command of Brigdr.-Genl. Crawford, 36th regiment, Capt. Monkland being under Lieut.-Col. Burne. After touching at various places *en route*, they, with the brigade to which they belonged, (the command of the expedition having now devolved on Lieut.-Gen. Whitelock). landed at Ensenada de Barragon, and sat down before Buenos Ayres at the end of June, 1807. Capt. Monkland was present at the affair of the 2nd July, and at the final attack on the town on the 5th. He afterwards formed a portion of the Garrison at Monte Vidue, where he did duty until he embarked for England, being the last officer of the expedition to quit the shore.

[1] Mr. Monkland's stepson, **Mr. W. E. Surtees**, D.C.L., of Fairfield, Taunton, was educated at the Bath Grammar-School, and afterwards at Winchester and University College, Oxford. As an accomplished gentleman and an author of repute, he claims a notice. Mr. Surtees is a connection of the Eldon family, and his "Sketch of the Lives of Lords Eldon and Stowell" is a very interesting and able biography, of which Lord Campbell largely and thankfully availed himself in writing his work on the "Lives of the Chancellors."

of Nelson, who engaged Dean Willis, afterwards Bishop of Winchester, and several other persons of distinction, to aid and assist him in this arduous and charitable undertaking; the Corporation having liberally contributed towards it, as well by their subscriptions as by a grant of the ground on which the former schools were erected.

The objects of the charity are the children of honest and industrious parents, inhabitants of the city of Bath; and the number of boys and girls one hundred. They receive a complete outfit once in the year, and are daily instructed in the principles of the Christian religion, reading, writing, and accounts. The girls are also taught sewing, knitting, and housewifery business. They are admitted, upon the recommendation of subscribers, between the age of six and twelve years, and at the age of fourteen are, by the trustees, put out apprentices to trades, or placed out in such services as appear most suitable to their several capacities; a sum not exceeding six pounds being given as an apprentice-fee with every boy, and forty shillings with every girl.

These schools are in some measure supported by annual subscriptions, but chiefly by collections made twice a year at the doors of the several churches and chapels in this city.

The government of this charity is intrusted to the care of fifteen trustees; the Mayor, the two annual justices, and the Rector of Bath, being always of the number.

The first school-house was finished in 1722, and occupied a part of the site of the present building, at the north-east angle of the *Sawclose*, or, as it is sometimes called, *Gascoyne Place*. The present frontage is a little in the rear of the former. The building is a little longer than its predecessor, and the playground has been enlarged by the removal of two small houses in Bridewell Lane. The foundation stone was laid on Saturday, June 30, 1859, by the Mayor, R. W. Falconer, M.D., in the presence of a large number of the friends of the institution. At the close of the ceremony, an oak box was given to each boy, and an oak pin-cushion to each girl attending the school—the box and pin-cushion having been made from the oak timber of the old building. The building, of which Messrs. Manners and Gill were the architects, is in the Elizabethan style, and whilst creditable to the architects is well adapted to the purposes of the school.

Robert Nelson was a zealous Churchman, and though a layman, one of the most earnest writers of his time on Church subjects. His work on the "Fasts and Festivals of the Church" will ever remain as a testimony of his learning and piety. One of the latest gifts to the Abbey Library was a copy of this work, in four vols., 8vo., 1808, by Mr. Joseph Todhunter. The book has been stolen,[1] the fate, indeed, of many others in this collection. Most libraries have answered the purpose either of ornament or use, some both ; here is a library which has answered neither, unless its use be the cause of humanity—in feeding the worms.

No. 4, HARINGTON PLACE, and No. 4, NORTHUMBERLAND BUILDINGS ; HENRY HARINGTON, M.D.—A man of ancient lineage, bearing an honoured name, a skilful physician, a valued public man, and a refined gentleman, possessed of varied accomplishments. Such was Dr. Henry Harington. He was directly descended in the fifth degree from Sir John Harington, whom in some of his intellectual endowments he strongly resembled. He was born in the ancestral house of his distinguished ancestor at Kelston, on Michaelmas-day, 1727. Dr. Harington was the contemporary of Dr. Parry and Dr. W. Falconer, to whom he stood in strong contrast. " The minds of the latter," Warner says, " were chiefly marked by force, depth, and comprehensiveness ; " that of Dr. Harington reflected lights of an equally delightful, though less splendid hue ; genius original, but mild ; taste correct and refined." It may be observed that the name of Harington has been associated with the city of Bath longer than that of any other city or county family. From the reign of Henry VIII. to the present time the fortunes of the city have been always closely identified with the Haringtons. In art, in literature, in politics, in municipal government, the Haringtons have exercised a useful influence. The courtier, the statesman, the philanthropist, Sir John, as he was, in a sense, the first of the family, so in all probably he will ever remain the most conspicuous for deeds of genius, philanthropy, chivalry, and intellectual distinction. During three centuries, although there have been many distinguished members of this family, none can compare with Sir John himself, indeed a rare character in an age of great men. The vast estates which he possessed have all passed away from the family since the third generation, but there was vitality in a family that, despite the loss of large territorial wealth, could ever maintain the position of great social distinction, and high and deserved respect for their ability. The names of Dr. Edward Harington, Dr. Henry Harington, and his not less distinguished son, Sir Edward Harington, and the late Chancellor Harington, attest the truth of this assertion. Dr. Henry Harington was so closely identified with Bath and its institutions, that, on this account, and

---

[1] The remainder of the books in the same collection are only a rich feast for the worms. Various attempts have been made to induce the authorities to use the books, but to no purpose. Perhaps it may be that by this time the worms have acquired a vested interest in them, and that it would be unjust to " disestablish and disendow " them. Far be it from the author to interfere with the rights of property !

because of the versatility of his talents, and the admirable qualities which always disposed him to use them for the delight of the city in which he spent the greater part of his long life, and which he loved with a never varying affection. Notwithstanding his professional and extra-professional engagements he found time to attend to public business ; and in 1793 he filled the office of Mayor with dignity and advantage to the city. In appearance he was singular looking. Warner says, " In form he was tall, thin, and rather stooping ; " and as he wore a costume of the most *antique cut*, [1] the style of which he never varied, he always looked older than he really was. But his face, when lit up in the presence of his friends, was full of animation ; " his manners and conversation were so ' full of sunshine,' that he was irresistibly charming. " Warner states that he had " more than once heard it observed, in reference to this charm of manner, that it exercised a curative influence over his patients ; that as was his prescriptions on healing the body, so was the charm of his manner in tranquillising and encouraging the mind. " His fund of anecdote never failed ; and the point and quaintness which he threw into every story, and the dry and quiet humour with which he narrated it, were quite his own. The confidence he inspired as a physician was equalled only by the respect and love felt for him as a man.

Dr. Harington's special accomplishment was music. He was well versed in its theory, and well skilled in composition. He lent much of his own enthusiasm to the musical taste of the period. The correctness of his taste, and the soundness of his judgment, did much to render Bath at the close of the last, and the early part of the present century, the very centre of musical attraction. He was the author of catches, glees, duets, &c., of great merit, but it was not so much what he did *in* music as what he did *for* it. As Warner says, Dr. Harington composed *Eloi* [2] at the age of seventy, and " that it met the applause of every competent judge among our musical professors and amateurs." But it was his generous and intelligent enthusiasm which did so much for the science. Warner, one of his friends, but at the same time a judicious critic, and a discriminating friend, writes thus :—" Dr. Harington was master, both of the theory, and the composition of music. He would often be seen gliding into the principal music-

---

[1] He wore the triangular hat, and the powdered, full-bottomed wig of the physician of yore ; the court-fashioned coat, and the deep-pocketed waistcoat. The whole of his dress, cut from the same piece of cloth, was, of course, uniform in colour, and usually of a stony hue ; and to complete his picture, he was never seen walking in the street without a white pocket-handkerchief appended to his mouth, to guard his chest from the influence of the cold external air.— *Warner.*

[2] When this appeared, Dr. Gardiner, of the Octagon, made an angry attack upon the author, whom he arraigned for his presumption in setting such words to music, and for permitting his work to be performed at a place of public entertainment. The controversy ran very high. Public opinion has now pretty well settled the question as to these Sacred Oratorios, and their effect upon the religious sentiments of a nation. For many years the *Eloi* was sung on Good Friday at the Abbey.

shop of Bath, when it was void of company, and, silently sitting down to the piano-
forte, would, under the influence of the spirit of harmony that stirred within him,
strike out the most magnificent or moving *chords, voluntaries,* and *fugues.* Compared
with his powers, however, his compositions were but few and slight. But genius is
rarely accompanied by industry. It delights in creating, and not in imitation.
Its own imaginings come spontaneously, and its stores are poured out without
effort ; and, free as light itself, it shrinks from that patient labour, which it must
necessarily exercise, if it would place its stores in the possession of others.

"The enjoyment which Dr. Harington received from the performance of
those who could play well, was by no means diminished by his own exquisite
taste and singular skill in *off-hand* composition. No man ever experienced more
intense delight than himself from this rational source of intellectual pleasure. He
invited me one morning, many years ago, to accompany him to the Bath concert-
room (supposed to be one of the best apartments in England for the circulation of
sound) to hear a performer on the pedal harp, who had been prevailed upon by
the family with whom he was staying to afford to the public an opportunity of
hearing his unrivalled powers on that noble instrument. We went early to secure
a *good place.* The Doctor looked round the room and noticed the spot on which
the performer was to be stationed. He then took me into the *gallery,* and planted
me next to the wall against which the harper was to stand on the floor below.
'Here,' said he, 'you will hear the vibration of every note.' The performer
appeared, a *Count Marat,* one of the most magnificent and most noble-
countenanced men I ever beheld. He seized his harp as if it had been a feather
with the grasp of a giant, swung it round with a rapidity and ease that made its
chords whistle in the air, and commenced a prelude of such powerful and varied
harmony as appeared to realise the conceptions of the poet :—

> ' Now the rich stream of music winds along,
> ' Deep, majestic, smooth and strong,
> ' Through verdant vales and ceres' golden reign,
> ' Now rolling down the steep amain,
> ' Headlong, impetuous, see it pour ;
> ' The rocks and nodding groves rebellow to the roar.'

"He then asked if any person present had a printed musical air. Several
were handed to him. He declined selecting one himself, and begged it might be
chosen by an indifferent person. It was placed before him. He played it over,
threw away the sheet of notes, and commenced a series of *impromptu variations,*
increasing in difficulty and complexity as he proceeded ; so varied in time,
measure, and character, but still completely impregnated with the original air, as

not only astonished his audience, but actually moved the greater part of them to rise from their seats and listen to him standing. I expressed my wonder to the Doctor. He nodded assent. Very few words passed between us ; but I saw that his spirit was deeply impressed. We met a few days afterwards. I mentioned his silence. He allowed it, and confessed that every faculty had been absorbed by the ecstacy which he experienced from the music he had heard.

" Dr. Harington was ' a stricken deer.' His sorrows had been, at different periods of his life, severe ; and to fill up his cup of misfortune, it pleased God, some years before his death, to afflict him with the loss of sight. Previously to the occurrence of this calamity, he felt it to be a prudent step to dispose of his small, but curious and valuable library. He communicated his intention to me. The reason which he alleged for the sale was the gradual decay of his vision. I knew, however, that *other* motives might be added to this apparently reasonable one ; and really believe that I felt a pang almost equal to his own at the moment of this communication, when I reflected on the sadness with which he must anticipate the loss of those long-cherished and highly-valued friends, the companions of his silent, solitary hours ; which had been wont to add lustre to his days of brightness, and to tranquillise and heal his spirit when fretted with the vexatious, or wounded by the afflictions of mortality."

But neither vicissitude nor misfortune could overwhelm the mind of Dr. Harington. [1] It had been deeply imbued, in early youth, with the principles of religion, virtue, and benevolence ; every day of his long life was a practical comment upon these principles ; and under all "the changes and chances " of it, even to its very close, he felt that support from them, which they are mercifully intended " by the God of all consolation " to afford. He died at Bath the 16th of January,

[1] The following Note was given to the Author in 1877, the writer being an old Bath resident. It is quoted here to show the great change since 1815 in the conduct of the city, as well as in the administration of justice. The writer's impression as to Dr. Harington being a *little* man, if by that term is meant *short*, is erroneous :—

" March 22, 1877.—Mr. Hibbert was born in 1805. He well remembers Dr. Harington. He says he was a little, thin, spare man. It was often the case to see men put in the stocks ; and he once saw a woman put in the stocks. He saw several men flogged, and the blood ran down their backs. They were usually flogged from the Market Place to the Old Bridge, *but not over*, as that was out of the Mayor's liberty. He once saw a man flogged on the Quay. He saw a woman flogged from the White Lion. It was thought she was going to be taken to the Old Bridge, but a gentleman, like a magistrate, came up and had her released at the bottom of Union Street. He saw two men pinioned at different times. The mob flung mud, eggs, and fish entrails, etc. One of the men had his face cut, and blood ran down on his face. This was in the Market Place. He remembers it was quite common to see pigs roaming about the streets all over the town, and at night they would return to their homes. People in Pulteney Street, etc., would put ash-boxes out at their doors, and the pigs would go to the boxes and root them over, and sometimes fling the ashes over the street ; and he saw a child once catch hold of a pig's tail, which frightened the animal, and it ran off and dragged the child with it. Most of this would be about 1815."

1816, aged 89 years.   He was buried in the Abbey, and his monument was erected by public subscription, which called forth a short poem by his accomplished son-in-law, ARCHDEACON THOMAS, who died in 1822, and whose remains rest also in the Abbey.

No. 12, BLADUD BUILDINGS; WILLIAM MELMOTH.—The name and reputation of William Melmoth as a scholar and philanthropist are a local possession.   A man of dignified presence, courteous bearing, and great learning, he was one of the most popular of the literary band of whom Warner and Falconer were the leaders, or chiefs.   He lacked the energy and versatility of the former, and force of character of the latter; but in classical knowledge, and in the elegance of his diction, he was their superior.   Melmoth's works were *Fitzosborne's Letters, Translation of Pliny's Letters,* and some of the works of *Marcus Tullius Cicero.*   Melmoth, the son of a barrister, was also himself a barrister, and in 1756 was made a Commissioner of Bankrupts.   Giving up his professional appointment he first retired to Shrewsbury, but for the last forty years of his life he resided at 12, Bladud Buildings, in this city.   Besides the works enumerated, Melmoth was a contributor to Dodsley's and Pearch's collections, and he wrote a life of his father, " Memoirs of a late eminent advocate, and a member of the Honourable Society of Lincoln's Inn," 1796.   Melmoth died in 1799, aged 89; and was buried at Batheaston, though a tablet to his memory is in the Abbey.

W. Melmoth was the eldest son of his father, by his second marriage with a lady named Rolt, daughter of S. C. Rolt, Esq., of Milton Erneys, Bedfordshire.   W. Melmoth himself was twice married.   1st. To Dorothy, daughter of the celebrated Dr. King, Principal of St. Mary's Hall, Oxford.   2nd. To Miss M. Ogle, who was related to the second wife of Richard Brinsley Sheridan.   She survived him.   He left no family, but he adopted a grand-niece, Sophia, daughter and co-heiress of Rev. John Skynner, who was a grand-daughter of a brother of the elder Melmoth.   Sophia Skynner married Thomas Walters, and was the mother of the late **Melmoth Walters,** so many years known in Bath as an eminent conveyancing barrister, and not less esteemed for his active and kindly benevolence. A sister of this lady married **John Swale,** and was the grandmother of Capt. Melmoth Gataker.   The Latin Epitaph in the Abbey, upon William Melmoth, is from the pen of the **Rev. John Skynner,** who was Rector of Easton, near Stamford, and son of **Capt. Skynner, R.N.,** who was killed in action whilst in command of the *Biddeford,* in an engagement with two French frigates, in 1760.   He was a nephew of W. Melmoth.

The Melmoths were men of singularly fine presence, especially the elder,[1] of whom Captain Melmoth Gataker, himself a descendant from the Melmoths, possesses a remarkably fine portrait. Hunter, than whom a more discriminating critic could not be found, says of the younger Melmoth that his "elegant and beautiful translations would gain him the character of one of the finest writers of his time, did they not place him in the higher rank of those who raise the moral character and the intellectual purity of the age in which they live."

In **BATHAMPTON CHURCHYARD**, a gravestone is to be seen on which is inscribed—

"Here rest the remains of **JOHN BAPTISTE DU BARRÉ**.
Obiit 18th November, 1778."

This unfortunate gentleman was slain in a duel on **CLAVERTON DOWN**. The particulars are as follows:—In the year 1778, many foreign nobles made Bath their residence, and, among others, were the Viscount du Barré, his wife, and her sister, two ladies of great beauty and accomplishments, and **COUNT RICE**, a gentleman of Irish extraction, who had borne arms in the service of France. A house was taken at **No. 8, ROYAL CRESCENT**, where for a time the party lived together on the most amicable terms. They kept open house, where play was allowed to a ruinous extent. Quarrelling at cards, words ran high between Du Barré and Rice, and an immediate challenge was given and accepted. At one o'clock in the morning, a coach was procured from the *Three Tuns*, in Stall Street, and Claverton Down was reached in moody silence, at the first dawn of day.

A contemporary account describes the combat as follows:—"Each armed with two pistols and a sword. The ground being marked out by the seconds, the Viscount du Barré fired first, and lodged a ball in Count Rice's thigh, which penetrated as far as the bone; Count Rice fired his pistol, and wounded the Viscount in the breast. He went back two or three steps, then came forward again, and both, at the same time, presented their pistols to each other; the

---

[1] It appears that there was some doubt as to the authority of Melmoth's work, "The Great Importance of a Religious Life Considered." It was ascribed to the Earl of Egmont, but in an edition, edited by his son and published in 1790, he claims it as his father's work, which it indisputably was. The first edition was published in 1711, and as the book was enlarged at different periods, it is most probable Lord Egmont edited and enlarged an edition. The Earl of Egmont, formerly Sir John Percival, was the friend and correspondent of the illustrious Bishop Berkeley, and the fact of this book having been attributed to him implies no small praise in itself.

pistols flashed together in the pan, though only one was discharged. Then they threw away their pistols, and took to their swords; when Count Rice had advanced within a few yards of the Viscount, he saw him fall, and heard him cry out, 'Je vous demande ma vie,' to which Count Rice answered, 'Je vous la donne;' but in a few seconds the Viscount fell back and expired. Count Rice was brought with difficulty to Bath, being dangerously wounded, though now he is in a fair way of recovery. The coroner's inquest sat on the Viscount's body last Saturday, and after a mature examination of the witnesses and the Viscount's servants, brought in their verdict ' Manslaughter.' "[1]

The Viscount's body was left exposed the whole day on the Down, and was subsequently buried in Bathampton Churchyard. Count Rice recovered; was tried at Taunton for murder, and acquitted. He died in Spain in 1809. At that part of the Down where the Yeomanry were formerly reviewed, a bank slopes towards the wall. It was on the *other side* of this wall, and a few yards from the gate, that the duel took place, where a stone slab marks the spot. The ivory hilt of the sword once belonging to Count Rice is now attached to the city seal in the Town Clerk's office.

[1] Thicknesse, in that extraordinary combination of slander, indecency, and amusing gossip, *The New Prose Guide to Bath*, 1788, gives his version of the facts, or rather of his theory, which was sure to be ill-natured, and must be taken *cum grano.* He says :—
"The most probable conjecture is that these two gamblers, being invited to dine with Col. Champion, and having picked him after dinner of £650, Rice, finding that there were six other pidgeons to pull, claimed Du Barré's share in part of payment of the old debt, and Du Barré, perceiving that he would no longer support his style of living, and that Rice had brought him into a strange kingdom, under promises of finding large play and plenty of pidgeons, determined to break up the party. Certain it is that jealousy had no share in the misunderstanding; and what was very singular is that it appeared that Du Barré was totally disqualified as to commerce with women, in the opinion of all the women of Bathampton, where his body was for many days inspected by all !
The money won by Du Barré and Rice of Col. Champion was in playing at faro, and Rice and Champion held the bank, and therefore Rice lost £650. Also I took occasion a few days after to hint to Champion that perhaps she was not quite right when they lost their money. However unfortunate this affair turned out for Rice and Du Barré, it was a very lucky hit for Bath. A brace of gamblers with a lovely woman at stake could not have set out on a better plan ; and it was pleasant to observe that the blacklegs of the lower town never offered to join the upper ; but the *privateers* of different nations did not touch upon one another."

The following also is given by Thicknesse :—"The cause of this fatal quarrel is *now* probably known to *one* person. The post-boy found in Count du Barré's great-coat pocket 20 diamond waist-coat-buttons and a French letter. He attempted to conceal the buttons, but discovered them in his cups, and they were delivered up. The letter, which we saw but read very hastily, was from a Frenchman. It had no name to it, was written with respect, and the writer, after saying *that he had only* 50 *Louis d'Or in his escritoire*, added that he would either come to Path or return to France (as the Count should direct) ; it is probable that this man was his London banker. There were also in this letter a certain number of propositions which seemed intelligible only to the person to whom the letter was addressed. Mr. *Dutens*, a French Protestant parson —*whose fortune in this country has been very remarkable indeed !*—seemed to be Mme. du Barré's privy counsellor, and it is said a noble Duke (with whom he has some influence) offered the lady a purse of 500 guineas. Dutens is a native of Paris, and his relations there are all good Catholics, but he, being a moderate man, lives in a friendly correspondence with them. He was left by Lord Bute's brother Chargé d'Affaires in the last war in Turin, with a salary of £700 per annum, and has now some tolerable pickings in our Church. It is doubtful whether he be naturalized."

In the time of Louis XV., the Du Barry family consisted of three brothers and two sisters :—1. Jean Baptiste,[1] Count de Cérés, who had an only son, Jean Baptiste, born 1749 (the Viscount). 2. Count Guillaume, who married Jeanne Vaubernier, "la du Barry." After her death he married again, and, by this second marriage, had a son, who became a very distinguished officer, and was decorated both by Napoleon and Louis XVIII. 3. Elie, Count d'Hargicourt, who died 1830, aged 90. His only child was the Countess Narbonne Lara. The two sisters, Isabelle and Françoise, never married, and died at an advanced age, at Toulouse. Although Count Guillaume du Barry went through a formal marriage with Madlle. Vaubernier, it was for the purpose merely of giving her a title, and was at the direct instigation of the King (Louis XV.). The Count and the woman who had become his wife after this shameless fashion, never lived together as man and wife. The King, it was understood, did not wish to confer upon her, by his prerogative, an independent title ; he preferred, in fact, an addition to his iniquity rather than commit an act of imprudence !

Jean Baptiste, Viscount du Barry, only son of Jean Baptiste, Count de Cérés, married (1773) Madlle. de Tournon, of the distinguished family of Soubise, by whom he had one child, who died in infancy. It will be seen, therefore, that the Viscount who fell on Claverton was the nephew of the husband of Madame du Barry.

In 1778 the Viscount, accompanied by his young wife, her sister, and Count Rice, an Irish Jacobite, whose grandfather went to France with James II., came to Bath, when he met his untimely fate. His young widow returned to Paris, resumed her maiden name, and entered a convent.

For sixty years, it was commonly believed that the wife of the slain man was the notorious Madame du Barry,[2] but this, as the author demonstrated twenty years ago, was impossible.

---

[1] This is the Viscount du Barry who, with "Madame," figures in Dumas' "Memoirs of a Physician."

[2] The story of Madame du Barry may be worth a note. "1791, Feb. 6.—This evening Mr. Stephen Clark, City Marshal, with proper assistants, apprehended on an information, at the Cross Keys Inn, Gracechurch Street, five Frenchmen, charged with feloniously breaking and entering the palace of the Countess du Barré, near Paris, and stealing thereout money, plate, jewels, etc., to the value of £50,000 and upwards. On them were found 1,500 guineas, and diamonds to the value of between £40 and £50,000 sterling. · When taken, they attempted to throw a number of diamonds into the fire. Several were found among the cinders. Four of the men charged were conveyed to the Poultry Compter, and one to the New Compter. who has petitioned to give evidence against the rest." The men were prosecuted, and the property for the most part recovered. In April, 1791, Madame du Barry, for the first time, came to London with a regular passport, in consequence of this stolen property, and Mr. Pitt and others of the highest distinction called upon her. On December to of the same year application was made in the Court of Chancery "for further direction as to the re-delivery of Madame du Barré's jewels, and the payment of the expenses incurred in their recovery. The Lord

WARNER, or WARNER'S COTTAGE ; The Rev. RICHARD WARNER.

—It is very commonly supposed that the house called at the present time " Warner," formerly " Warner's Cottage," was built by the late Rev. Richard Warner ; but this is not so. The house was called originally **HANGING LANDS HOUSE;** and it derived its ugly name from the locality, which, from its peculiar configuration under the ridge or scarp of the hill on the east side of Lyncombe Vale, was called **Hanging Lands.** The house was built before Warner came to the city, and he bought, enlarged, and lived in it ; and as the name Hanging Lands House seemed to those who were not familiar with local nomenclature indicative of its having been at some former period a place of execution,

---

Chancellor made some pointed animadversions on the scramble for the reward and expenses, and it was finally settled that £3,000 should be deposited by Madame du Barré to answer all demands, which are to be liquidated by arbitration, and the jewels immediately delivered up."

Madame du Barry returned to her palace at Louveciennes, and in 1793 the municipality of that place granted her a passport to England on her promising to return to France, and she again visited London, during her stay in which she attended the funeral service of Louis XVI. in deep mourning, and this was the crime for which she lost her life. She was foolish enough to keep her promise to return to France, though, it was said, Mr. Pitt warned her of the fate of Regulus. One motive by which she was impelled was doubtless the fact mentioned by Madame la Brun, namely, that her friend the Duke de Brissac was at that very time concealed in her house at Louveciennes.

The following historic note may prove interesting to the reader :—The family of Du Barré, or Barri, were originally nobodies. Louis XV., or his satellites, persuaded Lord Barrymore—who, tradition says, was a scamp or a fool—to acknowledge them as members of his ancient family, descended from the Kings of Ireland ! It just served the purpose, and the heralds made a fine pedigree, giving them the rights of noblesse, etc., and on the strength thereof Mme. *du Barry* was presented at court. Could Rice—a man of really good family, though poor—have taunted " Lolo," as the young du Barry was called, with this—his mean origin, the scandal attaching to his name, and his inability to pay his "debts of honour, now that his aunt and former protectress was herself struggling vainly to free herself from a crushing load of common debts ? "

Mlle. de Tournon was married, a mere child, during the heyday of prosperity of the du Barry family, when riches and honours somewhat obscured the shame of the alliance. Now, she found herself the wife of a gambler, ruined, and without the hope of substantial help from her own family, for its head, the Prince de Guéménée, husband of his cousin, the co-heiress of Rohan-Soubise, had become bankrupt for 34,000,000 (thirty-four million) livres. Also, the Cardinal de Rohan had already given unpardonable offence to Marie Antoinette. Mlle. de Tournon's relationship with these illustrious persons was not nearer than the fourth degree. She retired to the Convent of the Filles, or Hospitalières de S. Thomas de Villeneuve, Rue de Sèvres. It was a compound establishment—a reformatory for women and girls sent there by royal order ; a School for Young Ladies at 300 to 400 livres per annum ; and a Boarding-House for Ladies, single and married, at 450 livres *en pension.* She married her first cousin once removed, Jean Baptiste Marc Antoine de Tournon, Marquis de Claveron, and died, childless, in 1785. Her husband died the following year. Her only sister, Sophie, made an insignificant marriage with the Marquis de Montdragon, and died in 1800. Their brother, the Viscomte de Tournon, also died childless in 1787. Mme. la Viscomtesse du Barry was baptized Rose Marie Hélène. Her father was Hugues François, Comte de Tournon, who was married in 1755, and died in 1789.

Mme. de Simiane, grand-daughter of Mme. de Sévigné, must have been closely related to the Marquis de Claveron.

Mme. la Vicomtesse du Barry was in a great hurry to resume her name of de Tournon, and she consoled herself with a second husband of that name, her cousin. *Anciens démêlés—old quarrels.* This is no aspersion on Madame la Vicomtesse's character, nor is there any sort of accusation of lightness brought against her—rather of coldness and indifference.

the name was changed to Warner's Cottage, in honour of the eminent man by whom it was occupied.[1] "Warner" is at present the property and residence of A. G. D. Moger, Esq., and is one of the most charming residences in the city. The prospects from its windows excel in grandeur those from any other residence in Bath, which abounds with such an infinite variety of scenery. Since Warner's time the house has undergone a complete metamorphosis, and is now approached by a beautiful drive, instead of by the former rough and difficult road.

The associations of Richard Warner, and his literary life and labour, are so interwoven with Bath history and social interests of the latter part of the last and the early part of the present century, that they will go down to distant posterity. The annals of Bath existed only in fragmentary and detached forms until Warner put them into historic shape, and with great industry and admirable literary skill produced his History of Bath. With all its faults it remains the great authority upon subjects relating to those parts of the city which were then comprehended in the *liberties*. The work was published in 1801 ; but since that time Bathwick, Lyncombe and Widcombe, and a large part of Walcot have been incorporated with the ancient *liberties*, under the provisions of the Reform Act of 1832, and the Municipal Corporations Act of 1835.[2]

It will be remembered that under the Letters Patent of Queen Elizabeth, the several parishes of Bath, except Walcot and Bathwick, were consolidated into one Rectory, which also included the Vicarage of Lyncombe and Widcombe, comprising an area of 1,941 acres, with an aggregate population of 21,995, the patronage being vested in the Corporation. After the passing of the Municipal Reform Bill, in 1835, the advowson was purchased by the Rev. Chas. Simeon, for £6,330, the transfer having been completed about one month before his death, in Nov., 1836. It was subsequently vested in the Trustees appointed by him. The first Rector appointed under this new patronage was the Ven. Henry Law, Archdeacon of Wells (now Dean of Gloucester). He was succeeded, in 1839, by the Rev. W. J. Brodrick, afterwards Viscount Midleton. The

---

[1] Warner gave this cottage to his daughter, **REBECCA WARNER**, who became a convert to the Roman Catholic faith ; and on her death she bequeathed the property to a lady of the same faith. Rebecca Warner was a remarkable woman, of great intellectual power; and in 1818 she published a work entitled *Epistolary Curiosities*, in two series. She lived in " **Beech Cottage**."

[2] It is to be hoped that some able author, in conjunction with an enterprising publisher, may be induced to edit Warner, and to bring down the History to the present day. Warner fell into many errors, some of which are of a nature to excite surprise, seeing that there were many sources of information open to him, by using which he might have avoided those errors. What occasions so much dissatisfaction with Warner's works, however, is that he never gives an index. To consult a large 4to. book of 500 pages without the aid of an index is one of the most provoking tasks a reader can encounter ; and in the case of so voluminous a writer as Warner it has diminished his usefulness and importance incalculably.

increasing population and parochial and ministerial responsibilities of so large a district, rendered some sub-division of labour inevitable, and the early attention of Mr. Brodrick was directed to the task of re-arrangement. The first concession made by him was the parish of St. Michael, which he resigned to the trustees in 1843, when the Rev. John East, formerly curate of the parish, was presented to the living.

In 1855 the Vicarage of the large and important parish of Lyncombe and Widcome was handed over to the Trustees, and subsequently divided into two distinct ecclesiastical districts, viz., that of **Widcombe**, including the Old Parish Church, dedicated to St. Thomas a' Beckett, with the new church of St. Matthew's, of which the Rev. Mourant Brock was the first vicar ; and **Lyncombe**, with St. Mark's as the parish church, to which the Rev. J. W. Sproule was presented. A further division was made in 1867, and a new Vicarage formed in **South Lyncombe**, the church of which is dedicated to St. Luke ; the Rev. J. A. Watt was the first Incumbent.

In the year 1861, during the incumbency of the Rev. Charles Kemble, the Rectory of Bath was divested of the last of the originally combined parishes by the separation of **St. James's**, which is now an independent Vicarage. The Rev. H. T. Cavell was the first Vicar.

Under the old *régime*, the curacies were *quasi*-independent, and partly for that reason and partly by the social advantages they offered, many eminent men were attracted to these ecclesiastical appointments. The Rev. John Richards, the Rev. Philip Dart, the Rev. — Lawrence (brother of Sir Thomas), the Rev. Thomas Falconer, M.D., the Rev. W. L. Nichols, and many others, were men of whom any city might be proud. But of all the men whose names have done honour to Bath, the name of **RICHARD WARNER** stands pre-eminent.[1] The Rev. Richard Warner was the son of a tradesman in Marylebone, in which parish he was born October 18th, 1763. While Richard was still a youth, his father and mother removed to Lymington, and of this place he gives some account in his *Literary Recollections*. He was educated at Christ Church and St. Mary's Hall, Oxford, which he left without taking his degree, and was ultimately ordained by Dr. Markham, Archbishop of York. Warner's first curacy was at Boldre, in Hampshire, the rector of which was the Rev. W. Gilpin, whose works on landscape scenery are still so much admired. It seems probable that Warner acquired a taste for similar literary pursuits from Gilpin's example. In some of Warner's *Walks*, he evidently

---

[1] Intellectually, Thomas Falconer would be an exception, but he could scarcely be regarded as one of the ordinary clergy, active as he was in his co-operation with Warner and others in their labours. [See article on Falconer.]

has adopted the same method of treatment, both in his style and illustration, as his ingenious master, although it must be observed that Gilpin's illustrations are much finer and incomparably more artistic. Warner, without being a genius, evidently possessed great latent mental power, and it is due to the *stimulus* afforded him by Gilpin that those powers were developed and grew to their full maturity. After a few years, Warner removed to Fawley, in the same county, and then he accepted the curacy of All Saints' Chapel in this city, from whence, in a few months (April, 1795), he was transferred to the sphere in which he so greatly distinguished himself, namely, St. James's, which he occupied for twenty-three years. He was presented to the living of Great Charfield, Wilts, by Sir Harry Burrard Neale, Bart.; but, notwithstanding, he continued to hold the curacy of St. James until 1817. In 1825, he was presented by Bishop Law to the living of Timberscombe, and in the following year he obtained the living of Croscombe. He held Timberscombe and Croscombe for a short period only. The living of Chelwood was afterwards given to him, and that, with Great Charfield, he held until his death at the latter place, in 1857, at the age of 95. Details of this kind are sparingly given.[1]

Richard Warner was more intimately acquainted than any other man with the literary men of his day, and from his culture, great general and local knowledge, and independence of character, he was always (excepting Dr. William Falconer and his son, the Rev. Thomas Falconer, M.D.) the most distinguished Bath man of letters of his generation, and that, too, a generation which will bear comparison with any preceding or subsequent for intellectual eminence. The independence of Warner has been illustrated in various ways. In 1804, he preached a sermon[2] against war. If Warner had lived in these days, he would have denounced Jingoism. He hated war, though he was not prepared with a theory for the maintenance of peace. The tradition about this famous sermon is that Warner invited the *Volunteers* to his church, and then proceeded to demonstrate the wickedness of their calling. This is an erroneous representation. The sermon was preached on a *Fast-day*. Possibly the subject of the sermon might have got abroad, for "a few minutes before I commenced the service," he says, "a large body of military (without previous notice to myself, and contrary to my expectation) were marched into the church; and it was naturally enough, though

---

[1] The Bibliography of Warner will be found in the Appendix.

[2] Warner had cultivated the art of oratory. His sermons were models of pulpit eloquence, and, what is more, they were broad and liberal. He hated Calvinism with a cordial hatred, and although he worked well, as a rule, with the High-Church party of the period, he did not agree with them. He leaned, it was said, more to the latitudinarianism of Hoadley.

most erroneously, imagined by those who disliked the sermon that I had written it for the especial *edification* of these sons of Mars."[1]   The result was a paper-war of a most bitter character, Dr. W. and the Rev. T. Falconer taking a prominent part in it.   It stopped Warner's preferment, or he thought so, but it was not altogether the sermon, although the Lord Chancellor, for the time being, quoted it against him ; but Warner was a Whig when to be a Whig tended not to the good things which a Lord Chancellor had to bestow.   The singular part of the story is, that Warner magnanimously justified the Lord Chancellor for refusing to confer preferment upon him, holding, as he did, views of which the great functionary disapproved.   Yet it is curious to observe that, Whig as he was and continued to be, and sincere as he was, he opposed, by speech, sermon, and pamphlet, the *Catholic Emancipation Act.*   The versatility of Warner was very remarkable : topography, history, antiquarianism, poetry, satire—all came alike to him.   *The Rebellion in Bath* (1807) and *Bath Characters* (1807) were examples of his satirical powers. The latter was a pungent series of dialogues upon living characters, in which the *weak spots* of each were brought out with admirable effect.   Each name was caricatured by some designation or *vraisemblance* which could not be mistaken.

The book was attributed to Dr. William Falconer, who bore his martyrdom heroically, but, being with a group of friends in the tea-room at the Assembly Rooms, Warner amongst the number, the last-named joined with the rest in *chaffing* his friend.   Falconer said, "No, my friend, I am not the author.   But I could put my hand upon him," at the same time laying his hand on Warner's shoulder, who denied not the soft impeachment.[2]   The public, down to the death of Warner, were not clear as to the authorship.

The associations of Warner with the two Falconers, the Parrys, Maclaine Graves, **DR. PARR**, and others, are full of interest, and give a vivid picture of the intellectual life of Bath in Warner's time.   Parr and Warner were on terms of the closest intimacy.   Warner understood the great Leviathan, admired his inte-

[1] "An incident of a more comic character arose out of the preaching of this inauspicious and incautious sermon.   During the time of its delivery, I observed some disturbance in one of the pews. It was occasioned by the abrupt departure of *two gentlemen* from the church, whose *political sensibility* was completely overcome by the subject of my discourse.   I paused till they had made good their retreat. The rest of the congregation *sat it out.*   On the ensuing Fast-day, I prepared another sermon for the occasion, on the text, James iii. 17—'The wisdom from above is first pure, then *peaceable,*' &c. While announcing this beautiful passage, I observed that the pew-opener—a worthy man, who felt a very laudable pride in preserving order and decency in the church—was busily employed in the middle aisle.   Before I had preached for ten minutes, a commotion arose in the seat occupied by the two gentlemen above mentioned.   They appeared to be endeavouring to open the door, but could not effect it.   On returning to the vestry, I enquired of the pew-opener, whether he could account for the disturbance in the strangers' seat.   'Oh, yes, sir ! very well.   When I heard your *text,* I didn't know *what was coming;* and afeard the gemmen might again *bolt,* I *lock'd 'em in.*' "

[2] The late Dr. R. W. Falconer related this to the author.

grity and sincerity, his kindness and benevolence. At times he admits that Parr's foibles lowered the dignity of his moral bearing, and lessened the charms of his social converse, but the noble qualities of the man were, like the *Oases* of the Arabian deserts, refreshing spots of brightness and joy in the wilderness of the moral world. Warner visited the Doctor at his parsonage at Hatton. No cloud hung over them during these happy times, except the cloud of the Doctor's pipe. Warner tells how much Parr was beloved by his people. In 1805, Dr. Parr lost his favourite daughter, Catherine. She died of consumption at·Teignmouth. On his return, he remained for some time at the **WHITE HART.** Warner tells how much this strong-minded man felt his bereavement; how he pressed his hand in speechless sorrow. In 1807, Dr. Parr again came to Bath on a visit to Mr. Cottle,[1] at **1, SEYMOUR STREET.** He wrote to his friend the following character-istic letter :—

" DEAR MR. COTTLE,—

" Mr. Warner will tell you of the blunder which I made with ———, and which threw me back a week. I shall strive ; strive ; strive ; to reach Bath on Monday se'nnight, and to reach it by five o'clock in the afternoon, so as to dine with you.—And now, dear sir, I must desire you and Mrs. C. to attend to what I am going to say.—Keep yourselves quite at ease ;—Let me be quite at my own ease—and these two important ends are to be attained, by your permitting me to take just the same food, and no other, which you are accustomed to take yourselves.—Many people *talk* this ; but I do really *mean* it : and indeed, my old pupil, you would make me wretched, very wretched, by admitting the slightest alteration in your way of living on my account. Believe me, this is the only way of making me comfortable; and it is the *very best* way in which you can show your regard for me. I certainly shall take the liberty of telling your good lady one or two luxuries to which I am addicted ;—the first, is a shoulder of mutton, not over-roasted, nor under-roasted ; and richly encrusted with flour and salt ;—the second, is a plain suet-pudding;—the third, is a plain farmerly plumb-pudding;—the fourth, is a kind of high-festival dish, adapted to the stomach of a pampered priest, and consists in hot boiled lobsters, with a profusion of shrimp sauce ;—and the catalogue of dainties will be closed, with a request, to be one day indulged with a cranberry tart—and when I dine with my brother Warner, he is to treat with soals, which are excellent in your part of the world,—and I charge you, to charge him, to charge——— and my favourite, to receive me in a plain way. Show me your faith by your deeds. Now, my dear Mr. Cottle, I am going to Bath, solely for the friendly purpose of shaking you once more by the hand, before I die; and I do assure you, with my wonted sincerity, that, having *such* a purpose before me, I shall undertake my journey with great and *peculiar* satisfaction ; and I beg leave to add, that Mrs. Parr, entertaining for you the same regard which I do, is extremely bent on this my expedition ; and would have accompanied me, if her presence at Hatton had not been necessary to attend her only remaining daughter, who expects every hour to lie in.—This is the plain truth.—I am coming to see Mr. and Mrs. Cottle—I am *not* coming to diffuse myself among the belles or the beaus, nor among the grandees, nor among the scholars

---

[1] Cottle was a West India proprietor, the owner of an estate called *Roundhill*, in the island of Nevis, a correspondent of Parr's, and at this time was residing in *Seymour Street.*

of Bath. I must live quietly and privately; and Mr. W.'s very good sense will enable him to enter thoroughly into my views.—Oh ! he is a naughty varlet and has secretly goaded you to employ your influence for carrying a point, of which he would himself have despaired. I never *preach* except at the call of *duty;* and that call I hear in my own parish church, and in the churches of neighbouring villages, when my clerical neighbours are ill, or when they go out for their amusement.—But, I preach volunteers, neither in towns, nor cities, nor villages ; and I believe that *Bath* is the very last place in the world, where I could be prevailed upon to mount a pulpit. If Fox, Pitt, and Burke, were to employ their eloquence in English ; if it were to be enforced by Cicero, in Latin ; and by Demosthenes, in Greek ; if Aristotle, Thomas Aquinas, and Duns Scotus, assailed me with all the subtleties of their logic—if the Pope of Rome ; the Patriarch of Constantinople; and the Primates of England and Ireland, were to hold up the terrors of ecclesiastical authority—if the three furies were to try the force of their angry menace—if the three graces were to address me, with the soft and sweet allurements of persuasion—all these contrivances and efforts, conjointly and separately, would be insufficient to vanquish my reluctance to preach a sermon at Bath. I am an old-fashioned, and long-winded preacher :—the old would fall asleep ; the young would titter ; the middle-aged would be listless and weary ; and some witlings would scribble epigrams in your Bath newspapers, upon the length, and the dulness, and pedantry of my discourse. Woe be to that crafty priest, Richard Warner, for drawing you into a snare.—He knows my habitual unwillingness to preach, except in my own church ; and he also knows my opinion about the popular pulpiteers in your town ; and I desire you, to bid him to prepare himself for a most tremendous castigation from me.

"I hope that Mr. W. has favoured me with very minute directions to find your house. Pray do not wait beyond five o'clock on Monday se'nnight ; for my movements are, in some measure, dependent upon —————. I must stop at Glo'ster, and give some directions at the foundery about my bells. I am very eager to be with you on the day above-mentioned ; and yet I dare not fix the hour. I hope my brother Warner will be in the way, to assist me about the choice of some person, who is worthy of shaving my consecrated beard, and dressing my orthodox wigs. I think we shall all be *very happy* together ; and Mr. W. will expect to find me fraught with indignation, against the oppressive and frantic expedition, which is going on in the north. I presume that neither ——, nor ——, nor ——, overflow with political zeal ; and if I should discover any lurking partialities towards the eloquence of Canning ; the piety of Percival ; the honesty of Castlereagh ; the sincerity of Lord ————— ; the innocence of Lord M——— ; the heroism of ————— ; or the patriotism of —————, I shall remember, that, in times of old, the priest was skilled in the duties of exorcism ; and shall employ the utmost force of my knowledge, and argumentation, and refutation, in expelling from your minds, all the demons of credulity, bigotry, and intolerance. But, I trust, that you will give me very little trouble in this way ; and that the ladies will put neither julep ; nor opium ; nor worm-wood ; nor arsenic, into my glass of wine, when I drink to the immortal memory of Charles Fox ! I leave Hatton on Monday ; and, perhaps, I shall write a line or two before I quit Birmingham."

The great man's estimate of a shoulder of mutton was more exalted than that of the young lady who regarded it as the material from which the appropriate product was *glue.* He dined with Warner at his Cottage, and puffed the strong shag tobacco, told his stories; and finally astonished his friends by informing them he cherished a secret predilection for bull-baiting. "You see," said he, baring his muscular arm, "that I am a kind of *taurine* man, and must therefore be naturally addicted to the sport." The Doctor played *penny whist.* Warner was his partner, and, says he, "ambitious as I was to impress him with an idea of my consummate knowledge of the game, I made a *finesse.* It failed, and we lost the rubber. The doctor, knitting his mighty brows, *inflicted* upon me one of his gorgon looks, and most caustically exclaimed—' Dick, you have all the *cunning* of a Bath sharper, without his *skill.*' Happily for my reinstatement in his favour, his next hand of cards was a brilliant one. The features of his disturbed physiognomy assumed their natural arrangement, and, in a tone of conciliation he mildly said—' I acquit you of *trickery*, Richard; would that I could of *stupidity;* however, I believe your intention was good, and that's no mean praise.' "

After all, Warner could not coax the great man to "fill his pulpit," but he read the communion service in his own impassioned, and somewhat pompous manner. Before the service began, however, he took the clerk on one side, and admonished him not to repeat the responses audibly after him. The latter was a nervous man; moreover, he was a Somerset man, and he had no more notion than the great Doctor of hiding his light under a bushel. It may be more readily conceived than described what were the Doctor's feelings to hear himself, and his grandiloquent style, followed up in the commandments in stridulous accents, and in unmistakeable *Zummerzet*, by the worthy clerk. Only those who are accustomed to hear a real *Zummerzetshire* man, can appreciate a parish clerk's method of entreating the Deity, first to "have mercy upon us," and then to "incline our hearts to keep this law." A refined stranger listening to such a functionary for the first time, would require an ingenious translator. On this occasion poor Mr. Warner was most to be pitied; he knew the Doctor,.and he knew his clerk, and the result was indescribable. As the clerk said in justification of his special emphasis on that day, "Na business to interfere wi' I, Zur;" whilst the Doctor poured out his indignation upon "Richard Warner."[1]

Warner accompanied Cottle and Parr to Bristol and Clifton, and amongst other questions Warner asked Parr as to the authenticity of the anecdote of his celebrated reply to Mr. M., respecting Coigly. Turning sharply round, "Where did you hear that, Richard?" said he, "Oh, from many quarters." "Well, I

---

[1] Warner's reflections upon the Doctor's manner, however, are that the *energy of passion* should never be thrown into the repetition of any written or public form of prayer, but that a calm solemnity of manner is infinitely more judicious, satisfactory, and effective, than a highly impassioned one. Perhaps few people will be found to deny this. Since Parr and Warner's day, Churchmen have, amongst other things, found out that they do not require Parish Clerks to do their worship by deputy.

believe it is pretty correct, but he provoked me to it." [1]

"Our walk to Clifton, from Bristol, and back, rendered it necessary for us to seek refreshment, and we seated ourselves in a dining-room, at the Bush Tavern, where, in a few minutes, 'a clumsy beef-steak' (as the Irish labourer in *Rosina* expresses himself), with a broad yellow salvage to it,' smoked before us. The doctor rubbed his hands with satisfaction, and ate his lunch with appetite ; and, on the removal of the cloth, called for his *pipe*, the necessary adjunct to all his meals. The attendant bowed ; begged the gentleman's pardon ; but 'must inform him, that no smoking was permitted in their house.' ' Not smoke, sir I send up your master.' A spruce gentleman soon appeared. ' Do you keep this inn, sir ? ' ' No, sir ; but master is busy. I am the head waiter.' ' Well, then, Mr. Head Waiter ' (with considerable emphasis, and a dark scowl under his bushy eyebrows), ' can I have a pipe here ? ' ' No, sir ; we do not suffer it at the Bush.' ' Admirable I *you* do not suffer it at the *Bush*. Bah ! Why, sir, I have smoked in the dining-rooms of half the nobility in England ; and the Duchess of Devonshire herself has told me, that I might do the same in every apartment in her mansion, except her dressing-room, And not *suffer a pipe* in this dark hole of a *Bristol public-house !* Ama—a—zing ! Bring the bill, sir ! ' "

Warner introduced Parr to **DR. STOCK, Bishop of Killalla**, and afterwards of Waterford. He gives an amusing description of the meeting of these two distinguished men. The bishop was simple, natural, and a man of "halcyon" spirit. He met the Leviathan as if he had been a small fish, and the Leviathan could not quite understand the playful, almost quizzing manner of the good Bishop. As Parr and Warner left the Bishop, Warner says, "the latter gave me a *queer* look, which seemed to say, Bozzy, I have seen your ' Doctor.' " Dr. Stock was Bishop of Killalla during the invasion of Ireland, in 1798. *Humbert*, it will be remembered, landed his troops at Killalla, and the conduct of the Bishop was admirable ; cool, brave, dignified, and loyal, amidst scenes calculated to try the courage of the stoutest-hearted. The Bishop won the respect of the French commander, and set an example of calm endurance, which, if it had been

[1] The anecdote is given as Warner gave it. "Dr. Parr and the brilliant character in question met, one day, at a large party, and the conversation turning upon the execution of Coigly, the Irish priest, which had lately occurred, a difference of opinion arose among the company, respecting the equity of the sentence and the legality of his punishment. Mr. M. argued warmly in defence of the proceedings which had taken place ; and Dr. P. as strenuously against them. Heated by the dispute, Mr. M. at length attacked the *personal character* of the unfortunate culprit, and declared that he *could not conceive* one of more black or atrocious a die. ' Yes, Jemmy,' retorted the indignant Grecian (preluding this *coup de grace* by a mighty cloud of tobacco-smoke), ' a much worse man may be *easily conceived ;* for, he was an *Irishman*, and he might have been a *Scotchman ;* he was a *Priest*, and he might have been a *Lawyer* ; he was a *Martyr*, and he might have been an *Apostate*." [The "brilliant" Mr. M. was Macintosh, afterwards Sir James Macintosh. Warner uses the word *Martyr*, but the word used by Parr was *Traitor*.]

followed by the people, would have reflected credit upon them. In Lever's *Maurice Tierney*, the account of that memorable period is interesting from the graphic manner in which he describes the events and the several persons who took part in them; more especially the excellent Bishop himself. The Bishop's own narrative is the best account written of the invasion; it is characterised by that modest, clear, and unaffected style which distinguished this excellent prelate. His visits to Bath were frequent, and he sometimes lived at the **White Hart**; he and Warner were like David and Jonathan.[1] Warner relates an anecdote, very characteristic of the Bishop. A clergyman, encumbered with a large family, waited upon the Bishop in the first year of his residence at Killalla, and petitioned to be continued as the curate of the living which he served, his Rector having been killed by a ball from the French, when they landed at Killalla. His lordship invited him to remain to dinner, and as soon as the cloth was removed, he proposed the health of the late curate as *Vicar of Cross Molina !*

Warner's relations with Dr. Parry and Maclaine, and the two Falconers, were close, friendly, and hearty. There were occasional passages of arms between them, and they "gave and received" like men and gentlemen. There was a fine and sturdy independence of character about these men, and the mutual respect they felt for each other never induced them to flinch when the interests of truth were involved. A signal instance of this fact is afforded by the incident of the Sermon on War. The elder Dr. Falconer wrote and published a scathing "Remonstrance" to his friend, "Dick" Warner;[2] and his son, the Rev. Thomas Falconer, M.D., who was Warner's (gratuitous) coadjutor in the parish, addressed A Letter,[3] abounding with polished but unanswerable arguments on the one-sided views advocated by Warner. Men of this calibre must have been high-minded and magnanimous, who could thus afford to differ, and yet retain a hearty and faithful respect for each other.

It was not so with Warner always. Some of his contemporaries he held in contempt, and he took no pains to conceal it. Moreover, he wielded the lash sometimes with terrible severity, and no little bitterness. The "Bath Characters" is a work exhibiting wit, humour, and satirical power of no ordinary merit. But if he spared not the subjects of his satire, he spared not himself. The tenor of this book excited at the time of its publication much anger and bitterness,

[1] Dr. Stock died in his wheel-chair, Aug. 14, 1813, regretted by no one more than his friend "Richard" Warner. His published works were, Isaiah and Job, with the Hebrew texts; English Translations and Notes. These works were printed and published by Richard Cruttwell.

[2] A Remonstrance, addressed to the Rev. Richard Warner, on the subject of his Fast Sermon. May 27, 1804. "Justum est bellum; quibus necessarium et pia arma, quibus nulla, nisi in armis, relinquitur spes."—*Livii, Lib. ix., Oratio C. Pontii.*

[3] Letter to the Rev. Richard Warner, respecting his Sermon on War, 1804.

and, if the truth must be told, much satisfaction to those whose "withers were unwrung." The concluding portion of the introduction in the form of "Codicil to the Will of *Zachary Goosequill*, late of Grub Street, St. Giles's, author, deceased," is quoted rather as a key to the characters, than from any intrinsic merit it possesses. The wit is vulgar and unworthy of the writer, or of the general character of the book itself :—

"I give and bequeath to the said Timothy Goosequill, my FULL-BOTTOM'D WIG, in which, for these twenty years past, I have visited my employers the booksellers, and appeared at the literary table in the cyder-cellar, hoping that the use of it may impart to my said nephew a little of the GENIUS and LEARNING, which its curls have been accustomed to encircle. And, lastly, I give and bequeath to the said Timothy Goosequill my SILVER INKSTAND, (the gift of my loving grand-father (and lately rescued from the fangs of the pawnbroker), trusting that as often as he dips his pen therein, he will be reminded of the HONEST LABOURS of his uncle, who preferred a garret, and the cause of truth and virtue, to purple, fine linen, and daily sumptuous fare, and the prosti-tution of his talents in the service of humbug and vice. And it is my earnest and last request to my said dear nephew, that he will more especially direct the POWERS of the afore-mentioned WIG and INKSTAND to the CORRECTION of the CITY OF BATH, which offers such an ample field for satire and reprehension, and never cease endeavouring the reformation of its manners, till he have effected the following consummations, most devoutly to be wished, viz. :—Cured Ramrod [1] of his SOLEMN FOPPERY, and Rattle [2] of his BAREFACED IMPUDENCE ; taught Mrs. Vehicle [3] a little MODESTY, and infused into Sir Gregory Croaker [4] a scruple of DIFFIDENCE ; purged Signora Rattana [5] of her VANITY and AFFECTATION, and cleansed Bow-Wow [6] from INDECENCY and SCURRILITY ; inspired Sir Clerical Orange [7] with a grain of HUMILITY, and divested Sour-Crout [8] of PEEVISHNESS and SARCASM ; instructed Borecat [9] in LATIN SYNTAX, and stripped Mixum [10] of MEDICAL HUMBUG. That my said nephew can effect any reformation in the remaining characters I have no hope ; and therefore I do not make it a condition of this my codicil, or even urge it as my request, that he should exhaust his time and labour in endeavouring to attain the following impossible objects, viz. :—To inspire Chip [11] with a SENSE OF DECENCY ; to cure Drawcansir [12] of PRIDE, POMP, and BIGOTRY ; purify Gaffer Smit [13] from the filth of the WARBURTONIAN SCHOOL, and teach him CANDOUR, CHARITY, and BENEFICENCE ; to break Morose [14] of SWEARING and SCOTCH SNUFF ; Vegetable [15] of CARD-PLAYING and SERVILITY to the GREAT ; Sable [16] of DEMO-CRACY and LONG SERMONS ; and Skipper [17] of PETULANCE, CONCEIT, and CALVINISM."

1—King, M.C. 2—Matthews, the admirer of Miss Linley, who married Sheridan, with whom Matthews fought a duel on her account. 3—Mrs. Carr, the Actress. 4—Sir G. Colebrook, Hart. 5—Miss Wroughton. 6—Rev. Mr. Bowen. 7—Rev. Mr. Lemon. 8—Dr. Crawford. 9—Dr. Birkett. 10—Bowen, Apothecary. 11—Rev. Mr. Wood, an immoral, indecent, shameless old parson, who was a disgrace to his cloth and the city. 12—Archdeacon Daubeny. It is not obvious why Warner presents Daubeny in the character of *Drawcansir*. The Archdeacon, it is true, was one of the cold, dignified, *high and dry* school of Churchmen, and his controversial style was tinged with a tone of arrogance ; but he was a high-bred gentleman ; moreover, he was not one of the Warner coterie, and the Hoadley latitudinarianism was the Archdeacon's abhorrence. But to compare him with the *Drawcansir* of the *Rehearsal*, was not only unjust, but an ill-natured injustice. 13—Rev. Stafford Smith, who was formerly chaplain to Bishop Warburton, and married his widow. 14—Counsellor Morris. 15—Rev. Dr. Gardiner, of *the Octagon*, towards whom Warner was either in a state of open warfare, or armed neutrality. Warner, in the body of the book, is very hard upon Gardiner, but it is singular that the doctor should have fixed upon Dr. W. Falconer as the author, and resented the reflections cast upon him accordingly. In vain Dr. Falconer repud-iated the authorship of the book ; the injured divine was resolved he should endure his displeasure as

Warner makes some very characteristic errors in his History of Bath, which may take rank as "curiosities in literature." He gives from Wright's Rutland, as an historical fact, with most circumstantial details, the story of Queen Elizabeth's visit to Bath, and her visit of state to Sir John Harington at Kelston, in 1591.[1] No such visit took place. The tradition most probably was founded upon the Queen's visit to the city, in 1574, of which he makes no mention. But what will be felt by most readers who are acquainted with the historical facts, and who know anything of the process of historical enquiry, is surprise that so acute and able a man as Warner should have failed to consult a book so readily accessible as *Nichols's Royal Visitations* (1788), by which he might have ascertained the facts. But apart from the *direct* evidence, if Warner were unacquainted with it, there is the negative and indirect evidence, almost as conclusive as the direct, namely, that Sir John Harington nowhere makes any reference to a visit from his Royal Mistress, which, if such a visit had occurred, he would have rendered immortal by his eloquent pen. It would have been as well known, indeed, as her visit to Cecil, at Stamford,[2] or the more famous visit to Kenilworth. Warner was well acquainted with the *Nugæ Antiquæ*, which contains so much about Sir John, and it is curious to remark that to his acquaintance with, and reliance upon, that book is attributable another great and strange blunder into which he fell, with respect to the representation of Bath at the most critical period of its history. A fair amount of research into the value of the authority by which he was guided, and into the documents ready to his hand, would have enabled him to test its accuracy, and would have saved him from the perpetration of historical misstatements of an almost ludicrous character. Warner appears to have followed the *Nugæ Antiquæ* with implicit faith, notwithstanding that the editor himself, the Rev. H. Harington

---

such. 16—Warner himself. 17—Rev. Dr. Shepherd, a seceder from the Church of England, and at this time (1808) an adherent of the Lady Huntingdon sect, a bigoted *Calvinist*, but a capital schoolmaster. These are not all the characters who are made to take part in the dialogue in the book. Lady Belmore as *Lady Loftiname ;* Sheridan as *Mr. Merriman ;* Rauzzini as *Resin ;* Miss Linley as *A Little Linnett ;* Dr. W. Falconer as *Dr. Vellum ;* Dr. Harington as *Dr. Harmony ;* Bowles the Poet as *Billy Sonnett ;* and many others who were well known at the time, but some of whom have been forgotten in connection with Bath at that period.

1 "The year ensuing the date of Elizabeth's charter (1590), that Princess conferred an additional mark of favour on the city of Bath, by honouring it with her presence. Sir John Harington, the godson and favourite of Elizabeth, had received the promise of a Royal visit at his country mansion, at Kelweston, near Bath ; and that he might afford the Queen a proper reception there, had fitted up his house in a style of elegance and magnificence suitable to the taste of the age. The Queen kept her word, arrived at Sir John's house *on her way to Oxford,* A.D. 1591, and dined right royally under the fountain which played in the court.* Elizabeth took this opportunity of visiting the city of Bath."—*Warner's " Civil History of Bath,"* p. 187.

* Such is the tradition.

2 Not to Burghley, which was not built, but to Cecil's house in St. Martin's.

(a descendant of Sir John), admits his own uncertainty. This should have led the historian to make more careful investigation as to the matter involved. The reader will understand that the object here is not to criticise, for the sake of criticising, Warner's History, but to point out certain erroneous statements, and to present the true statements as involving important and most interesting historical facts and associations connected with Bath during the revolutionary epoch. In 1641 Bath was represented by two members, namely, Charles Berkeley, Esq., and Alexander Popham, Esq. ; afterwards Berkeley was superseded by William Bassett, Esq. As to the following election, which took place in September, 1645, but which the *Nugæ*, with all its strange contradictions and ambiguity, says was 1646, Warner quotes the following letter :

" To our muche honoured and worthie Friend, J. H., Esq., at his House at Kelston, near Bathe.
   " Worthie Sir,

   " Out of the long experience[1] we have had of your approved worth and sincerity, our Cittie of Bathe have determined and settled their resolutions to elect you for Burgess of the House of Commons in this present Parliament, for our said Cittie, and do hope you will *accept the trouble thereof;* which if you do, our desire is, not fail to be with us at Bathe, on Monday next, the eighth of this instant, by eight of the morning, at the furthest, for then we proceed to our election. And of your determination we entreat you to certifie us by a word or two in writing, and send it by the bearer to

   Your assured loving Friends,

                                                          JOHN BIGG, the Major.
   Bathe, December 6, 1645."   WILLIAM CHAPMAN.

   [1] It will be noticed that the words, " Out of the long experience we have had of your approved worth and sincerity," could only apply to the father, and yet at that very time he was one of the representatives of the county, George Horner being the other.   John Harington, the father, sat for the county from 1645 to 1654.   He died in April of the latter year, and was succeeded by his son John, who sat until 1656.   He was elected for Bath with Ashe in 1658, and sat until 1659.   Both father and son were tainted with Republicanism, or were said to be, and both were exposed to much danger from this cause in times of reaction.   After 1659 the name of Harington disappears from the roll of Parliament for Bath and Somerset.   It would be desirable to get at the origin and meaning of the letter written by Bigg, but it is clear that neither the editor of the *Nugæ* nor Warner had got at the true meaning of it, if it be anything more than a species of literary forgery of the younger John Harington, which is most unlikely. There is another discrepancy which adds to the puzzle.   The letter purporting to be written to Harington bears date December 6, 1645, and yet the election took place in the preceding September.   There is another hypothesis as regards the " Note," namely, that the date 1646—about which the editor of the *Nugæ* admits a doubt— was 1654, and that the election was for the county, and not the city.   It was in 1654 that the elder John Harington obtained permission to retire from the House on the ground of ill health, and it was known that he would not again offer himself for re-election.   This was early in the year 1654, and it is certain that he was to be succeeded by his son.   John Harington died in April, and his son was elected in his stead.   But then, assuming that the wrong year is given by the editor of the *Nugæ*, how can the dates be explained ?   What had the Mayor of Bath to do with the county election, and how is the explicit statement to be got over, that, " on Monday, Dec. 28th, went to Bath ; met Sir John Horner; we were chosen by the citizens to serve for the *city*," and all the rest of the narrative? That Sir John Horner and John Harington were chosen to represent the *county* at the election in 1654, is an historical fact, and it is equally certain that Sir John Horner *never represented Bath at any time.* There is another theory—a theory supported by the opinion of Professor Earle—and it seems almost conclusive, namely, that Harington, who lived until 1700, before his death, made some Notes of his experience and past life, and from loss of memory made many errors.   This, added to the editor's want of knowledge of the events of the day, and his deficiency in literary arrangement, occasioned the utter confusion into which he fell.

"A SPECIMEN of the MODE of Electing MEMBERS for PARLIAMENT in the last Century. Taken from a Memorandum MSS. of J. HARINGTON, Esq., of Kelston, in Somersetshire. Dated 1646.

"A NOTE of my BATHE BUSINESS aboute the PARLIAMENT.

"Saturday, December 26th, 1646, went to Bathe, and dined withe the Major and Citizens; conferred about my election to serve in Parliament, as my father was helpless and ill able to go any more;—went to the George Inn at night, met the Bailiffs, and desired to be dismissed from serving; drank strong beer and metheglin; expended about iijs., went home late, but could not get excused, as they entertained a good opinion of my father.

"Monday, Dec. 28th, went to Bathe; met Sir John Horner; we were chosen by the Citizens to serve for the City. The Major and Citizens conferred about Parliament business. The Major promised *Sir John Horner and myself a horse apiece,* when we went to London to the Parliament, which we accepted of; and we talked about the Synod and ecclesiastical dismissions. I am to go again on Thursday, and meet the Citizens about all such matters, and take advice thereon.

"Thursday, 31, went to Bathe; Mr. Ashe preached. Dined at the George Inn with the Major and 4 Citizens; spent at dinner vj sh. in wine.

	s.	*d.*
Laid out in victuals at the George Inn	xj	4
Laid out in drinking	vij	ij
Laid out in tobacco and drinking vessels	iiij	4

"Jan. 1. My father gave me 4l. to bear my expenses at Bathe.

"Mr Chapman the Major, came to Kelston and returned thanks, for any being choosen to serve in Parliament, to my father, in name of all the Citizens. My father gave me good advice, touching my speaking in Parliament as the City should direct me. Came home late at night from Bathe, much troubled hereat concerning my proceeding truly for men's good report and mine own safety.

"Note, I gave the City Messenger ijsh. for bearing the Major's Letter to me.· Laid out in all, 3l. vijth. for victuals, drink, and horse-hire, together with divers gifts.

"N.B. The Editor is not quite certain that this Election was in 1646, as the Date is obscure in the MSS; but it was within a Year or two of that time."

The "Note" does not appear in the first edition of the *Nugæ,* but in the second. It does not answer to any historical fact; no trace of either can be found in the records, nor was either Sir John Horner or John Harington elected to represent the city. In 1645, Bassett was in some way legally "disabled" from "this Parliament,"[1] and James Ashe was elected in his room, 16 votes being recorded for him, and 3 for Edward Popham. It will be seen, therefore, that up to this time the city had been represented by two members, to which it was legally entitled under the charter of Queen Elizabeth. In 1648, for some reason not explained, one member alone was

---

[1] "Disabled" is the word used in the minutes of the Council. It means really that Bassett was a Royalist and a true gentleman, and so he was expelled to make room for Ashe, who was neither.

elected, and that was William Prynne, who was also appointed Recorder. In 1654 there were three candidates, namely, James Ashe, "Collonell" Alexander Popham, and — Clift, Popham being elected solely.[1] " In the Council iiij day of Aug., 1656. Business—Who shall be a Citizen of this Citty to sitt in Parlt. as Burgess for the same City accordg. to a Warrant to us in that behalfe directed, bearing date the 25th July, 1656. Agreed [one vote only shewn for Mr. Bigg] that Mr. James Ashe, Esq., Recorder,[2] shall be citizen of this City to sitt as Burgess in Parlt. for the same City as above said." In January, 1656, two members were again returned, and this, be it observed, is the first time the name of John Harington is mentioned as one of the representatives, Ashe, who was still Recorder, being the other. In 1660 Popham and Prynne [3] were elected (" nem. con."). This was the election after the restoration, when the two members were returned in accordance with legal privilege.

[1] Ashe was elected Recorder instead of Prynne. He was a violent member of the Parliamentary party and of the rump Parliament. The fact of the Council electing such a man as its Recorder and Member says little either for its discrimination or its independence. In 1661, Prynne was restored to the Recordership.

[2] One of the peculiar blessings conferred by these revolutionary Parliaments was to cut and carve and manipulate the representation according as it suited them. Bath was no exception. Sometimes the elective body pleased the Parliament ; sometimes it indulged in the luxury of a little independence, for which the noble and liberal government bereft the city of a member. Ashe was a rumper and a pious prig, but he was held to be good enough to supersede Prynne both in Parliament and as Recorder. There is little or nothing in the Records to show *how* this pressure was brought to bear, but it is quite certain that the Biggs, and the Chapmans (except Henry), and the Atwoods, and the other leading men of that day were not likely spontaneously to lop off a member, even if they could legally have done so, much less to disfranchise the city altogether, as was done during part of the period of the Long Parliament and the Rump. It is also a circumstance to be remarked that, notwithstanding the part the municipal body was obliged to play during the revolutionary contest, sometimes on one side and sometimes on the other, there is not a single reference to these important events in the Municipal Records.

[3] It was on this occasion that Henry Chapman attempted to establish the right of the Freemen to elect their own members, but was ultimately defeated in the attempt. Chapman had been up to this time a rampant Republican ; as soon as Charles II. was firmly established on the throne, he became a cringing Royalist. He was a man of energy, ability, and ambition, but wholly selfish and unprincipled. In 1812 a similar movement was attempted by a very notorious person, one Allen, a pawnbroker, a man of property, whose ambition it was to sit in Parliament. The constituted authorities had no desire to elect Allen, and he therefore appealed to the Freemen, claiming for that body precisely the same privileges which Chapman claimed for the Freemen in 1660, and basing his claim upon the same constitutional principle, notwithstanding the fact that Parliament had contemptuously rejected the claim and refused to recognise any such principle. An amusing account of the affair was written by C. Hibbert in 1813. Allen is called " The Man of Pledges," " The Child of Promise," " The Disturber of Corporations," and a portrait is given of him, in which, with his right hand, he is holding the Corporation shield, upside down. Allen, at the time of this lively episode, lived in Philip Street, from whence his address is dated, and it would be difficult to conceive a more truculent or a more impudent production. There was a good deal of rioting, a few broken heads, *not* including Allen's, and a few victims were sent to prison, of whom Allen was not one. Lord John Thynne and Colonel Palmer were elected in the usual way. The vapouring of Allen about sacred rights and liberties and upstart usurpers, and the use of such like expressions, meant only the difference between the Corporate Elective Body and the "sworn citizens," or any limited number of Freemen, of whom 28 recorded their votes for Allen.

Warner published his History of Glastonbury Abbey [1] during his residence at **PROSPECT COTTAGE, NEWTON ST. LOE,** in 1823, and a very able work it is. The most curious work, however, of which he was the author is the *Antiquitates Culinariæ*, a 4to book, a l.p. copy of which sold at Sir R. Colt Hoare's sale for £15 15s. Warner's career as an author ceased when he left Bath, about 1823. His life in Chelwood was calm and happy; he loved his work, looking with satisfaction upon his past activity and usefulness, and forward with cheerful hope to his great reward. In the next History of Bath the name of Richard' Warner will occupy a distinguished place. His daughter died before him, but Mrs. Warner survived him.

GOVERNOR HOLWELL, WESTHALL.—If the reader has not recently read Macaulay's Essay on Lord Clive, perhaps he will again read in it the description of the fearful episode of the Black Hole of Calcutta, before he reads this notice. Holwell was one of the 23 who survived that night's horrors. Mr. Monkland says that Holwell built *Beaulieu Lodge,* but this statement rests upon the evidence of "two informants," and after all is opposed to the evidence on which he originally arrived at the conclusion that Holwell built *Westhall,* and that it was his residence. This is the correct statement. Tickell built *Beaulieu Lodge. Westhall* stood on a site near the turnpike-gate, and when built there were no other houses near. Holwell wrote a history of the Black Hole tragedy, and many other tracts and works relating to Hindostan. At the close of his life he wrote a very foolish and extravagant work on the transmigration of souls. He held that the mortal bodies of men were but tabernacles, or the temporary abodes of fallen angels. On this theory, the body of *Surajah Dowlah* must have been the abode of a whole legion.

JOHN MORRIS, No. 4, BELVEDERE,[2] born 1789, died 1869. Educated at Mr. Holdstock's school, with G. P. Manners, Mr. W. Hunt, etc.; afterwards the pupil of Dr. Shepherd, who figures in *Bath Characters* as *Dr. Skipper,* along with Archdeacon Daubeny as *Mr. Drawcansir.*[3] Joined Mr. Moline's Chess Club, along with Professor Davies, Mr. G. Rosenberg, G. P. Manners, etc. Also the Eclectic Society, founded by C. Godwin, in 1830, from which emanated the Bath and Bristol Magazine, which engaged the pens of James Montgomery, Rev. W. L.

---

[1] In this book, singularly enough, he fell into one of those peculiar errors which seemed to beset him as an author, and which were the result partly of carelessness and partly of a desire to startle by some new theory. In this instance, he, in Banwell Church, mistook some modern masonic devices, which would scarcely deceive a child, for works of antiquity.

[2] In this house he was born, brought up, and died.

[3] See Warner.

Bowles, Rev. E. Mangin, Mr. G. W. Homer, and others, and to which Mr. Morris was also a contributor. This magazine only continued for three years, but Mr. Morris continued in the columns of the *Bath and Cheltenham Gazette* a series of Somersetshire Worthies, including Dr. Tobias Matthew, Richard Edwards, Humphry Sydenham, Sir John Harington, and Samuel Daniel; at a later date this last was extended, at the suggestion of Mr. Monkland, into a volume bearing the title, "Selections from the Writings of Samuel Daniel," to which was prefixed the life of neither the least, nor the last, of the Worthies of Somerset.

RAUZZINI, PERRYMEAD VILLA,[1] 13, GAY STREET.—From 1780 to 1810, the great Musical Dictator of Bath was **VENANZIO RAUZZINI.** He exercised undisputed authority in the region of Music in this city, when Music and the Drama were supreme. Rauzzini was a man of remarkable character and ability. As a preceptor, singer, composer, and conductor, he ranked above all others in his day. He was the friend of Herschel, and it was his privilege to have been the mentor of the first English tenor of his time—perhaps of any time—the great **BRAHAM.** A Roman gentleman by birth, cultivated in taste, and early distinguished in his profession, Rauzzini had experienced the highest applause at Vienna, where he became the intimate friend of **METESTASIO,** and where he was also "the idol of the cognoscenti, the favourite of princes, and the delight of all who heard him." From Vienna Rauzzini removed to Munich, and there he met with Dr. Burney, who lauded him with unstinted praise. In 1774 he came to England, and notwithstanding his great eminence as a singer and an actor, he retired from the lyric stage in 1780, and settled in the city of Bath. Perhaps this act of self-sacrifice may be accounted for by his unconquerable sensibility, as he never made his appearance as a public performer without trepidation. Garrick conceived a high opinion of Rauzzini's acting, and praised him accordingly. He longed, however, for a more calm and less exciting career, and what he longed for, that he found in Bath. The period was precisely opportune for the career of such a man. About 1780 he came to this city, and at once became pre-eminent as a professor of singing and music. With La Motte he became joint conductor of the public concerts. Rauzzini was not only the instructor of Braham, who was his articled pupil for three years, but he was also the preceptor of Madame Mara, Mrs. Billington, Signor Storace, Mrs. Mountain, Incledon, and other distinguished singers. It was said of Rauzzini that, "accomplished in all the learning, and all the graces of his art, he imparted the light of his mind to every professional student" of ability, and that "a singer untutored by him" was only

[1] One of the four villas of which Warner's Villa was one, on the site of Hanging Lands.

half taught. Braham lived with his distinguished master, and it is related of him that when the instructor requested the young aspirant to sing, himself accompanying him on the piano, Rauzzini closed the instrument in silence, paused; and at length, turning round to his pupil, said in his broken English, "That will do— Master Braham will make a first-rate singer." A feeling of mutual esteem grew between master and pupil, which was interrupted only by death. Rauzzini died in 1810, and was followed to his grave, in the Abbey, by many of his distinguished pupils, his accomplished friend Dr. Harington having written his epitaph. Playful and simple as he was accomplished, he sometimes became a little impatient. A female pupil in rehearsing the sacred song of Handel, "Pious Orgies, Pious Airs," dwelt so much on *pi* that Rauzzini exclaimed, "Vat pie, my dear, *plum pie* or *apple pie ?*" One, butcher Matthews, a chorus singer, wanted to sing a solo, and became importunate, but Rauzzini said, "Go home, Mr. Maddew, and kill de sheep." When it was stated to him that Bartleman had not the defects of other singers, Rauzzini said, "True, but he has plenty of his own."

ESTCOURT, SIR T., Nos. 11 and 12, BROAD STREET.—In 1695 one of the Parliamentary Representatives of Bath was Sir Thomas Estcourt. Broad Street, though it was not within the "liberties" of the city, was virtually a most important part of it. The houses, chiefly Elizabethan in date and style, were occupied by the aristocracy of the period. The gardens on the western side extended as far as the site of Milsom Street, and on the eastern side towards Walcot Street. The last house preserved until a recent period was that in which Sir T. Estcourt resided. It stood immediately above the Grammar School, and on the same side; and in its stead, stand two modern houses, one used as a hairdresser's shop, and the other as a grocer's. The two oldest buildings now in the street are a gabled house, (No. 38,) built in 1709, and the *Saracen's Head*, built in 1713.

THE TWO DOCTORS OLIVER, BATH WATERS, BISCUITS, AND GOSSIP.—There were two Doctors Oliver, both of whom were residents in Bath, and both Fellows of the Royal Society. Both wrote on the same subjects, and each has frequently been mistaken for the other. Dr. Watt confounds them in his *Bibliotheca Britannica.* Dr Oliver, the elder, studied medicine in foreign universities, and for a time gave up his pursuits, in 1668, to join the Prince of Orange. After completing his medical education, he was appointed Physician to the Fleet, and later he was appointed Physician to the Hospitals of Chatham and Greenwich. The latter appointment he held at the time of his death, which occurred April 14, 1716. It is not quite clear what this Dr. Oliver's connection with Bath was. He does not seem to have practised in Bath; indeed, the supposition is forbidden by the fact that his official appointments were quite incompatible with any other professional engagements. It is nevertheless clear that his spirit of investigation, and love of knowledge, induced him to make a special study of the climate of Bath, and the Bath Waters, on which he wrote two distinct works:— in 1704, "A Treatise on Fevers and the Bath Waters;" in 1707, "A Practical Dissertation on Bath Waters." He wrote "Relation of an extraordinary Sleepy Person at Timsbury, near Bath," which was published in the later editions of the Dissertation. This narrative of the Sleeping Man is a somewhat cold-blooded story. The physiological phenomena connected with the case are curious, and as there appears to have been no probability of collusion or fraud, there can be little doubt as to the facts, of which the chief are related :—

"May the 13th, An. 1694.—One Samuel Chilton, of Timsbury, near Bath, a Labourer, about twenty-five years of age, of a robust habit of body, not fat, but fleshy, and a dark-brown hair, happen'd without any visible cause, or preceding sign, to fall into a very profound sleep ; out of which no art, used by those that were near him, could rouse him, till after a month's time. Then he rose of himself, put on his cloaths, and went about his business of husbandry as usual ; slept, could eat and drink as before, but spake not one word till about a month after. All the time he slept, victuals stood by him ; his mother, fearing he would be starv'd in that sullen humour, as she thought it, put bread and cheese and small beer before him, which was spent every day.

"From this time he remain'd free of any drowsiness or sleepiness, till about the 9th of April, 1696, and then he fell into his sleeping fit again, just as he did before. After some days, they were prevail'd with to try what effect medicines might have on him ; and accordingly one Mr. Gibbs, a very able apothecary at Bath, went to him, bled, blister'd, cupp'd, and scarify'd him, and us'd all the external irritating medicines he could think on; but all to no purpose, nothing of all these making any manner of impression on him ; and after the first fortnight he was never observed to open his eyes. Victuals stood by him as before, which he eat of now-and-then, as he had occasion ; and sometimes they have found him fast asleep, with the pot in his hand in bed, and sometimes with his mouth full of meat. In this manner he lay for about ten weeks, and then could eat nothing at all ; for his jaws seemed to be set, and his teeth clinch'd so close, that with all the art they had, they could not open his mouth, to put anything into it to support him. At last, observing a hole made in his teeth, by holding his pipe in his mouth, as most great smokers usually have, they, through a quill, poured some tent into his throat, now-and-then. And this was all he took for six weeks and four days, and of that not above three pints or two quarts. He had made water but once, and never had a stool all that time.

"August the 7th, which is seventeen weeks from the 9th of April (when he began to sleep), he awaked, put on his cloaths, and walk'd about the room, not knowing he had slept above a night ; nor could he be persuaded he had lain so long, till going out into the fields, he found everybody busy in gathering in their harvest, and he remember'd very well, when he fell asleep, they were sowing of barley and oats, which he then saw ripe, and fit to be cut down.

"There was one thing observable, that though his flesh was somewhat wasted with so long lying in bed, and fasting for above six weeks, yet a worthy gentleman, his neighbour, assur'd me, when he saw him (which was the first day of his coming abroad) he look'd brisker than ever he had seen him in his life before ; and asking him, whether the bed had not made him sore, he assured him and everybody, that he neither found that, nor any other inconveniency at all ; and that he had not the least remembrance of anything that pass'd or was done to him all that while. So he fell again to his husbandry, as he us'd to do, and remain'd well from that time till August the 17th, Anno 1697; when in the morning he complained of a shivering and coldness in his back, vomited once or twice, and that same day fell into his sleeping fit again.

"Being then at the Bath,[1] and hearing of it, I took horse on the 23rd, to inform myself of a matter of fact I thought so strange. When I came to the house, I was by the neighbours (for there was nobody at home at that time besides this man) brought to his bedside, where I found him asleep, as I had been told before, with a cup of beer and a piece of bread and cheese upon a stool by his bed, within his reach. I took him by the hand, felt his pulse, which was at that time very regular; I put my hand on his breast, and found his heart beat very regular too, and his breathing was very easy and free ; and all the fault I found was. that I thought his pulse beat a little too strong. He was in a breathing sweat, and had an agreeable warmth all over his body. I then put my mouth to his ear, and, as loud as I could, called him by his name several times, pull'd him by his shoulders, pinch'd his nose, stopp'd his mouth and nose together, as long as I durst, for fear of choaking him, but all to no purpose ; for in all this time he gave me not the least signal of his being sensible. I lifted up his eyelids, and found his eyeballs drawn up under his eyebrows, and fixed without any motion at all. Being baffled with all these tryals, I was resolv'd to see what effects Spirit of Sal Ammoniac would have, which I had brought with me to discover the cheat, if it had been one ; so I held my viol under one nostril a considerable time, which being drawn from quick-lime was a very piercing spirit, and so strong I could not bear it under my own nose a moment, without making my eyes water ; but he felt it not at all. Then I threw it, at several times, up that same nostril. It made his nose run and gleet, and his eyelids shiver and tremble a very little, and this was all the effect I found, though I poured up into one nostril about an half-ounce bottle of this fiery spirit, which was as strong almost as fire itself. Finding no success with this neither, I crammed that nostril with powder of white hellebore, which I had by me, in order to make my farther tryals ; and I can hardly think any impostor could ever be insensible of what I did. I tarry'd some time afterwards in the room, to see what effects all together might have upon him ; but he never gave any token that he felt what I had done, nor discover'd any manner of uneasiness, by moving or stirring any one part of his body, that I could observe. Having made these my experiments, I left him, being pretty well satisfied he was really asleep, and no sullen counterfeit, as some people thought him.

"Upon my return to Bath, and relating what I had observed, and what proofs this fellow had given me of his sleeping, a great many gentlemen went out to see him, as I had done, to satisfy their curiosity in a rarity of that nature, who found him in the same condition I had left him in the day before ; only his nose was inflamed and swelled very much, and his lips and the inside of his right nostril blistered and scabby, with my spirit of Hellebore, which I had plentifully dosed him with the day before. His mother, for some time after, would suffer nobody to

---

[1] This shows that the Doctor was only an occasional visitor to *the* Bath.

come near him, for fear of more experiments upon her son.[1] About ten days after I had been with him, Mr. Woolmer, an experienced apothecary at Bath, called at the house, being near Timsbury, went up into the room, finding his pulse pretty high, as I had done, took out his launcet, let him blood about fourteen ounces in the arm, tied his arm up again, nobody being in the house, and left him as he found him ; and he assur'd me he never made the least motion in the world when he prick'd him, nor all the while his arm was moving.

"Several other experiments were made by those that went to see him every day from the Bath ; but all to no purpose, as they told me on their return. I saw him myself again the latter end of September, and found him just in the same posture, lying in his bed, but removed from the house where he was before, about a furlong or more ; and they told me, when they removed him by accident, carrying him down stairs, which were somewhat narrow, they struck his head against a stone, and gave him a severe knock, which broke his head, but he never moved any more at it than a dead man would. I found now his pulse was not quite so strong, nor had he any sweats, as when I saw him before. I tried him again the second time, by stopping his nose and mouth, but to no purpose. And a gentleman, then with me, ran a large pin into his arm to the very bone, unknown to me ; but he gave us no manner of tokens of his being sensible of anything we did to him.

"In this manner he lay till November 16, when his mother, hearing him make a noise, ran immediately up to him, and found him eating. She asked him how he did. He said, 'Very well, thank God.' She asked him again which he liked best, bread and butter, or bread and cheese ? He answered, 'Bread and cheese.' Upon this, the poor woman, overjoy'd, left him, to acquaint his brother with it ; and they came straight up into the chamber to discourse him, but found him as fast asleep again as ever, and all the art they had could not wake him. From this time to the end of January, or the beginning of February (for I could not learn from anybody the very day), he slept not so profoundly as before ; for when they called him by his name, he seemed to hear them, and be somewhat sensible, though he could not make them any answer. His eyes were not now shut so close, and he had frequently great tremblings of his eyelids, upon which they expected when he would wake ; which happen'd not till about the time just now mentioned, and then he walked perfectly well, not remembring anything that happened all this while. 'Twas observed he was very little altered in his flesh, only complained the cold pinched him more than usually, and so presently fell to husbandry, as at other times.

"I have no reason to suspect this to be a cheat, because I never heard of any gain to the family by it, though so near the Bath, and so many people went thither out of curiosity to see the sleeper, who, when awake, was a support to his old mother by his labour, but now a certain charge to her. Besides, there was seldom anybody in the house to attend any profits that might be made by it, he being left alone, and everybody at liberty to go up to his bedside."

What will strike the reader in this narrative is the cool manner in which these old *quid-nuncs* experimented upon the poor man. The reference to the *hellebore*, and the swollen lip and nose, is cruel enough, but the "gentleman with me" running a pin up to the bone was an act of revolting barbarity.

---

[1] These experiments, so cold-blooded and cruel, are related by the worthy doctor as if they were a fine joke. The reflections which follow the relation are neither profound nor edifying. There is much affectation of learning, and a vast deal of nonsense about the "seat of the soul," references to ancient philosophy, and such like, but no rational explanation as to the phenomena he witnessed. Mr. Woolmer, the "experienced apothecary," deserved a flogging.

In taking leave of *Dr. Oliver, No. 1, Dr. Oliver, No. 2,* at once presents himself. He was the illegitimate son of the elder, and, like his father, was a physician, an F.R.S., and he was something more than this—he was the inventor of that immortal farinaceous tit-bit, known as "Oliver's Biscuits." There have been many eminent physicians in, as well as out, of Bath; one less or twenty more probably would have made little difference, but the physician biscuit-maker must be ranked amongst the *immortals*. No stomach was ever so robust as to hold the crisp delicacy in disdain, none so delicate as not to relish and digest it. Ah! that great benefactor of the human race; surely he deserves a place by the side of Jenner and all the great discoverers! But if Oliver was great, he was not less generous; he made the discovery, but he disdained to profit by it. He used it as the grand *pabulum* for his patients, and when his time drew near to "shuffle off this mortal coil," he left his secret for others to profit by, and to perpetuate the blessings thereof to posterity.

Dr. W. Oliver, the younger, practised in Bath for upwards of 40 years, and attained to the first rank in his profession. He was commonly known, *not,* as is occasionally supposed, in contradistinction to his father, but simply because of his own eminent gifts and success, as the *famous Dr. Oliver.* He was, moreover, the intimate friend and medical adviser of *Borlase,* the historian, who was in Bath in 1730, and on that and subsequent occasions took an active part in public matters. Dr. Oliver was not only distinguished as a physician,[1] but he was a warm-hearted, enlightened philanthropist. Dr. Oliver was appointed physician to the Bath General, or Mineral Water Hospital, May 1st, 1740, and at the same time **JERRY PEIRCE**[2] was appointed Surgeon. They both resigned

[1] He was the author of the following books :—In 1751 he published a "Practical Essay on the Use and Abuse of Warm Bathing in Gouty Cases," 4to; in the "Partium Genitalium in Muliere Structura Præternaturalis;" and for 1755 another on "Some Cases of Dropsy cured by Sweet Oil."

[2] Jerry Peirce, if not a direct descendant of Dr. Peirce, of the Abbey House, was one of the same family. He was one of Ralph Allen's personal friends and medical advisers. With Dr. Oliver he attended Allen during his last illness, each of them receiving a complimentary legacy of £100. Oliver died shortly after Allen. Peirce was somewhat peculiar in his habits. Wood built him a house, in 1738, which he mentions in his *Description of Bath.* The edifice stood on, or very near to the site of the house now called "Battle-Fields;" whether it was pulled down entirely, or whether any part of its walls were incorporated with that house cannot now be ascertained, but be that as it may, Lilliput Castle, as it was called, has disappeared.

"The House that enriches the End of *Mons Badonica* goes by the Name of *Lilliput* Castle, and bearing North North West, half Northery from the Center of the Body of the City, is about four Miles distant from that Point: The Villa stands about a Quarter of a Mile below the Monument erected by my Lord *Lansdown* in Memory of his Grandfather, Sir *Bevil Granville;* it fronts principally towards the West ; and it was built with the Free Stone raised upon the Summit of the Hill above it : A Square of one and twenty Feet contains the whole Structure ; and the predominant Precept of the Building being Strength, this very fairly entitles it to its Sirname of Castle.

"LILLIPUT consists of a Cellar Story, almost sunk into the Earth, and this sustains a Principal and half Story, wherein there is a Hall and a Dining Parlour; an Alcove Bed Chamber,

May 1, 1761.   In the Board Room of the Hospital there is a picture, painted by W. Hoare, containing a portrait of these two excellent men.   They are in the act of examining a patient.   Hoare seems to have caught just that expression of sympathy and compassion which was so characteristic of the doctor and surgeon in their professional conduct.   Oliver died in 1764, and was buried in the Abbey.

He left two daughters, the younger of whom married the celebrated physician, *Sir John Pringle.*   Before Oliver's death he called to him a favourite coachman, and thus addressed him : "My good Atkins, I wish to put you in a position to obtain a livelihood when I am gone.   I give you the *recipe* to make my *biscuits;* I give you a supply of 10 sacks of finest wheaten flour, and One Hundred Pounds."   Atkins took a small shop in Green Street ; and there he established himself as the sole proprietor and maker of *Oliver's Biscuits.*   He thrived ; he made a fortune ; and when, many years after, he died, he bequeathed a large fortune [1] to his children, one of whom, a short, deformed gentleman, lived

with a light Closet ; and a Room sufficient for holding a second Bed : The lower Story yields proper Cellars, a Pantry, and a Kitchen ; and the Precept of Convenience may be very justly said to shine so eminently in every Part of this little Box as to render it the *Multum in Parvo* of all *Bath.*

"The windows in the Westward Front are dressed with Architraves ; and those of the principal Story are crowned with Freezes and Cornices, the central Window having the Addition of a Pediment to distinguish it ; All the Ornaments were intended to have been such as were proper to the *Dorick* Order ; and the Building being crowned with an Entablature. the whole was at first covered with a Pyramidal Roof ; in the Center of which the Funnels of the Chimneys rose up in a small Pedestal.

"The Figure of the Structure thus finished was such, that the Wits of *Bath* soon gave it the Name of *T Totum;* and I have only two Things to Lament concerning the Edifice : The first is that such a Toy of Architecture was not put into the Hands of our most accurate Workmen ; and the second is, the Hospitality of the Builder, a Virtue that hath twice brought our little Castle, in all outward Appearance, to the very Brink of Destruction, and rob'd it of its chief Beauty : For from an unreasonable Use of the Kitchen Chimney it took Fire ; and such a Pillar of Flame, Smoak and burning Soot each time surmounted poor *Lilliput* as was sufficient to have warmed and kindled any other Structure into one universal Blaze ; yet our Castle defied the raging Element : But nevertheless the Horror of a Conflagration, on the like Occasions, instantly condemned its Roof to everlasting Banishment ; the Base of the Pyramid was then spread over with Lead for a Covering to the Building ; and the Walls were disgraced with an ill-proportioned Balustrade, improperly divided, and as improperly set up to conceal the Funnels of the Chimneys in the Pedestals of it.

"The Ground in which *Lilliput* is situated bears the Name of *upper Rogers;* but *Rogers* seems here to be a manifest Corruption of *Rogus,* a word importing a great Fire wherein human Bodies were burnt to Ashes : Here therefore we may suppose those People to have been sacrificed which the Druidical Religion condemned, or allured to the Flames ;—*Cæsar,* in the 6th Book of his *Commentaries,* informs us of the cruel Custom ; and our Author assures us that as often as the Gods were appeased with publick Offerings of the human Species, the Victims were put into hollow Images, bound about with Oziers, to which the *Druids* set Fire, and thereby suffocated the People inclosed in the Cases."—*Wood's Description of Bath, pp.* 234—236.

[1] It has been said that he acquired money by other means. The story is pretty well known, but it rests upon no better evidence, perhaps, than the story told by Thicknesse of Allen.

for many years at 16, Kensington Place, and there he died in 1859. Atkins was succeeded by others,[1] some of whom made fortunes, and the business is still carried on, on the same premises, by **MR. JAMES FORTT**, who, imbued with the spirit of modern progress, has enlarged and improved them. For 120 years, therefore, these far-famed biscuits have been associated with the same shop, and it is not too much to say that they maintain their pristine reputation and their wonted crispness.

SIR C. J. NAPIER, No. 37, HENRIETTA STREET.—At the close of the year 1836, the doughty warrior whose name heads this monograph for the second time settled in Bath.[2] He was at this time Lieut.-Col. Napier, but in the following January he obtained the rank of brevet Major-General. Sir William, in his Life of Sir Charles, says :—" At Bath, Charles Napier entered warmly into the politics of the day, which were perilous; and Bath was at that time the most vigorous reforming city of the empire, being then unsurpassed in generous patriotism. He attended public meetings and dinners, aided the formation of reforming associations, and avowed himself a Radical. Yet he always endeavoured to repress a tendency to public violence, which, *for their own party purposes, was so much encouraged by the Whigs !* " In one of his speeches he animadverted upon the conduct of O'Connell, for opposing an Irish Poor Law, upon which a paper-war ensued. O'Connell called Napier "a ridiculous blockhead," and accused him of "heaping filthy vituperation " upon him (O'Connell). O'Connell in the meantime had become a convert to the Poor Law, and Napier rejoined, "Possibly, a blockhead I may be ; and as I am forced by conviction to go along with you on the subject of a Poor Law for Ireland, I confess alarm, knowing the danger which attends a blockhead when he travels with a consummate knave ; but as to vituperation, I have not used it, nor would it be wise to do so against so perfect a master of the art. I once asked a dirty fellow, black as a chimney-sweep, if a coal-pit could be descended without soiling my clothes. ' Lord bless you, I goes down ten times a-day, and never minds my clothes.' Do you, Mr. O'Connell, make the application ? " O'Connell retorted by calling Napier a "*doldrum general.*" In the same year occurred the election in which Roebuck was defeated by Lord Powerscourt. Sir W. Napier, in the Life of his brother, published in 1857, quotes his letters relating to the incidents of that

[1] Norris, Carter, Munday, Ashman, Fortt.

[2] On the first occasion he remained only a very short time, and he then resided in apartments at 9, *Henrietta Street.*

election, which are here reproduced. The quarrel between the Whigs and the Radicals was a spectacle not very creditable to either party, especially as it may be assumed that the two elements of Whiggery and Radicalism, or the latter exclusively, constituted the "generous patriotism" so peculiar to Bath at that period, according to Sir William Napier. A similar split between the two parties occurred in 1847, when Roebuck was rejected, and took his final political leave of this "vigorous reforming city."

"August 7th.—Roebuck was cast 1°. By bribery. 2°. By the Dissenters, who split on account of his speech about the Sabbath. 3°. The Whigs set up Captain Scobell, which drew votes from Roebuck, and made another split ; Scobell then resigned, having done the mischief which his set designed in setting him up. 4°. Intimidation to a furious length, which made many tradesmen vote against their opinions and a still greater number refuse to vote at all. To these causes of failure, one party says, may be added mismanagement of his committee, directed by Tutton[1] the auctioneer. This I do not believe had any influence whatever; my belief is that it was all well done. That not very wise man, H————,[2] is at the head of the accusing party ; but if men choose to vote, no mismanagement of the committee could have hindered them.

"To describe the rage and grief of the people is difficult. The chairing was a funeral procession amidst groans and hisses ; and since the election many Whigs even have expressed their regret for Roebuck's failure. Hobhouse worked hard for him, and voted for him. Roebuck and he are friends now, and Tom Falconer[3] told me, as did Roebuck, that nothing could be more handsome than Hobhouse's conduct. The reasons thus given to you for Roebuck's failure are those generally ascribed, and truly; yet I am myself of opinion that his support of the new Poor Law was a fifth. Neither he nor Falconer will admit this, but it had some effect, though not much. The noise was so immense that speaking was out of the question, or I would have tested this. Roebuck did not attempt to speak on the hustings ; the others did, but though almost touching Lord Powerscourt, I could not even hear his voice, much less catch the words. He seemed like one making faces ! They may flatter themselves that their advocacy of the new Poor Law does them no harm, but it does. Had the sun been a political œconomist, Joshua could never have stopped him ! They are now proposing subscriptions to give Roebuck a piece of plate, no one to subscribe more than ten shillings. I shall subscribe. The address to be presented with it is not to pledge one to any particular opinions, but merely to express approbation of his general conduct and detestation of the personal abuse heaped on him by a certain set at Bath.

"With regard to the elections generally, I am in hopes they will turn out the Whigs, and that the Tories will give us something as a gratuity, an instalment, to get in ; then the Whigs, being out, will be of some use as curs to bark at the Tories ; when we have done with them, they

[1] Tutton was a dapper little man, who dressed very much like a clergyman of the establishment. Brummell himself could not have surpassed the faultless necktie, either in the manner of its folds or the purity of its whiteness. He was a shrewd man, but illiterate and conceited, without influence, and not likely to be equal to such an occasion as that indicated by Napier.

[2] H————, "that not very wise man," was the late Mr. R. Hellings, an attorney, whose capacity was equal to fault-finding and nothing else.

[3] "Tom Falconer" was the Rev. Thomas Falconer, M.D., whose only daughter was married to Mr. Roebuck.

may be hanged, as all curs should be. All things considered, matters seem favourable to the people. But the state of Bath is pitiable.[1] The Tories, especially the women, are making a run against all the Radical shops; it is *a hateful system*, yet *I have been driven to adopt it in justice to the Radical tradesmen.* And the tradesmen have amongst themselves begun a system of exclusive dealing. This is very disgusting and barbarous, but what can be done? Can we let a poor devil be ruined by the Tories because he honestly resisted intimidation and bribery? Nothing can exceed the fury of the old Tory ladies. Old Barry swears he knows an old lady who subscribed three hundred pounds to assist in bribing voters.[2]

"Roebuck was going to be very violent with Lord Powerscourt, but I stopped him and would not let him push it to a duel as he wished. He accused Lord Powerscourt of bribing, who denied it, and I believe he did not bribe or personally know of bribery, but he certainly treated. Roebuck called him a 'barbarian of weak intellect,' and therefore, if any challenge was necessary, it ought to have come from the other side, and I think I did right in quashing the quarrel. A letter came here for you, having the Bath post-mark. I opened it and found the most abusive anonymous attack you ever read ; very amusing though. The writer calls himself *Anti-Jacobin.* You are hiding your head at Freshford. Roebuck is shirtless, the spawn of a gipsey ; you are only Catiline, malicious against British officers, with a due portion of treason.

"August 11th.—The Tories have made a desperate rally, carrying by force of money all before them. At Devizes Sir F. Burdett was elected, and the riot was tremendous ; several were killed, we hear. At York, also, Feargus O'Connor says there were fifty thousand combatants, pretty equal on each side ; some were killed, report says. The result is that the Tories have the majority, and it seems to be the general opinion that Lord Melbourne will resign. So far as I can judge, the Tory reaction is all humbug ; it is money and the people's apathy about Whiggism that has caused the defeat of the latter, for the Radicals are stronger and more determined than ever. I am, however, afraid there is one bad effect springing from the success of the Tories, viz., that the Radicals are ready to believe all the Whigs say, and in this town they are resolved to unite. Crisp and Tutton fight like dogs,[3] yet agree on this. That they are right I do not believe, yet they know their own game best. I have advised them, if they coalesce, to do so

1 This state is not quite consistent with Sir W. Napier's statement that Bath was pro-eminent at this time in "reforming vigour" and in "the generosity of its patriotism."

2 All this about the Tories and their intimidation and exclusive dealing is grossly exaggerated. It was carried on as much by one side as the other, and ceased altogether with the occasion. Party feeling ran very high, but the bark of both sides was worse than the bite. "Old Barry" was a foolish, credulous partizan, who said anything and believed anything against his opponents. Barry was an Irishman of small independent means. He lived in Norfolk Buildings. Sir William says he was "driven" to adopt a "hateful system" on the principle of two wrongs making a right, as involved in "reforming vigour" and "genuine patriotism."

3 Crisp was a hatter, and it is not easy to say which he hated most, the Whigs or the Tories. That these two "patriots" fought like dogs is indisputable, for Dr. Watts's reason probably, "For 'twas their nature to." Napier omits all mention of another hatter, who was an ardent Radical—the late Mr. G. Cox, who lived in Stall Street. He was a man of short stature, and wore a white, fulled cambric neckerchief ; a nonconformist and a zealous local preacher. Commonly, he was known as "Bishop" Cox. On one occasion, during the incumbency of the late Bishop Carr as Rector of Bath, Cox met the amiable prelate, and taking off his hat addressed his Lordship as a "brother bishop." Bishop Carr smiled, as was his wont, and, perceiving the joke, expressed his gratification at meeting him. Cox reminded the Bishop at parting that he was a step in rank above him. "For many years," he said, "I was a bishop, but since I preached under a railway-arch I have been an archbishop."

on the condition that the members they take up shall pledge themselves to the ballot, short par-liaments, extended suffrage, and protection for the factory children ; if the Whigs will not join in this, to cut them.

"12th.—I went to a private meeting. The question was, 'Shall the Radicals join the Whig association?—the latter being secretly against Roebuck.' I and one or two others were averse to a junction, but all the rest in favour of it. Crisp said, that unless it takes place, a mass of timid citizens will join the Whig association from fear of our supposed violence; but if the Radicals join the Whigs, those timid people will adhere to the former on all important occasions.[1] We finally voted that a deputation of Radicals should meet the Whig committee and offer a union, on condition that they should not take part in any election against Roebuck, and that half the committee of management should be named by Radicals. I demanded that a test of Radicalism should be established, and it was agreed that these committee-men should be such as were pledged to vote for Roebuck at the next election.

"The deputation met a Mr. Wilson,[2] spokesman for the association. We had a good deal of conversation, in which he said the association wished to exclude two classes, extreme Tories, and extreme Radicals and Republicans, which he seemed to consider the same. I objected to all exclusion : and as to extreme Radicals, it would exclude our members and the deputation who had the honour to meet him. Republicanism and Radicalism were not one. I was an ultra-Radical and not a Republican. The others expressed like opinions, saying, that at all the meetings they had attended at Bath for many years, no man had ever heard a wish to establish a republic. Mr. Wilson said he would submit our resolutions to the society, and appoint a day for our further proceedings. The discussion lasted until past nine o'clock. I asked Crisp why we should not form a Radical society, and let the Whigs join us if they chose? He said we were not strong enough."

In 1838, Napier was made a K.C.B., and in the same year he applied for the Governorship of Jersey, but was refused, and at the close of the year he left Bath and "proceeded to Dublin, intent to devote his energies in furtherance of Capt. Kennedy's project for raising the scale of civilization in Ireland by com-bining useful education with an improved system of agriculture."

It must not be supposed that Sir W. Napier devoted the whole of his time to petty, undignified, political warfare. He did not; the marvel is that Sir William, twenty years later, brought up these reminiscences. The greater part of Sir Charles Napier's time was devoted to authorship. It was during his two years' residence in Bath that he wrote his work on *Military Law ;* and it is not surprising that he should have chafed and fretted at being condemned, as he thought, to a

[1] Crisp was right ; in 1841 the two sections were united, and the Whig and Radical were returned ; in 1847 recriminations were revived, and Roebuck was rejected. Crisp was one of the first Aldermen under the New Corporation Act.

[2] Wilson was the late Mr. Walter Wilson, who lived at 12, **Pulteney Street.** He was a natural son of the original Mr. Walter, of "The Times." The leaders of the Whigs were the late Mr. G. Norman, Mr. Wilson Brown, Mr. Simon Barrow, Admiral Gordon, and Mr. W. Hunt, who is living. These gentlemen usually acted on the principle involved in the epigram—
"The Whigs resemble nails. How so, my master?
Because, like nails, when beat, they *hold the faster*."

life of ignoble professional inactivity. Personally, he was agreeable in manner, accessible, and kindly disposed. The house in which he lived is small, but, one side of it looking into Laura Place, pleasant, sunny, and cheerful. Sir Charles kept little company, lived frugally, as became a man, as he said, with little or nothing beyond his half-pay.

SIR W. P. NAPIER, FRESHFORD HOUSE and 19, GREEN PARK.— At the close of 1831, this distinguished man, with his family, took up his residence at the mansion belonging to the old Somersetshire family of the Joyces—" Freshford House." He was already known as a hero, and as the author of a History, which bid fair, although only one volume was published, to be a grand and noble work. Moreover, he was known as an eloquent speaker and as a vehement reformer. On the 7th of June, 1832, he was urged by a section of the Liberal party in Bath to offer himself as a candidate for one of the seats in Parliament, the deputation conveying the offer undertaking to pay all expenses.[1] On the 14th he addressed a letter to Mr. J. Crisp and Mr. Hellings, who made the offer to him in the name of the Bath Political Union, declining it on the ground of straitened means. In that letter he gave expression to political opinions, which he lived long enough to modify and in some sort to retract. If he himself refused the nomination offered him, he took an active part in the contest which ensued. In 1835, he spoke with the vehemence and eloquence which characterized his speaking in 1831 at Devizes. His power over a multitude was irresistible. His noble presence, his grand impetuosity of style as a speaker, his personal disinterestedness and irreproachable private character, and his emphatic condemnation of all means save those of constitutional and legitimate agitation to achieve the great object in view, rendered him one of the most formidable *tribunes* of that memorable period. Few men in Bath were so well known as General W. Napier. His grand, erect person; his frank, but somewhat stern manner, could not fail to attract attention to him, wherever he went. Amongst his intimates, his energy of manner, his ready eloquence of expression, and his sincerity, made him very popular. His form and carriage were perfect, and his countenance, which was capable of expressing terrible anger, was also, especially in the presence of children, full of gentle tenderness. When he came to Freshford, he was engaged upon his history, the first volume of which was published by Murray in 1828, and the other five at later intervals by Boone, so that, with the exception of a portion of the last volume,

---

[1] It is curious that his biographer should use such an expression as that " he received the offer of a seat for Bath, free of expense." It had not quite come to that, at any rate, at the first election after the Reform Bill. All they could or did do, was to run him as a candidate free of expense to himself.

those five volumes were written in the charming retreat at Freshford.   Notwithstanding the immense labour involved in his history, Napier found time for speech-
making, newspaper controversy, and private correspondence.   In 1835 and 1836 he
spoke at public meetings, and he sometimes put his heavy heel on the tender corns
of his friends with as little remorse as he did upon those of his opponents.   He hit
away right and left in the newspapers, abused the Whigs, exposed their " treason "
in tampering with his loyalty before the Reform Bill in urging him to take command
of a force to overawe the Parliament.   At one of the meetings of the Bath
Working Men's Association, in 1838, he refused to attend, because one of the
speakers had at a previous meeting declared that the objects of the Association
were to "destroy all priestly and kingly institutions, and to establish democracy on
their ruins; to bring America hither," and the like.   The secretary of the Association
was a Mr. Bolwell, a very strong Radical, but he received Napier's remonstrances
with good sense and good temper.   It was one of Napier's most valuable attri-
butes that he had the moral courage and the honesty to tell his party when he
thought they were wrong, and to point out to them the consequences of departing
from certain fundamental principles.

In 1841 General Napier left Freshford, and took No. 19, Green Park.   In
the same year a general election aroused his zeal and energy to the highest point.
His pugnacity was, as usual, directed more against the Whigs than the Tories.
At the declaration of the poll—Lord Duncan and Mr. Roebuck being elected—
the General made a speech from the hustings, in the course of which he com-
mented severely on the late Whig Ministry, stating that they had excited the
people to insurrection in 1832.   Some voices behind him called out that this was
false, on which the speaker turned round and declared it to be true, as he had the
proofs.   One individual, however, reiterated that it was false, and a "falsehood,"
several times, and with a manner so offensive that General Napier lost his temper,
and struck the man a blow which knocked him backwards.[1]   This person entered
a criminal prosecution against General Napier for the assault, and the case came
on at the spring sessions of the following year, but a compromise was effected in
court, both parties paying their own costs, the prosecutor first expressing his
regret for having used insulting language to General Napier, and General Napier
then expressing his regret that he had repelled the insult in the manner he had
done.   The actual words were :—" Mr. S. regrets to have made use of expressions
offensive to General Napier ; but he disclaims all intention of having given
offence to General Napier by such expressions."   " In consequence of the above

---

[1] Mr. Saunders, a miller, a very highly respectable citizen, a nonconformist, and a member of the
Whig Committee.   He was the father of Mr. Saunders, of the Central News Association.

expression of regret on the part of Mr. S——, General Napier regrets the mode in which he repelled the language used." These political amenities were but a hollow truce—as unreal as the disclaimer was unmeaning when Saunders declared that by imputing falsehood to Napier he meant no offence.

In 1842, Napier was appointed Governor of Guernsey, and Bath saw him no more. He continued, however, to correspond with some of his Bath friends. One, an old Tory associate, received from him in constant succession, for several years after 1842, letters, some longer, some shorter, containing characteristic comments upon the public men and public measures of the period. It was the privilege of the author to read these letters, so full of pregnant wisdom and striking observation ; but it must be admitted, in other cases, so abounding with prejudice and egotism. But taking Sir W. Napier for all in all, Bath will never look upon his like again.[1]

EDWARD GIBBON, THE HISTORIAN, was a frequent visitor to Bath early in life, but of those visits very little is known, except that he formed a strong attachment to the city. In 1789, he contemplating settling here. Writing from Lausanne to his friend, *Lord Sheffield*,[2] on the subject of pecuniary matters, he says : " I have passed an anxious year, but my anxiety is now at an end, and the prospect before me is a melancholy solitude. I am still deeply rooted in this country ; the possession of this paradise, the friendship of the Severys,—a mode of society suited to my taste, and the enormous trouble and *expense* of a migration. Yet in England (when the present clouds are dispelled) I could form a very comfortable establishment in London, or rather at Bath." At this time Mrs. Gibbon (Gibbon's step-mother), to whom he was much attached, lived in Belvedere, and afterwards at **No. 22, CHARLES STREET.** Gibbon, in 1793, visited this venerable lady, himself staying at the **YORK HOUSE,** whence he wrote the following letters to Lord Sheffield :—

" Sunday afternoon I left London and lay at Reading, and Monday in very good time I reached this place, after a very pleasant airing ; and am always so much delighted and improved with this union of ease and motion, that, were not the expense enormous, I would travel every year some hundred miles, more especially in England. I passed the day with Mrs. Gibbon yesterday. In

---

1 At the time Napier was in Bath, he, Landor, Leader, Sir W. Molesworth, Roebuck, Dr. Thomas Falconer and others, used to meet at the library of the late Miss Williams, in Milsom Street. In the midst of them was this famous woman, and the more radical the sentiments uttered the more she applauded. She outlived her friends and her prosperity in this " vigorous reforming city," and died almost in poverty.

2 Formerly Colonel Ho'royd, created Lord Sheffield in 1781. Lord Sheffield edited an edition of Gibbon's Works, in 5 vols., in 1814.

mind and conversation she is just the same as she was twenty years ago. She has spirits, appetite, legs, and eyes, and talks of living till ninety. I can say from my heart, Amen. We dine at two, and remain together till nine : but although we have much to say, I am not sorry that she talks of introducing a third or fourth actor. Lord Spencer expects me about the 20th ; but if I can do it without offence, I shall steal away two or three days sooner, and you shall have advice of my motions. The troubles of Bristol have been serious and bloody. I know not who was in fault ; but I do not like appeasing the mob by the extinction of the toll, and the removal of the Hereford militia, who had done their duty. Adieu. The girls must dance at Tunbridge. What would dear little aunt[1] say if I was to answer her letter ? Ever yours, &c.

> York-house, Bath,
>   Oct. 9th, 1793.
>
> "I still follow the old style, though the Convention has abolished the Christian æra, with months, weeks, days, etc."

> "York-House, Bath, October 13th, 1793.
>
> "I am as ignorant of Bath in general as if I were still at Sheffield Place. My impatience to get away makes me think it better to devote my whole time to Mrs. Gibbon ; and dear little aunt, whom I tenderly salute, will excuse me to her two friends, Mrs. Hartley and Preston, if I make little or no use of her kind introduction. A *tête-à-tête* of eight or nine hours every day is rather difficult to support ; yet I do assure you, that our conversation flows with more ease and spirit when we are alone, than when any auxiliaries are summoned to our aid. She is indeed a wonderful woman, and I think all the faculties of her mind stronger, and more active, than I have ever known them. I have settled, that ten full days may be sufficient for all the purposes of our interview. I should therefore depart next Friday, the eighteenth instant, and am indeed expected at Althorp on the twentieth ; but I may possibly reckon without my host, as I have not yet apprised Mrs. Gibbon of the term of my visit ; and will certainly not quarrel with her for a short delay. Adieu. I must have some political speculations. The campaign, at least on our side, seems to be at an end. Ever yours."

In 1780, Gibbon wrote to Mrs. Gibbon two letters, here quoted, on the subject of the Gordon riots. From the opening sentence, it is probable the good lady felt some misgivings from her own experience at Bath, where for many days symptoms of rioting had shown themselves, which culminated in very serious acts of violence :—

> "DEAR MADAM,   "London, June 8th, 1780.
>
> "As a Member of Parliament, I cannot be exposed to any danger, since the House of Commons has adjourned to Monday se'nnight ; as an individual, I do not conceive myself to be obnoxious. I am not apt, with duty or necessity, to thrust myself into a mob : and our part of the town is as quiet as a country village. So much for personal safety ; but I cannot give the same assurances of public tranquillity : forty thousand Puritans, such as they might be in the time of Cromwell, have started out of their graves ; the tumult has been dreadful ; and even the remedy of military force and martial law is unpleasant. But government, with fifteen thousand regulars

---

[1] "Dear little aunt" was Lord Sheffield's sister, Miss Holroyd.

in town, and every gentleman (but one) on their side, must extinguish the flame. The execution of last night was severe; perhaps it must be repeated to-night: yet upon the whole, the tumult subsides. Colonel Holroyd was all last night in Holborn among the flames, with the Northumberland militia, and performed very bold and able service. I will write again in a post or two.

I am, dear Madam, ever yours."

" DEAR MADAM, " Bentinck-street, June 27th, 1780.[1]

" I believe we may now rejoice in our common security. All tumult has perfectly subsided, and we only think of the justice which must be properly and severely inflicted on such flagitious criminals. The measures of Government have been seasonable and vigorous ; and even opposition have been forced to confess, that the military power was applied and regulated with the utmost propriety. Our danger is at an end, but our disgrace will be lasting, and the month of June, 1780, will ever be marked by a dark and diabolical fanaticism, which I had supposed to be extinct, but which actually subsists in Great Britain, perhaps beyond any other country in Europe. Our parliamentary work draws to a conclusion ; and I am much more pleasingly, though laboriously, engaged in revising and correcting for the press, the continuation of my History, two volumes of which will certainly appear next winter. This business fixes me to Bentinck-street more closely than any other part of my literary labour ; as it is absolutely necessary that I should be in the midst of all the books which I have at any time used during the composition. But I feel a strong desire (irritated, like all other passions, by repeated obstacles) to escape to Bath.

Dear Madam,

Most truly yours."

CLAVERTON ; Rev. RICHARD GRAVES, SHENSTONE, &c.—As Twickenham is to London, so is Claverton to Bath. A spot incomparably beautiful ; consecrated to many memories ; and truly may be called classic ground. "Of the village, church, and old mansion of Claverton, much might be written, for each was peculiar, and all were and are replete with interesting associations. The scene is truly romantic, wild, and picturesque. An abrupt declivity from the table-land of the Down descends to a narrow, evergreen valley, through which the river Avon meanders silently and sluggishly towards the west. This steep hill consists of rocks and woods, interspersed with natural terraces."[2] " Situated in a spacious valley, diversified by all the accompaniments of wood, water, and graceful undulations of ground, its little church with its ivy-mantled tower nestling among trees at the foot of a grassy slope; its Manor House crowning the hill above, and its elegant and commodious rectory occupying a site near the church below, while the whole overlooks the varied and tasteful domain of Warleigh rising from the opposite bank of the Avon,—it presents a combination of picturesque features rarely centreing in one locality. Many of us recollect the old rectory standing on the same site as the present, but of a far humbler character, a long low build-

[1] The letters are not given in chronological order. [2] Britton.

ing, beneath the level of the road, possessing nevertheless an air of comfort and respectability suited to its appropriation. This old house was for more than fifty years the residence of the Rev. Richard Graves, rector of Claverton."[1] In the old Manor House, of which the stately terraces leading to it still remain, lived the **BASSETTS**, whose loyalty brought upon them the heavy hand of Parliament. It was one of these Bassetts who represented Bath during a part of the Rebellion. In 1609 Sir T. Estcourt sold the Manor to William Bassett, whose son, William, above referred to, represented Bath from 1640 to 1645. The Parliament in that year expelled Bassett, not for any proved or even alleged offence, but on account of his loyalty. It was this same William Bassett who, in 1643, when sitting at dinner with Sir E. Hungerford and others, received an unwelcome visitor in the shape of a cannon-ball directed from the opposite hill by the Parliamentary forces; it pierced through the outer wall of the hall, and, passing over the table at which they sat, lodged in the breast wall of the chimney without doing any further mischief; another ball fell into the churchyard, where it was found some years ago. On the same occasion, and in the same skirmish, three soldiers of the Parliament and one of the Royalists were killed in the meadow by the river-side, and were buried in the churchyard. The son of this William Bassett, who was also William, was knighted by Charles II. Sir William[2] is represented as having been extravagant, largely encumbering the property; but the truth is, the race was an unthrifty one, and the encumbrances were cumulative, father, son, and grandson each doing his part to heap up the mortgage-debt beyond equity of redemption. In 1701, the property was sold to Robert Holder, Esq.,[3] whose son in 1714 sold it to William Skrine, Esq., and his son in 1758 sold it to Ralph Allen, who, dying in 1764, bequeathed it to his first wife's niece, Mrs. Warburton, wife of Bishop Warburton. When Allen died, he bequeathed the Manor of Claverton, as well as the Prior Park Estate, to his first wife's niece, who was the wife of Bishop Warburton. This lady, after the death of the Bishop, married the Bishop's Chaplain, the Rev. Stafford Smith. In 1817, that lady's representative sold the manor to **JOHN VIVIAN, Esq.**, who was Solicitor to the Excise. Mr. Vivian pulled down the old manor-house, and erected the present mansion. When the house was nearly complete, Mr. Vivian, who was his own architect, discovered that he had forgotten

---

[1] Kilvert's Essay on Graves. The old Rectory was partly built in 1760, by Ralph Allen, and a large room, used as the School-room, with dormitories over, was added by Graves. Graves died in 1804, so that the house was occupied by him not 50, but 44 years.

[2] He represented Bath from 1678 to 1681, and again from 1685 to 1690.

[3] The grand-daughter of this Robert Holder was the second wife of Ralph Allen.

Cl. 1 ... 100

KINGSTON HOUSE, BRADFORD-ON-AVON.

the kitchen![1]   On Mr. Vivian's death, he left Claverton to his second son, the late Mr. George Vivian, a gentleman of great learning and varied accomplishments, who published an account of the old manor-house,[2] with illustrations. The façade of this house forms the subject of the frontispiece of the present volume. The property was sold in 1870, shortly before Mr. Vivian's death, to the late Mr. Isaac Carr, who resold it to the present owner, Henry Duncan Skrine, Esq., the representative of the senior branch of the Skrine family.[3]   William Skrine,[4] of whom mention has been made as a former proprietor, in the last century, was descended from a younger branch. He resided chiefly at *Laver House, Bathford,* which, with other property, has now reverted to the squire of Warleigh

[1] Wyattville was the nominal architect, but Mr. Vivian was a self-willed director.

[2] The late Mr. Edward Davis, an able Bath Architect, writing in 1845, in reference to Hetling House, says :—"Whilst Sir Walter Hungerford was building this, his Town residence, *John of Padua* was engaged at Longleat ; at a house at Bradford, known (for the last century) as the Duke's House ; and at Claverton ; all within a few miles of each other, and of this (Hetling House)." If the building of all these mansions was going on simultaneously under the direction of John of Padua, Claverton would have been begun about 1570 ; but according to Mr. Vivian it was not finished until 1625, inasmuch as when the house was pulled down in 1820, "a leaden pipe-head was discovered, bearing the escutcheon and initials of William Basset." The fact stated by Mr. Davis would show also that Sir Walter Hungerford, who died in 1596, was the owner of Claverton previous to the Estcourts, and was building Claverton at the same time that he was building his Bath Town House. The reasons assigned for the demolition of the old Manor House of Claverton was the unsafe condition of the walls. There is a small portion of the manor house still left, which was used as the dairy, and was a part of the west wing. On each gable there is a very beautiful coat-of-arms, and of these, together with that on the house of Mr. Harding, a representation and description will be given in the new edition of *Rambles about Bath.* The Bradford mansion has experienced a far different fate. Mr. Vivian, writing in 1837, despondingly says :—"The house is becoming daily more dilapidated and there appears no prospect that it will ever again deserve the praise bestowed on it by John Aubrey, who visited it in 1686 and declared, in his quaint language, 'that it was the best house for the quality of a gentleman in Wiltshire.'" Fourteen years after that prophecy, the late *Mr. Moulton,* all honour to his enterprise, his intelligence, and his skill, bought the property and restored it stone by stone, detail by detail, until it stands now in all its original beauty, and worthy still of the quaint commendation of John Aubrey. The **WOODBURYTYPE** represents the house in its present state.

[3] "About midway in this ascent, overlooking Warleigh and the river, the pleasing village of Claverton seems to hang suspended, where its large Gothic mansion (renowned in the civil wars) and its little church, with the pyramidical tomb of the late much-esteemed Mr. Allen, are striking objects. Neither is its parsonage less pleasing, the little grounds of which are laid out in a truly classic taste by the Rev. Mr. Graves, the friend and literary rival of Shenstone, and where that worthy veteran closes the placid evening of his days in the retirement he has so happily embellished, deservedly beloved and respected."—"*Skrine's Rivers of Great Britain,*" by Richard Dixon Skrine, of Warleigh ; Grandfather of Mr. Henry Duncan Skrine. The author of the above description was a private pupil of Mr. Graves, who prepared him for Winchester, and was on the most friendly terms with the Skrine family, to whom he addressed several pieces of poetry.

[4] William Skrine was a medical man of repute in Bath. He married a Mrs. Savil, to whom Hetling House was assigned by Lord Lexington, in lieu of a legacy of which he had the payment. Lord Lexington married a Hungerford, and thus inherited the property, which had been the residence of the lady's father. After the two Princesses (Princess Caroline and Princess of Hesse) ceased to occupy the house, between 1750 and 1760, it fell into much neglect. The name, "Hetling House," is of recent date, a wine merchant named *Hetling* having occupied it during the early part of this century (see *Historic Houses,* 1st series, p. 10). William Skrine's grandfather was Thomas Skrine, a physician in Bath and an Alderman in 1660. He was a loyalist and a supporter of Prynne in his opposition to Cromwell. He was one of those who, with many others, signed the loyal address to Charles II. on his restoration.

and Claverton, above mentioned, of whom it may be said :—

> " Loke who that is most virtuous alway,
> Prive and apert, and most entendeth ay
> To do the gentel dedes that he can,
> And take him for the gretest gentilman."

If Mr. Skrine's motto were not "*Tutamen*," it might be "*ut prosim aliis.*" Of the history and traditions of Claverton much might be written, but this work is limited in its scope and object. The author has trenched as little as possible upon the vocation of the historian, the antiquary, and the archæologist. The parish of Claverton in itself lies without the limits of the author's ground, but it has been for the past two centuries and more intimately associated with Bath ; in one sense, so inseparably connected and identified with it, that it may be regarded as an integral part of the city. Its squires and its clergy have to all intents and purposes been Bath citizens.

Perhaps the most conspicuous amongst the Clavertonians was the Rev. Richard Graves. The peculiar interest felt in the old Claverton rector is, in the opinion of the author, attributable more to the singular individuality of the man than to any striking literary genius he possessed. Presented to the living in 1748 and dying in 1804, during that long period he was never a month at a time absent from his parish.[1] Collinson says Graves was the incumbent and the patron of the living, but he was certainly presented to it by the then owner of the manor, Mr. William Skrine. He bought the advowson of Mrs. Warburton in 1767 after his own induction ; and it was afterwards repurchased by the representatives of Ralph Allen, and formed a part of the estate, when the property was sold to Mr. Vivian in 1817. Richard Graves was born at Mickleton, in Gloucestershire, in 1714, being the second son of Richard Graves, the accomplished friend of Hearne, the famous antiquary. The name of the elder branch of the family was spelt Greaves. A distinguished member was John Greaves, whose younger brother was Sir Edward Greaves, an eminent Bath physician, and who was afterwards physician to Charles II.,[2] whom he accompanied to Bath when that monarch and Catherine of Braganza came hither in 1663, and abode at the Abbey House.

The Rev. Richard Graves "was educated partly at home under the Rev. Mr. Smith, curate

---

[1] This is stated by most writers as a remarkable fact in itself, but it is repeated here to show that Graves was always amongst his friends, and was therefore such a favourite personage with the Bathonians. His lines were cast in pleasant places ; he had health and ample means, light and simple duties, except what he chose to impose upon himself as a schoolmaster, and none of these at any time prevented him from enjoying the society of his joyous literary and other friends in Bath whenever he chose. Graves remained at home not because it involved any act of self-denial, but because he was more happy there than he was anywhere else. A less cheerful and contented person than Graves might, in Graves's circumstances, find Claverton a place in which the full meaning of "*otium cum dignitate*" might be realized.

[2] The late Rev. F. Kilvert says Charles I., but that is an error.

of Mickleton (with whom he read *Hesiod* and *Homer* at 12 years old), and partly at Abingdon school, then in good repute as a place of education, whence at the age of 16 (being then, to use his own words, 'a pretty good Grecian'), he was elected scholar of Pembroke college, Oxford. Soon after going into residence he joined a party of young men who met in the evening to read Epictetus, Theophrastus, and other Greek authors seldom included in the university course; their only beverage (then a solecism at Oxford) being water. A short time after this he became the associate of Shenstone, Whistler, and Jago. This party, less abstemious, though not less devoted to intellectual cultivation, 'supped Florence wine and read poetry, plays, Spectators, Tatlers, and other writings of easy digestion.' His intimacy with Shenstone, which continued to the death of the latter in 1763, was maintained by frequent interchange of letters, many of which have been published. There does not appear to have been a perfect coincidence between them in matters of taste, but in general there was a congeniality and a harmony of opinion resulting in a friendship which added considerably to the happiness of both. In 1736 he was elected fellow of All Souls, where he became intimate with Sir William Blackstone, then fellow of the same college, of whom he has recorded some interesting anecdotes in a little posthumous work called *The Trifler.* With the great jurist Mr. Graves lived in habits of the most unreserved intercourse, and their college friendship continued uninterrupted and undiminished to the latest hour of Sir William's life.

"Instead of pursuing the study of divinity according to his original design, he now turned his attention towards medicine, and attended in London two courses of anatomy under Dr. Nichols.[1] A severe illness however, which incapacitated him for pursuing so laborious a profession, induced him to resume his divinity studies; and in 1740, after taking his master's degree, he entered into holy orders. About the same time he accompanied Mr. Fitz-Herbert, father of the first lord St. Helen's, with whom his elder brother had been acquainted at the Temple, to the estate of that gentleman at Tissington, near Ashbourne, in Derbyshire, as family chaplain; where he besides performed the clerical duties of the parish, a small donative in the gift of the Fitz-Herbert family. In this elegant retirement he enjoyed for three years the pleasures and advantages of refined society, including among others the distinguished names of Charles Pratt, afterwards lord Camden, sir Eardley Wilmot, Nicholas Hardinge, clerk of the House of Commons, &c. &c. In his *Spiritual Quixote* he has characterised Mr. and Mrs. Fitz-Herbert and Dr. Johnson's friend Miss Boothby, under the names of sir William and Lady Forrester, and Miss Sainthill. His reference to their characters is generally respectful. The localities of Tissington are also very accurately described."—*Essay by Rev. Francis Kilvert.*

The personal appearance of Graves was remarkable: short in stature, and slender in form, a large, expressive blue eye, prominent nose, small mouth, well-cut chin and intellectual forehead, and withal a singularly kind and benevolent expression. His movements were eccentric; his walk, or rather his *trot*, was almost ludicrous. Usually when he was on the move, both hands were held straight out before him, and in his right he held a large gingham umbrella, and in his left a stick or other object he might be carrying at the time. His costume, when at home in his village, was the clerical coat of the period much too large for him, black smalls and silk hose, and fulled white cambric neckerchief. When,

[1] A good physician may have been lost in an earnest but never a very efficient parson.

as he advanced in years, he came to Bath, as he did most days, except Sundays, he wore a Spencer over his coat, top boots, with black cloth coverings buttoned over the tops, and a low, square-crowned beaver hat, much battered, similar in shape to the modern " deer-stalker." His utterance was clear and rapid, his manner cordial, demonstrative, but always that of a well-bred gentleman.

After leaving Tissington, Graves became curate of Aldworth, near Reading, and there he married Lucy Bartholomew, a young and beautiful, but uneducated lady. [1] If he pleased himself in this matter, he offended his relations, and it is needless to say it involved the surrender of his fellowship of All Souls. It followed that he was much straitened in his pecuniary circumstances. If Mr. Graves had been a " splendid *roué,*" instead of marrying a woman he loved, and who was worthy of that love, perhaps he might never have known the " pinchings of poverty." Happily, the cloud soon passed, for Mr. William Skrine, who had recently purchased the Claverton estate, presented him with the Rectory in 1748, and Graves was inducted in July, 1749. Although his sermons, of which he published a volume, read smoothly, making allowance for the mannerisms and pedantry of the times, he was a dull preacher. As a Churchman he was zealous, and a lively opponent of dissent in any form; he was a Liberal, *i.e.,* a Whig of the period, but he did not object to pluralities. The year before Allen's death he, it is said, procured the vicarage of Kilmersdon, near Radstock, for Graves, and 30 years after Graves obtained the rectory of Croscombe,[2] near Wells. Warner, who was himself afterwards rector of the latter place, relates the following "anecdote"—an unworthy artifice, if true—but there is every reason to believe it was understood to be nothing more than a joke, the best proof of which is that the form of pulling the bell-rope was not a condition precedent of the patronage being conferred upon him, but a part of the ceremony of induction, all legal requirements having been already complied with. Graves knew he was expected to be the helpless old man, and yet was conscious of his constitutional vitality, and hence the fun. Warner must have known all this; but he gave a twist to the facts for the sake of enhancing the joke :—

" The rectory of Croscombe, Somersetshire, had become vacant, and the patron felt desirous of alienating its perpetual advowson. This could not be effected, however, unless there were a living incumbent on the preferment at the time of the sale. He cast his eye, therefore, through the diocese, in search of the oldest clergyman within it, to whom Croscombe might be presented ;

---

[1] Graves, after marriage, sent this excellent lady to London to be educated. Her ability and great natural intelligence, added to an innate refinement, enabled her to acquire all the manners and address of a born gentlewoman. She died in 1777, aged 46, and he never married again. An urn to her memory was placed in the church ; it is now in the vestry.

[2] Value £250 per annum.   [3] Value £200 per annum.

ensuring thereby a speedy vacancy; and enhancing, in the same proportion, the amount of the purchase-money. Mr. Graves proved to be the rarest example of longevity, among his brethren of the cloth : to him therefore the rectory was proffered. Some years afterwards I chanced to be inducted into the same living; and learned from the churchwarden, that he was present when a similar ceremony had been performed in behalf of Mr. Graves. The old gentleman, he told me, in the true spirit of his character, could not, on this occasion, forbear discharging a few witticisms, on the *generosity* of the patron ; and his own *perfect competency* to fulfil the duties of the office he was about to be put in possession of : nor was it without a look and tone of his native drollery, that, on being introduced into the belfry, he exclaimed, ' Where is the bell-rope ; I *cannot see it ?*' and having pulled it with all his feeble might, again enquired : ' Does it ring ; for I *cannot hear it ?*'"

Graves had three sons and a daughter, and the narrowness of his circumstances obliged him to superintend their education in person, and this induced him to take other pupils. For thirty years he continued the occupation of schoolmaster with very great and deserved success. One of his pupils was the only son of Bishop Warburton, Ralph Allen Warburton, who died young. The Bishop was tenderly attached to this only child. On sending him to his friend, Graves, he wrote to Bishop Hurd :—

" Ralph (then about ten years old) is as good, though not so learned, perhaps, as you could wish. He is now going upon Erasmus' Dialogues, a book long out of fashion, which yet I have recommended to Mr. Graves as a guard against too much poetry within doors, and superstition without. But apropos of Mr. Graves, my wife has let him the great house at Claverton, for which he gives £60 a year; and the great gallery-library is turned into a dormitory, so that where literature generally ends it here begins." Mr. Graves's reputation as a teacher must have been great, for within a month the bishop writes : " The dormitory is already filled ; but what inspirations, as a library, it may give to the forty little sleepers therein must be left to time, which reveals all things."

Another of Graves's pupils was Malthus, the author of the *Essay on Population*, whose father-in-law, Mr. Eckersall, occupied the old Manor House, after Graves had relinquished teaching, and had given up the mansion.[1]

Of Graves's relations with Prior Park, it is manifest they were of the most cordial character. He was always received there with more than ordinary familiarity and kindness. Whoever might be absent on great state occasions Mr. Graves was always present.[2] With Mr. Allen, Bishop Warburton and Mrs. Warburton, he was a great favourite, and the reason is obvious. Not only was Graves endowed

---

[1] Malthus was present with Graves in his first and last illness, and administered the rites of the Church to his old and beloved master.

[2] It is difficult, having due regard to the present enclosures and the existing roads, to realise the difficulty, at the time of Graves, of getting from one place to another. The foot and bridle road from Bath to Claverton, which was reached by crossing the ferry at the East Gate, extended from the Bathwick meadow, bearing a little to the left, and extended nearly to the top of the hill through the field emerging now into the opening close to the road by "Claverton Lodge." The path then extended almost in the direct line of the present road to the top of the hill, and then continued on the line of what is now the carriage road across what then was an open down—a continuance, in fact, of

with an excellent understanding and a keen intellect, but he was generous and kind in disposition, and knew his part almost as one of the family. In his anecdotes of Allen he tells of most of the distinguished guests whom he met at the "squire's" hospitable mansion. Mr. Kilvert writes:—"I have heard the late Mrs. Stafford Smith say that having the privilege of dining in boots, on account of riding home, and of retiring early from the dinner table, because of the distance, it was a standing joke against him that, in his hurried way, he used to carry off his dinner napkins upon his spurs." Graves had acquired the habit of wearing boots almost from necessity, but he had "toned down" the objectionable boots by encasing the tops in sober black coverings. If Graves had presented himself even in these innocent clerified integuments at Nash's assemblies, neither his cloth nor his excuses would have saved him from exclusion. But there is no mention anywhere of any meeting between Graves and Nash, not even at the table of Ralph Allen. "It is evident," Mr. Kilvert says, "from various short pieces of wit and humour addressed to individuals by Graves, that he lived on terms of ease and sociality with most of the principal families round Bath. To Lady Miller's vase he was a frequent contributor. . . . . He seems indeed to have been an acceptable companion in all societies, and the secret of his universal welcome manifestly was his conduct, good humour, and cheerfulness, and the lively tone of his conversation, his colloquial impromptus being often as happy as the *jeux d'esprit* of his pen ; while both, though marked by greater licence than our modern sense of propriety allows, were the effusions of a sportive fancy and a guileless heart."

In 1765, Graves published his first volume,[1] which was a collection of

---

the down. This foot and bridle path was, about a quarter of a mile from the top of the hill, intersected by other paths, whilst that extending from Widcombe and Prior Park joined at right angles the Bathwick path at that point. The only carriage road from Prior Park into the city was the " carriage road " made by Allen himself, which was almost parallel with the *tram-way* [*] by which the stone was conveyed from Combe Down to the basin in Widcombe, and thence transmitted in boats by river, which had been rendered navigable to Bristol. With the exception of the *Julian Road* and the Holloway, or old Wells Road, there did not exist any one of the roads which at the present day lead in every direction.

1 BIBLIOGRAPHY OF REV. R. GRAVES.

The Spiritual Quixote ; A Treatise on Politeness, translated from the Italian of De la Casa, archbishop of Benevento ; Columella, or the Distressed Anchorite ; Euphrosyne, consisting of poetical pieces ; Eugenius, or Anecdotes of the Golden Vale ; Recollections of some particulars in the Life of Mr. Shenstone, Plexippus, or the Aspiring Plebeian ; the Rout-Fleurettes, a translation of Archbishop Fenelon's Ode on Solitude, &c. ; the Life of Commodus, from the Greek of Herodian ; Hiero, on the Condition of Royalty, from Xenophon ; The Meditations of Antoninus, from the Greek ; The Reveries of Solitude ; The Coalition, or Rehearsal of the Pastoral Opera of Echo and Narcissus ; Sermons on various subjects ; The Farmer's Son, as a counterpart to Mr. Anstey's Farmer's Daughter ; The Invalid, with the obvious means of enjoying Long Life, by a Nonagenarian ; and Senilities.

* It was known at that time as " Wagon-way," but it was the legitimate predecessor of the present *tram-ways*. The difference as regards the *ways* themselves is that the wagon-ways consisted of large stones laid down in parallel lines, and a groove hollowed out in the centre, in which the wheels worked.   There is no part of the above way remaining ; but of the *Wagon-way*, which was used for a similar purpose, from Hampton Down, across the Warminster Road Bridge, many fragments remain *in situ.*

epigrams, entitled "The Festoon,"[1] to which he prefixed a short essay on the subject. The work, however, by which Graves will ever be best known is his satirical story of "The Spiritual Quixote; or, the Summer's Ramble of Mr. Geoffry Wildgoose—a Comic Romance." The object of the book is obvious enough. Mr. Graves's objection to the excesses of the religious zealots of the times was quickened by what he saw in Bath, and by the results of the fanaticism which generally prevailed, and by a mind singularly capable of estimating the historical, as well as the religious, importance of all similar movements in all ages. But Graves was provoked, in all probability, to the attack by the incident he relates in his preface : "After a little time a journeyman shoemaker from Bradford came into his parish, brought with him a large congregation, and preached and sang psalms in a large old house ; and thenceforth he found his church almost deserted, and his flock seemed to treat him with much less respect than they had before done. On Mr. Graves going to the meeting, and reminding the preacher that as the house was not licensed he was liable to a penalty of £20, he desired to preach there for half a year, that it might be seen which would convert most drunkards and sinners of every description. He then asked Mr. Graves what was his definition of faith? and behaved with great insolence and impertinence, but never repeated his visit." No doubt that, whatever good might have been done by John and Charles Wesley, and men of that class, it was sadly marred by the ignorance and vulgar irreverence of the "journeyman shoemakers," and such like would-be teachers—fellows who, too idle to become good workmen, their opinions upon any subject not being worth one penny, yet assumed to be teachers of the holiest and deepest mysteries of religion.[2]

Graves anticipated the angry attacks likely to be made upon him, and explained his motives. Some went so far as to denounce all satire as a fitting weapon for putting down religious error, and that species of fanaticism which is held to be

---

[1] The success of "The Festoon" was, however, not great.

[2] What would Graves have said if his parish had been invaded by an "army" of "Salvationists?" Fiddlers and horn-blowers, accompanied by screeching women in every stage of hysterical fanaticism, and young fellows whose ardour is sometimes not regulated by discretion. The epidemic of the present day is precisely the same as that of Graves's day ; it has assumed a different phase, but its evils are the same, though in many respects more gross and immoral. What is so surprising is that many sober-minded people think it is doing good, and yet never join it, and do not even learn to play the fiddle, or the comet, or the drum, by way of a temporary qualification. The man who places religion upon a false basis is the greatest enemy to religion. If you preach up to ploughmen and artizans, that every singular feeling which comes across them, is a visitation of the Divine Spirit—can there be any difficulty, *under* the influence of this nonsense, in converting these simple creatures into active and mysterious fools, and making them your slaves for life? It is not possible to raise up any dangerous enthusiasm by telling men to be just, and good, and chaste ; but keep this part of Christianity out of sight, and talk long and enthusiastically before ignorant people, of the mysteries of religion, and you will not fail to attract a crowd of followers :—verily, the Tabernacle loveth not that which is simple, intelligible, and leadeth to good, sound *practice.*

dangerous to true piety, a due regard to reverence, and a just conception of things holy. The Rev. F. Kilvert, one of the most earnest, reverential, and religiously-minded men, writing in a more advanced age, and with a clearer guidance derived from experience, in his essay on Graves, sums up the question with admirable force. He does not defend some of the language and situations in Graves's book, but he puts the question generally very fairly in the following passage :—

"The work is skilfully planned and well executed, the plot probable and well sustained, the manners distinctive, the diction simple and natural, the episodes, especially that in which the history of his own marriage is given, well brought in, and the denouement dexterously effected.

"The main drift of the story may be guessed from its very title. Geoffry Wildgoose, a young man of respectable family and comfortable independence, educated at the university, withdraws to his family house in the country, where he lives with his mother, a widow, in much seclusion, but giving the law to the confined society in which he moves. A disagreement with the vicar of the parish, operating upon a nervous temperament, leads him to devote himself to the study of the old Puritan divines, of whose works he finds a large collection in a garret of his mansion. This line of reading coinciding in point of time with the preaching of Whitfield and Wesley, then in its zenith, induces him to throw himself into that movement, and set out, without the knowledge of his mother, as an itinerant preacher. In this expedition he is joined by Jerry Tugwell, a cobbler of the parish, a simple but shrewd and humourous fellow, owing an hereditary and devoted loyalty to his master, but a very loose and shaky adherence to that master's strict self-denying principles. The staple of the work consists in the various incidents, serious and ludicrous, prosperous and adverse, encountered by our adventurers ; and the attention is refreshed and the interest quickened by a variety of episodical narratives of the lives and fortunes of the parties they fall in with. Amongst these a part of the second volume is amusingly occupied by a detail of the author's own history, under the assumed name of *Rivers*, an old college friend of Wildgoose. But what would a novel on any subject be without a love story? Accordingly our Quixote is not left destitute of a Dulcinea. He finds her in a Miss Townsend, a hearer of his at Gloucester, who having escaped from the thraldom and persecution of a lady housekeeper whom her father, a widower, had placed over his household, has taken refuge there with a friend of her late mother, a votary of Mr. Whitfield. His attachment to this lady exercises, imperceptibly to himself, a powerful and salutary influence upon Wildgoose. And the struggles of religious enthusiasm with natural passion in a heart

'Where mixed with God's her sacred image lies,'

form perhaps one of the best and happiest touches in the work. After visiting in succession Glouce-ster, Bath, Bristol, Wales, and the Peak in Derbyshire with various success, our adventurers arrive at Warwick at the time of the races, where Wildgoose, in the midst of an unseasonable address on the race-course, receives a blow from a decanter launched at his head by a drunken reveller. He is received into the carriage of a Dr. Greville, a dignified and amiable clergyman of Warwick, is carried home and carefully attended to. The blow, though accompanied with some immediate danger from hæmorrhage, yet proves ultimately of the greatest benefit by relieving his over-charged brain, and restoring him to cooler and more rational views of religion. Dr. Greville proves to be an intimate friend of the Townsend family, and Miss Townsend happens at that very time to be on a visit at his house. 'The consequence,' to use a hackneyed phrase, 'may be more easily conceived than expressed.' And I will venture to say there is not one of my fair hearers whose imagination will not be able to supply every succeeding step in the courtship until it terminates in the happy union of the parties. And the curtain falls, according to the established rule of novels of the bygone time, on a stage peopled by joyous hearts and smiling faces.

"The author was evidently thoroughly imbued with the spirit of his master Cervantes, and has framed his two principal characters upon the precise model of Don Quixote and Sancho Panza. We admire in Geoffry Wildgoose the same upright earnestness of purpose, the same simple dignity of character amidst all his extravagancies which distinguish the Don; and in Jerry Tugwell the same mixture of shrewdness and simplicity, the same quaint humour, the same lurking suspicion that there is a screw loose in his master's wits, and yet the same quailing before that master's superior genius and earnest enthusiasm which characterize Sancho. One great secret of the success of this work is that many of the principal characters were drawn from real life. There is extant a key, assigning each of these to its original. The character of Wildgoose has by some been considered as a fiction, by others as representing either sir Harry Trelawny or Mr. Joseph Townsend, formerly rector of Pewsey, Wilts. But I have some suspicion that the true original may be found in Mr. Graves's brother,[1] above-mentioned. Perhaps it may have been a composition combining features taken from different originals.

"The mention of this work naturally raises the vexed question whether or no error in religion is a legitimate subject of satire.[2] As I am unwilling to dogmatize, I will content myself with stating the main arguments on both sides. A pious and able writer of the present day has said : ' Ridicule cannot be employed with impunity as a test of truth ; error and truth often lie so close together. Nay, most religious error has so much of truth mingled up with it that the very love of truth ought to preclude the use of jesting ; for, through this close connection of truth and error, mire cannot be cast at error without defiling the truth also.' The same writer proceeds to quote from bishop Warburton as follows :—' To see what little good is to be expected from this way of wit and humour, we may observe that even the ridicule of false virtue hath been sometimes attended with mischievous effects. The Spaniards have lamented, and I believe truly, that Cervantes' just and inimitable ridicule of knight-errantry rooted up with that folly a great deal of their real honour. And it was apparent that Butler's fine satire on fanaticism contributed not a little, during the licentious age of Charles II., to bring sober piety into disrepute.[3] The reason is evident : there are many lines of resemblance between truth and its counterfeits, and it is the province of wits only to find out the *likenesses* of things, and not the talent of the common admirers of it—to discern the *differences*.'

"These two extracts seem to embody the whole or chief of what is to be said on the one side. On the other it may be argued that fanaticism, even in its lighter shades, is so destructive of candour, generosity and charity ; and in its darker, so apt to generate both hypocrisy and cruelty, so fraught with hatred, malice, and all uncharitableness, as to require the strongest correctives ; and being of that class of social evils which the law cannot touch (except in its most frightful results), it seems legitimate to fall within the province of the satirist. As reasonably might it be asserted that Elijah was inflicting a blow upon natural piety and the worship of God when he mocked the priests of Baal, saying, ' Cry aloud, for he *is* a god ; either he is talking,

---

[1] Charles Caspar Graves, a younger brother, who had favoured Methodism and then "fell away."

[2] It is singular to find Warner on the side of those who disapproved of satire when directed against dangerous fanaticism, because in his Bath Characters he employed it unsparingly.

[3] No doubt, but the Bishop forgot that Butler *did* attack " sober piety " as well as its counterfeit.

or he is pursuing, or he is on a journey, or peradventure he sleepeth and must be awaked ;' as that the satirist, in levelling his shafts *bonâ fide* at mischievous religious error, must necessarily inflict a wound upon pure and undefiled religion."

In 1831 a writer in the *Christian Observer* delivered himself of the following diatribe :—

"Whatever might be the author's intention, and however plausible his reasonings, his warmest admirers must admit, that in ridiculing the practice of these 'irregular teachers,' he has done much to bring religion itself into contempt. He trifles systematically with all that is sacred, and his profane irony is displayed by an indiscriminate travesty of the language of inspiration, as well as of those peculiarities of expression, the use of which, in the opinion of the admirable essayist, *Foster,* [1] is to be considered as one of the causes why persons of taste have occasionally shown so lamentable an indifference to evangelical religion. A late writer remarks, that 'it is to be feared he (the author) descended into the grave without leaving behind him a single expression of regret for having polluted the clerical name with a performance which directly attacked Christianity, under the shadow of a pretence, merely to display the human weaknesses of such persons as Whitfield, Wesley, etc."

When Graves arrived at the grand climacteric, nothing gave him so much pleasure as to trot over the down on his cob to meet his friends in Bath. From 1760, until his death, Bull's Library was the great attraction for literary men, and Graves was one of the coterie. After the death of his wife, to whose memory he was so "touchingly true," and when he was free from the "carking cares" of pecuniary pressure he was seen most days about his well-known haunts in the Orange Grove. The Grove was as famous in its day as the *Pantiles* at Tunbridge Wells in the days of Johnson. The Libraries were a great attraction. There, or close to it, on the Parade, were the Libraries of Frederick, afterwards Leake, then Bull, and then Upham ; Meyler [2] established his well-known Library in 1781, and *The Herald* in 1792. Graves, after the death of Bull, was a member of Meyler's Library, which soon became the favourite resort of Harington, Graves, Parry, Warner, Falconer, and other local worthies. It was at the boarding-house of Mrs. Henderson, in the Orange Grove, where Graves first made the acquaintance of Shenstone, an acquaintance that ripened into a closer and intimate friendship, ending only with the death of the latter, in 1763. The letters addressed by Shenstone to Graves are interesting—more interesting than most of Shenstone's compositions, which are stilted and marred by egotisti-

---

[1] The terms which John Foster considered prejudicial and a hindrance to evangelical religion were the terms Graves satirized.

[2] Meyler was a clever, enterprising man, who wrote verses in his own paper ; sometimes contributed to Lady Miller's vase, and occasionally composed an address to be spoken by a favourite actor at the Bath Theatre. The first prologue spoken by Dimond in 1787 at the Bath Theatre was from the pen of Meyler. The Library he established in the Grove was afterwards removed to the Abbey Churchyard, and is at the present time conducted by Mr. J. Davies.

cal mannerisms. Besides Meyler, Graves was on intimate terms with Samuel Jackson Pratt,[1] who was an author and a poet—so he flattered himself; at one time he aspired to the laureateship. During the last year of Graves' life—when he was 90—a correspondence in verse took place between the veteran and his admiring friend, which the latter gives in Vol. 3 of "The Harvest Home":—

A POETIC DISPUTE.

'Proof rise on proof, and still the last the strongest.'

TO THE REV. MR. GRAVES,

OF CLAVERTON, NEAR BATH,

On receiving an admirable Letter, written after having passed the 90th Year of his Age.

"LONG-LOV'D and venerable Friend.
Thanks for the *Paradox* you send.
You talk of weakness and of age,
And then to *prove* it fill your page
With every mark of mental health,
Vigour and intellectual wealth,
And active, warm benevolence,
And all the energies of sense.

You tell me, too, you're deaf and blind;
Then show the *vision* of your mind
To be so little worse for wear,
In all those Genius pictures fair,
That, running sense and wit 'gainst time,
You little more than in your prime;
And had I not the date from you,
I scarce should think you fifty-two;
The point when Wisdom is mature,
And what remains of Fancy, pure;
Or, if you still dispute this truth,
We'll say you're in your *second youth* /
But even here you change the plan,
NOT TWICE a CHILD, BUT TWICE A MAN!"

SAMUEL JACKSON PRATT.

March 31st, 1804.

ANSWER BY GRAVES.

"ALAS! my friend, you're very kind
To say, that though I'm deaf and blind,
Of sight and hearing thus bereft,
My *mental vigour* still is left;
But while you'd contradict my senses,
My *feeling* stronger light dispenses,
And '*spite* of all your glowing diction,
Poets, I find, *will* deal in fiction;
Yet, though I think your praise invention,
I thank you for your kind intention.

You tell me too, I still am *young*,
Nor are you, Sir, entirely wrong.
If *follies* are of *youth* the test,
This obvious truth *must* be confest;
In this respect I'm still a child,
By every youthful whim beguil'd:
The lovely sex I still admire;
But, ah! what hopes can they inspire?
Love books—I nc'er can read, I fear;
Love music—which I cannot hear;
Love pictures—which I cannot see;
What greater follies can there be?
But, every scruple to remove,
These doggerel rhymes the fact will prove.

I'm also *twice* a man, you say,
Not *twice* a child—ah! lack-a-day!
I never was, say what you can,
But little more than half a man;[2]
And now, by age and grief worn out,
I still am *twice* a man, no doubt!
And that my faculties decay
I feel, alas! each fleeting day;
In short, if still you will dispute,
These rhymes your argument confute.
I'm hastening fast to ninety-one,
And ('tis full time) my work is done;
And hourly now I keep in view
My latter end.—Dear Sir, adieu!
R. GRAVES.

Claverton, April 2nd, 1804.

Pratt sent a rejoinder, so laboured and feeble that it is not worth reproducing.

---

[1] Pratt was a bookseller, in partnership with Mr. Clinch (from 1780 to 1787). Pratt, though of a versatile genius, is best known as the author of "Gleanings, or Travels Abroad and in England," and for his "Harvest Home," but he was also the author of Novels, Poems, and Dramas. His tragedy, entitled "The Fair Circassian," brought out at Drury Lane, 1780, had a continuous run of twenty-six nights. He published several Novels, under the assumed name of Courtney Melmoth; his Poems were of the *Della Cruscan* school. The Library which Pratt conducted was first started by Tennant, and kept by him up to the year 1780. In 1787 Marshall joined the firm, and, when Pratt

[Letter in the possession of Mr. C. E. Mathews, of Exeter.]

[Dr. Jeremiah Milles (Dean of Exeter from 1762-84) published a 4to. edition of the "Rowley Poems" in 1777; and the following letter, addressed apparently to a son of the Dean, was written, when Graves was 82 years old, in acknowledgment of the loan of a copy. The letter has not been published before.

It is to be noted that the writer passes in his letter from the *third* to the *first* person.

The letter is written in a fine bold hand on a half-sheet of crown 4to. paper. A descendant of Dean Milles—Major-General T. Milles—was recently living at Seaton in Devonshire.]

"Mr. Graves presents his compliments to Mr. Milles, and is much obliged to him for the use of the Dean's publication. He has certainly proved demonstrably the utter impossibility (morally speaking) of Chatterton's being the author of the poems attributed to Rowley; and the absurdity of the contrary opinion. That Chatterton, however, has occasionally inserted some modern expressions (perhaps where he could not decipher the original) seems highly probable (as I myself suspected when the poems first appeared). And I have always thought, that Sir Charles Bowdyn in particular, had undergone the same modernising with the original ballad of Chevy-Chase—either about Queen Elizabeth's time; or by Chatterton himself. The old ballad of Chevy-Chase, Dr. Percy thinks, was written about Henry VIth. time; but the language is more obsolete than any of Rowley's. On the whole, the Dean has displayed most elegant writing, as well as sound criticism and knowledge of antiquity; and I wish my old friend, Homer, and the Trojan War, may find as good an apologist as Dr. Milles, against the annihilating system of Mr. Jacob Bryant's late publication.

"But I did not intend a dissertation when I began a mere acknowledgment of a favour.

"I beg our respects to Mrs. Milles. I hope you received 'Mr. Burke's Letters' from the barmaid at the White Lion.

"Claverton, 19th November, 1796."

LADY DIANA BEAUCLERK, daughter of Charles, 3rd Duke of Marlborough, and wife of **TOPHAM BEAUCLERK**, eldest son of Lord Sydney Beauclerk, vice-chamberlain to George II.—This lady was a frequent visitor to Bath. Her beauty, her wit, and her vivacity, rendered her one of the most popular women of her time, especially amongst the "Duchesses." Topham Beauclerk, whom she married in 1768, was one of Dr. Johnson's most intimate friends. He was witty, humorous, and eccentric, but he possessed qualities which endeared him to Dr. Johnson almost, if not altogether, as much as the Herveys. Lady "Di" was very outspoken. Writing from Bath, in 1776, to George Selwyn, she says :—

LADY DIANA BEAUCLERK TO GEORGE SELWYN.

"Bath, Nov. 21st [1776].

"I am vastly obliged to you for your long letter; indeed, it was not at all a———; I dare

retired, it continued in the Marshall family till 1808, when it became the property of Mr. Henry Godwin, who, in 1822, consigned it to his brother, Mr. Charles Godwin,* who retired in 1852.

* Mr. C. Godwin accumulated a very remarkable collection of local books. He was not merely a man of great intelligence and a highly valued citizen, but he was a profound bibliographer, an admirable scholar, and a high-minded gentleman. After his death, his Bath Collection was sold to Mr. Shum, of Belcombe Brook, Bradford-on-Avon.

† Alluding to the shortness of his stature and slender form.

not write the word, because you seem to have such an objection to it; and as I am quite ignorant of its *sens radical*, it is better not to use it.[1]

"I have wrote once more to Mrs. Terry, and I hope that nothing but the children not being perfectly well will prevent them coming with you. I am perfectly at ease about their journey, approve of the calvacade, and still more of the private orders. I must insist upon Mary's sitting backwards, at least part of the way. I would not have Mie Mie crowded for the world, and should be quite unhappy if I thought my girls were the least trouble to you or her.

"Bob is here, and tired to death already. *Entre nous*, this is a most detestable place *(fie, fie*, Lady Di) ; and, to make it complete, the Princess Amelia[2] is here, poking about it in every corner. It is impossible to stir without meeting her, and as I have no hopes of her being gracious enough to take notice of me, I am obliged to avoid her. Perhaps you think that her taking notice of one would be a still better reason for avoiding her.

"The Fawkeners are gone ; I do not know where. Mr. B.[3] sends his compliments to you. I think my signing my name as unnecessary as your doing it."

THE FALCONERS:—WILLIAM FALCONER, M.D., F.R.S., 29, CIRCUS; THE REV. THOMAS FALCONER, M.D., 29, CIRCUS; THOMAS FALCONER, County Court Judge, 18, ROYAL CRESCENT; RANDLE WILBRAHAM FALCONER, M.D., 22, BENNETT STREET.

"William Falconer, M.D., F.R.S., was the younger of two surviving sons of William Falconer, Recorder of Chester, and the only son who married. He was born at Chester, Feb 13, 1744. In 1770 he chose Bath as his residence, and began at once his distinguished career. For a short time Dr. Falconer lived in Duke Street, and there his only son and child was born. Shortly after Dr. Falconer removed to **29, Circus.**

"Dr. Falconer married Henrietta Edmunds (born 22nd March, 1739, and died at Bath, 10th September, 1803), daughter of Thomas Edmunds, Esq., of Worsborough Hall, county of York. Her grandmother, Jane Edmunds, was the daughter of Francis Foljambe, Esq., of Aldwark. On the death of Mrs. Falconer's nephew, Francis Offley Edmunds (who married Mary, daughter of Francis F. Foljambe, Esq., of Aldwark), without issue, the estates of the Edmunds' family passed to the children of her niece, Maria Elizabeth, the wife of Henry Martin, Esq., of Colston Basset, Nottinghamshire, formerly M.P. for Kinsale, and a Master in Chancery."

Dr. Falconer was not a popular man in the ordinary sense of the word ; he was highly esteemed by those who knew him well, and who enjoyed his intimacy. He was too proud and too independent to stoop to the arts of his profession ; moreover, Dr. Falconer had a peculiar *brusqueness* of manner, which has been sometimes referred to as the *Falconer temper*. This constitutional infirmity—if it were not a virtue—characterized the son, the Rev. William

---

[1] The expression was probably *"a bore ;"* a term which has since been so familiarized to us that it has lost its vulgarity.

[2] See account of the Princess, first series, H. H.

[3] Topham Beauclerk.

Falconer, and his sons, the late Thomas Falconer and the late Dr. Wilbraham Falconer, than whom never were there kinder, more considerate men ; they could not stoop to what they regarded as the conventional courtesies of life, when plain speaking was demanded. If the *Falconer temper* revealed the sincerity of the men, in one and all it concealed a deep and tender nature, and a noble disinterestedness, of which ample evidence exists with regard to each in his day and generation. " They had hearts as sound as a bell, for which their tongue was the clapper, for what their hearts thought their tongues spake," if a little liberty may be taken with Shakespeare.   Dr. William Falconer was a sturdy Liberal in politics, and in his day he found, amongst his own class, few to applaud or to sympathise with him.   It was not that Dr. Falconer attached himself to the dynastic Whig party of the day, as distinguished from the Tory party.   He was a real, earnest reformer, and he regarded the Whigs as a party who cared less for reform than they did for office—

"Who gave up to party what was meant for mankind."

But withal he was true and loyal to the institutions of the country.   When the ludicrous incident connected with Warner's Sermon on War occurred, both Dr. Falconer and his son, the Rev. T. Falconer, M.D., who shared his father's political opinions, distinctly disavowed all sympathy with Warner, who denounced War under any and all circumstances as indefensible.   Moreover, Dr. Falconer shared Burke's opinion with reference to the French Revolution, as appears by the following interesting letter addressed to him by that great man :—

" Sir,—

" I am extremely thankful to you for letting me know to whom it is that we have been obliged for the temperate, judicious, and reasonable paper which appeared in the Bath prints some time since, and which was inclosed to me in a cover without any name.   I am happy in your thinking my little endeavour in any sort worthy of co-operating towards the good purposes which your able paper was so well calculated to promote.   It was very early my opinion, that even if the things which have been done in France were better done than they are, that the principles upon which the new legislators act are, in themselves, very pernicious, and cannot be adopted in any country without bringing it to shame and ruin.   I am proud in finding you in the same opinion.   I am perfectly sensible of my obligation to you for the pains you have taken in the various extracts which you have made for the support of our common principles, and for my instruction as well as satisfaction.   It is always of great moment to every man, who in affairs of consequence is obliged to dissent with several of his contemporaries, to show that in differing from them he agrees with other persons not less respectable.   The gentlemen of your faculty have long been distinguished for joining liberal erudition to professional skill.   I do not know any profession which may not be aided by it as well as adorned.   Your remarks show that you have gone further, and have joined to that liberal literature such a knowledge of our laws and constitution as make you valuable as a useful citizen as well as a man of letters and of medical knowledge.   I see that the managers of the Revolution Society, though they broke up in the most complete distraction and mutual ill-humour, have thought proper to publish such an account, as if their madness had been quite methodical, and that they had pursued their plans of anarchy in the very best possible order. There is a vein of fraud which runs through all their proceedings.

"If your business should ever permit you to visit London, I shall be very happy if you will add to the favour of your present communication, that of permitting me to cultivate a personal acquaintance with a gentleman to whom I am so highly obliged, and for whose learning and abilities, as well as for the use he makes of them, I have so sincere a respect.

"I have the honour to be, with the greatest possible attention and regard, Sir, your most obedient and faithful humble servant,

"EDM. BURKE.

"November 14, 1790.

"I beg leave to pray your acceptance of a new edition of my Pamphlet, in which you will find some particulars a little better methodised, and more clearly explained in the way of stating some facts and sentiments.

"*To William Falconer, Esq., M.D.*"

If Dr. Falconer did not do much *in* his profession, it was because he was independent of it, but he did much *for* it. He was a large contributor to the literature of his profession,[1] bringing to bear upon it in its various branches thoughtful learning, a mind singularly free from professional prejudice and pedantry, with a judgment based upon a simple, earnest, independent love of truth. In the days of Falconer, men of scientific pursuits were more dependent upon each other than they are at present; they formed a circle of friends; they met in friendly conclave at the Libraries, and they cultivated the art of conversation; they discussed professional questions, as well as subjects of the day, not solely or chiefly for amusement, but, as Falconer would say, for truth, and they became admirable talkers—ready, witty, full, and able talkers. There were many coteries; one perchance at Bull's, another at Meyler's, and another at Pratt's. Falconer was a man of good presence, dignified in manner, and ever ready with a retort, an epigram, or a witty rejoinder. Mr. Monkland, in his boyhood, remembers seeing him at Bull's Library. "There," he says, "was HARINGTON, seated in his *curule* chair, in his full-bottomed wig and three-cornered hat, one leg crossed over the other, and holding his handkerchief to his mouth, when not speaking, for he had delicate lungs; and FALCONER, pacing up and down, portly and erect of form, his nose with spectacles bestrid, and his hand resting in the bosom of his waistcoat; together with others I cannot at this distance of time call to mind; but this was the focus of all the INTELLECTUALS who resorted to Bath." Warner, in his "*Literary Recollections,*" gives some

---

[1] Dr. Falconer published 45 distinct works, larger and smaller.

interesting particulars of his friend :—

"I recollect it as an honour and a privilege, to have been on the list of the friends of the late Dr. Falconer : as it brought me into frequent intercourse with a man as remarkable for the gifts and acquirements of the mind, as for the virtues of the heart. Few students had read more extensively, or more successfully, than this gentleman. His knowledge of the Latin language was uncommon : his acquaintance with general literature comprehensive : his intellect bright and quick ; and his memory more than ordinary tenacious. I would say, however, that his prominent mental characteristic was (though a thorough gentleman in feeling and bearing) deep and incessant *thought*—but his mind was powerful and healthy ; and quite equal to the burden of its labour. That his *external* manner received a slight tinge from this not very common direction of the intellectual faculties, will be in the clear remembrance of all those who knew Dr. Falconer ; the little peculiarities which grew out of it, formed only a trifling deviation from the tame uniformity of customary personal habits—such as momentary fits of absence, occasional inattention to the men and things immediately around him, and ever and anon, an *inspection*, apparently so earnest, of the *trifling objects* of art or curiosity, as seemed to indicate that every faculty was concentrated in his admiration of these *nugæ*, while his thoughts were busily employed on subjects infinitely more important than the toys before him. Of this last trait in the Doctor's character, I remember a remarkable instance which was communicated to me by Mrs. Jefferys (the sister of John Wilkes), than whom no one entertained a higher regard for the subject of her anecdote.

"A friend of this lady had come to Bath for medical advice, and applied to Mrs. J. to recommend to her a practitioner of ability and integrity. She immediately named her friend Dr. Falconer, in terms which bespoke her own confidence in his attention and skill. The Doctor was accordingly requested to attend the stranger. He waited upon her : was admitted : and after the common forms of salutation, walked towards the fire-place, on the mantel-piece of which were arranged some little ornaments of china-ware. 'Favour me with the symptoms of your complaint, Madam,' said Dr. Falconer, and immediately took up one of the vases and began to examine it closely, and, to all appearance, with the greatest possible interest. The lady commenced her melancholy details of aches and pains, continued it for some time, and then suddenly *stopp'd.* 'Why do you not proceed, Madam?'—'Because I perceive, Doctor, that your attention is so completely occupied by the trifles on the slab, as not to allow you to direct the slightest portion of it to the subject of my ailments.'—' Say you so, my good Madam? You are exceedingly deceived. Not a syllable has escaped me ; ' and sitting down by her side, Dr. Falconer repeated to her, with minute exactness, every sentence she had uttered. The patient's prejudice instantly vanished : she was delighted with her *attentive* doctor, who soon increased her gratitude to him by her perfect cure.[1]

"It is not paradoxical to say, that this *habit* in Dr. Falconer, of *apparently* directing his

---

[1] This singularity of the Doctor was less impolitic than that of a more recent celebrated Bath medical man, who hated what he called the humbug of the profession. A lady who was about to make Bath her residence, enquired of her former medical adviser to whom she should go in Bath. Knowing Mr. —— only by repute, he said, "Go to Mr. ——." The lady was vain of her appearance, and on consulting Mr. —— for the first time, she said, "O, Mr. ——, what age do you think I am?" he, turning suddenly upon her, said, "Well Ma'am, God knows, perhaps a hundred !" On another occasion he visited a lady fifteen miles from Bath, and on entering her room he glanced at her, saw by intuition there was little the matter, walked up to a picture, looked at it, admired it, and then turning abruptly to the lady, waved his hand, and said, "Good day, ma'am, you'll do," and left without fee.

especial attention to an unimportant nick-nack, while the *thinking faculty* was employed upon speculations of a weighty or lofty nature, actually *assisted* him in fixing his thoughts more intently and exclusively upon the recondite topic.   The toy or trifle was just sufficient to *attract* his *attention*, and prevent it from being applied to, or distracted by, surrounding objects, without requiring any exercise of *thought* upon *itself;* and consequently, this intellectual faculty, undisturbed by foreign associations, was brought to bear solely and steadily upon that class of ideas which constituted the real subject of his mental contemplation. [1]

"Many of the results of Dr. Falconer's profound reflection and diligent reading are before the public in his printed works. Their subjects are, in some instances, ingenious and novel; in all, interesting and important : evincing his intimate acquintance with classical literature, with sacred and profane history, with the higher branches of natural philosophy, with grand views of the art and practice of medicine, with general and local law, with the theory of mind, and the abstractions of metaphysics. On civil and ecclesiastical law (a topic so little attended to and understood), his opinion was a satisfactory authority ; for he had not only studied it with great application, but written on it, copiously and elaborately. A few years before his death, he allowed me to peruse a commentary (or rather a voluminous mass of notes) which he had composed on the President Montesquieu's celebrated work. I was quite surprised by the reading displayed in it, which embraced references to many of the best productions of the ancients, and much of the less familiar literature of the middle ages, and was equally delighted with the strength of thought, acuteness of remark, and above all, the high tone of moral feeling with which almost every page of it was fraught.

" But among all the high qualities of Dr. Falconer's character, none shone with brighter lustre than a sober Christian piety, and a virtuous and honourable principle. With him, religion was a feeling, and not a name : it had its dwelling in his heart, and its exemplification in a conduct of uniform integrity and uprightness, kindness and beneficence. His love of sincerity was ardent, his regard for truth severe and uncompromising. A circumstance illustrative of this moral trait in the Doctor occurs to my recollection. Many years since, I dined at his house with a large party, among whom was my friend Dr. Parr. A discussion took place respecting Samuel Johnson's *conversational powers.* They were highly lauded by Parr. Dr. Falconer expressed no great esteem of them, and no envy at those who had had the opportunity (which never occurred to himself) of listening to them ; for, said he, ' Johnson was quite a monopoliser of the conversation : he would let no one talk except himself.' 'And pray,' returned Parr, ' what would you have gone into Johnson's company for, but to *hear him talk* ?' ' No, Sir,' responded Dr. Falconer with energy ; ' No, Sir, Johnson talked for *victory*, and not for *truth*—and all such talk I *utterly abhor* !'

"That Dr. Falconer's practice should have been proportioned to his real lofty claims to success, was not to be expected. He had been born for a wider sphere, and more scientific circle,

---

[1] " I met with a confirmation of the reasonableness of this hypothesis about twelve years ago, in the person of *George Bidder*, a child of eight years old, who exhibited in public an astonishing faculty of *off-hand* calculation, without the assistance of pen, ink, chalk, or any other implement for notation. In the course of from five to ten minutes, according to the difficulty of the question, this extraordinary lad would give accurate answers to the most complicated numerical queries. Having heard the question which was proposed to him, he ceased to look at the company, and directed his eyes to a *teetotum*, which he *spun* and *surveyed* as long as his mind was engaged in the *calculating process*. Unless he had this *merely amusing* object before him to divert his attention from the surrounding external objects and to enable him to throw the whole power of thought upon this operation, he was incapable of affording any solution of the question proposed."—*Note by Warner.*

than the little world of Bath ; for a metropolitan theatre, where the native force of his character could have been felt ; and the depth and variety of his attainments, accurately fathomed, and duly appreciated. To have numbered, however, the late Duke of Portland, Lord Chancellor Thurlowe, and William Pitt, among his patients, is proof sufficient that his worth as an able physician and a wise and experienced man, was correctly estimated by those whose confidence and good opinion were of far higher value and praise than mere vulgar popularity. *Laudatus a laudatis*, ought to satisfy the ambition of any reasonable man."

Dr. Parr, in his familiar letters to " Richard Warner," always refers in terms of affectionate respect to Dr. Falconer.   In December, 1820, he says—" Within these last few days I have been revising my will, and the contents of your letter, as read to me this morning, have increased the satisfaction which I felt in finding that I had bequeathed to you and Dr. Falconer a mourning-ring as a memorial of my esteem and respect." The respect he felt for Dr. Falconer he extended to the son. In 1805 he writes—" Mr. Falconer is an excellent man, and worthy of so enlightened and so virtuous a father." The relations of Dr. Falconer to Sir T. Lawrence, which have been referred to,[1] were highly credit-able to both parties.   In a reference to Lawrence in his " Literary Recollec-tions," Warner gives the following interesting fact :—" As the curiosity and interest of the public are still alive to the name and memory of that great deceased master in the art of painting, the late Sir Thomas Lawrence, it might not be irrelevant to add, in this place, a few circumstances connected with his residence and professional employ while he remained at Bath. If it were highly honourable to the character of Lawrence, that, during this period, he maintained his father and mother, by the exercise of his pencil, it was equally creditable to my great and good friend, the late Dr. Falconer, the patron of all that was ingenious and virtuous, to encourage and befriend the young man in this career of successful effort, stimulated by successful piety. Dr. Falconer gave him his advice, assistance, and friendship. Most of Lawrence's leisure was passed at the Doctor's house. Under his hospitable roof were begun and completed many of the best of the artist's early drawings. Among others, I have contemplated with delight two pencil ones, of Cassandra and a Christ's head, every line of which is radiant with genius, and full of the promise of future excellence and fame. Lawrence, to his praise be it spoken, never forgot his obligations to Dr. Falconer. They were expressed to the eldest of his grandsons,[2] in September last,[3] when he requested him to step into a parlour, and look at two drawings,

---

[1] " Historic Houses," first series, p. 113.

[2] The Rev. W. Falconer, Rector of Bushey, Herts, the translator of the Geography of Strabo, in Bohn's Library.

[3] About 1828.

which, he told him, were finished in the house of the young man's excellent grandfather."

In the **REV. THOMAS FALCONER, M.A., M.D.**, were combined the clerical and medical qualifications, both of which he exercised purely and freely for the good of his fellow-creatures. He refused preferment, and gave his friendly help to his clerical brethren without any other reward than that of doing good. He was an accomplished scholar, an excellent theologian, and a man in whom there was "no guile." When the Rev. Thomas Falconer deliberately gave his opinion upon a question of disputed scholarship, he generally proved to be right. Being the only child of his father, he possessed a competency which he might have enjoyed in inglorious ease. If he embraced the sacred profession from choice and with a sincere desire to do good, he saw also, by a true philanthropical instinct, how much that good might be enhanced by the ability to relieve the suffering body, whilst ministering to a mind diseased. But if he gave his aid in this twofold capacity in the cause of suffering humanity, he was "equally generous with his purse, which he used unsparingly." Like his father, he was said to be a "proud man," which put in other language means that he feared not any man.

The following sketch of Dr. Thomas Falconer was written by his second son, the late Thomas Falconer :—

"Feb. 18, 1839, died at his house in the Circus, Bath, after a very short illness, the Rev. Thomas Falconer, A.M. and M.D. He was born Dec. 24, 1771, in Duke street, in the parish of St. James, in this city, and was the only child of the late Dr. William Falconer, whose eminence as a physician, and whose great distinction as a scholar and a scientific inquirer, are well known. As a child he was remarkable for his studious and attentive habits, for his great kindness and humanity, for great cheerfulness of temper, and for his strict and undeviating regard for truth—excellences which he retained and exhibited to the last moment of his life. The early elements of his classical education he received under the tuition of the Rev. Mr. Morgan, of Bath. He was afterwards removed to the High School of Manchester, and was placed under the care of a most able scholar, Mr. Lawson, a layman, for whose kindness and attention he never ceased to express his gratitude. He was then removed to the King's School at Chester, of which Mr. Bancroft was the master, and some of his compositions were included in a work entitled 'Prolusiones Poeticæ,' printed at Chester in 1788. While at this school, and a little past the sixteenth year of his age, namely, on the 18th of January, 1488, he was elected a scholar of Corpus Christi College, Oxford, and became a Fellow of the same college on the 7th of November, 1794. In 1797 he published a translation, with many excellent notes, of the Periplus of Hanno. Having taken his degree of M.A., and been elected one of the Fellows of his college, he visited Edinburgh, and remained there for two sessions, during that time very regularly attending many of the medical classes. He had already entered the Church and taken priest's orders. At Edinburgh he became known to many of the most distinguished Presbyterian divines ; and though never hesitating to express his preference to that form of Church Government with which he was connected, was treated by them with great favour and attention. Mr. Dalzell, the Professor of Greek, was struck with his great acquirements as a scholar, and honourably mentioned him in one of the works he was engaged in preparing for the press, and afterwards published. On his return to England, he occupied himself in editing the Oxford edition of Strabo, the notes of which had been prepared for the press by his uncle, Mr. Thomas Falconer. This work he finished after overcoming many obstacles. It formed two large folio volumes ; and his share in it has always been spoken of with general approval. On some occasions he was elected a select preacher in the University of Oxford ; and published the sermons he delivered. In 1810, he filled the most honoured office that the University of Oxford can bestow upon a divine, namely, that of Bampton Lecturer ; and his appointment was communicated to him by the President of Corpus Christi College, ' to have been made with an unanimity that he should never forget.' In compliance with the regulations attached to this office, his Lectures were published. They were such as were worthy to be heard by a learned audience, and investigated several questions of extreme and great importance in relation to the evidences of Christianity. He afterwards published several minor works, among which the most remarkable was, ' A Defence of Eusebius, Bishop of Cæsarea,' from a charge of mutilating certain copies of the Scriptures that he had been directed to prepare. In 1823, yielding to a desire to practice medicine, which he had long studied, and the knowledge of which he had assiduously cultivated under the experience and direction of his learned father, he took the degree of M.D., at Oxford. He soon afterwards commenced to prepare for the press a translation of the Geography of Strabo, which he finished, and was engaged in arranging to print it at the time of his decease. The only parish duty that he performed was, during the short time that he held the office of curate of St. James', Bath. He never received any preferment. Dr. Fisher, Bishop of Salisbury, offered to him the Vicarage of West Anstey, in Dorsetshire, which he declined to accept. Upon all occasions he was very willing, and did frequently assist in the performance of divine service, though he preached but seldom. His writings were those of a gentleman, and a public scholar, correct, precise, and forcible. No man ever lived who had a stronger sense of justice, or felt more indignant at the violation of duty or morality. On such occasions alone, when justice or morality were attacked, was the gentleness of his character disturbed. He remembered no injuries, and was forgiving and kind. By his family he was deeply and affectionately beloved, and by his friends he was esteemed and admired. His great learning and extensive acquirements made his company at all times acceptable. He was no bigot, and being himself tolerant and kind, he neither relished nor sanctioned public displays of fanaticism or controversial disputes, believing that changes of opinion could only be effected by persuasion, and in a quiet, reflecting privacy. Towards the ministers of all sects he bore himself in a charitable and christian-like spirit, feeling that he and they were labourers in the same vineyard, and that He who shall come to judge all can alone make a just judgment."

Of the Rev. Thomas Falconer's daughters one died· young, and the elder, Henrietta, married the late **Right Hon. JOHN ARTHUR ROEBUCK, Q.C.,** the darling of the Radical party in Bath, and who represented the city in two Parliaments. In 1847 he was defeated by Lord Ashley. His next constituency was that of Sheffield, and by degrees he came to repudiate most of his old creed, and yet, whilst retaining the confidence of a section of the Sheffield Radicals, he gained the support of the Conservative party. ' He who had once denounced the Church lived to proclaim in the House of Commons his belief in it as the agent for the accomplishment of unmixed good. No one could—no one did— charge him with insincerity, and yet this *tribune* of the people openly assailed the Liberal party and its policy, and avowed his full confidence in the "patriotic policy" of Lord Beaconsfield. His sturdy honesty, his vigorous eloquence, and love of country, no man ever questioned. His hands never were tainted with ill-gotten public money, and all that he had he spent in what he believed to be the best service of his country.

THOMAS FALCONER was the second son of the Rev. Thomas Falconer, M.D., and, like his father and his grandfather, possessed a great capacity for intellectual labour. Educated to the law, he was called in February, 1830, and soon took a deep interest in public questions, and he wrote a prodigious number of pamphlets on subjects connected with the law, emigration, and colonial affairs, which no doubt exercised considerable influence in solving certain questions of difficulty. In 1850, Mr. Falconer was appointed one of the arbitrators to determine the boundary between the provinces of Canada and New Brunswick. In 1852 he was appointed by Lord Truro to be judge of the County Courts of the counties of Glamorgan and Brecknock, and of the district of Rhayader, in Radnorshire. His judgments in important cases were characterised by great learning, and difficult points of law were dealt with by masterly analysis and illustrated by most felicitous examples. He retired from the Bench in 1881, and shortly after returned again to the place of his birth, and died at his residence, 18, Royal Crescent, in 1882.

Dr. Thomas Falconer had two daughters and five sons, of the latter of whom **RANDLE WILBRAHAM** was the youngest, having been born 21st September, 1813; consequently, at the time of his death (in 1880) he was in his 68th year. He was educated at Edinburgh, and was afterwards articled to an eminent medical practitioner in York, and then pursued his medical education at Edinburgh, obtaining his degree of M.D. in 1839. For a few years Dr. Falconer practised at Tenby, and in 1842 he married Maria Wood, daughter of John Wood, Esq., of Cwm and Brynhafod, Carmarthenshire. This lady died in 1847. In the same year Dr. Falconer returned to his native city, and began that active career which was brought too soon to a close. So energetically did he devote himself to the public service, and to every useful project, in politics, science, literature, and local government, that, for a time, no doubt it obscured those professional claims which ultimately were so extensively recognised. He threw himself, in fact, into all the questions of the day, with an ardour and persistency that seemed to leave him little time for other duties ; and there is no doubt that his varied attainments, combined with a beautiful voice, a clear and faultless diction, a singularly engaging delivery, and an imposing presence, rendered him the most valuable, if not the most popular man in Bath.

In 1850 Dr. Falconer married, at Walcot Church, Sophia Harriet Frances Howard-Vyse, younger daughter of the late Major-General Howard-Vyse, formerly M.P. for Beverley and Honiton, and sister of Colonel Howard-Vyse, M.P. for the S.D. of the county of Northampton, and afterwards for Windsor. This lady survives her husband. In 1852 he carried out with great success the " Bath City Lectures ; " these lectures were not merely of rare merit, but they were produced at the nominal cost of 2s. 6d. for the course of twelve, and were adapted with great felicity to a mixed audience. In the same year he was elected a member of the Corporation, and soon became one of its most active and influential members, especially in relation to the Mineral Waters and their revival as a curative agent, and to those sanitary questions, on the promotion of which, as he so well understood, depended the welfare of the city he loved above all others.

Dr. Falconer was an earnest advocate for a Public Abattoir, and although the resistance was too great, immense improvement has been effected in the conduct of the slaughter-houses. He worked actively, in conjunction with his colleagues, to bring about the successful meeting of the Somersetshire Archæo- logical Association, his own special contribution to the proceedings being an abstract of a portion of the Records in the City Archives. He had bestowed no little research and trouble in the investigation of the manuscripts and documents belonging to the city, and although the abstract referred to is but a small portion, it is the first attempt to render the collection of practical value to the city. Dr. Falconer was the first who discovered the absence of all documents relating to the Civil War—a hiatus of significant importance, when historically considered. In 1849 he was elected Physician to the Bath Royal United Hospital, on resigning which he was appointed Consulting Physician ; and, in 1856, he was elected Physician to the Mineral Water Hospital. On the death of the Rev. Charles Kemble he was chosen in succession to that gentleman President of the Institution, a post he held to the last. In March, 1858, he was placed on the Commission of the Peace, having in the previous November been elected Mayor of the city, an office to which he was re-elected the following year, and it is needless almost to say that no man was better qualified to sustain the dignity of that office, and to advance the institutions and municipal interests of the borough.

During his Mayoralty, the Volunteer Force was organized under his direction and presidency, and his services were most valuable, more especially as they were rendered in the public interests without any regard to any personal views of his own. Dr. Falconer was one of the promoters of the Literary Club, in connection with which he read several valuable papers, and if he had been spared, he would have contributed another valuable chapter on Bath History in reference to Jones's Treatise of 1572, called "The Bathes of Bathe Aide."[1] In speaking of this just before his last fatal attack, he said, "The complete History of Bath has yet to be written, and no *one* man can do it."

Thirty years ago, having collected valuable materials, he contemplated writing a concise account of the city, the prospectus of which was issued— "Bath, Past and Present;" but his increasing engagements prevented him from accomplishing his purpose. About the same period, in conjunction with his friend Mr. Long, he made an attempt to establish a Public Library of Reference. The object contemplated was a Library of Reference, to be supported by voluntary contributions, of general books of reference, MSS. and documents elucidatory of local history, etc. Such a library would have constituted an important institution in this city. The effort failed, not from any fault of Dr. Falconer's, but because of the difficulty—or the impossibility it may be said—of uniting public opinion in favour of such a project. The feeling which prompted him to make the effort,

[1] The literature of the Bath Waters is in danger of being overdone. Treatise after treatise, teaming from the Press, whilst adding little or nothing to what is already known of the Waters, lead the public to believe that they are merely professional puffs. The present revival of the use of the Waters is one of many during the past three centuries, but it is more likely to be of permanent duration because the public are guided by results, and not by fashion. Physicians in the past wrote treatises, not so much to get at scientific truth, as to prove each other to be quacks and humbugs, and the effect was to drive patients to the Spas abroad. Mr. C. E. Davis, F.S.A., has lately made the Baths and Bath Waters the subject of historical disquisition, and he informs the visitors to the Health Exhibition, in his pamphlet, that the King's Bath was known in the thirteenth century ! This statement might have been regarded as a misprint, if it had not been reprinted in many editions of the pamphlet for free distribution, which forbids such a conclusion. The authority on which the statement is based would be valuable to the antiquary. Without mentioning the old Chroniclers,* some of whom make very vague references to the Bath Waters—and the earliest of these, the author believes, was in the 13th century—there is practically no sort of information to be obtained with regard to these Waters. Læland, in point of time, is the earliest authority, although little was known of his book until Ilearne edited and published it in the 17th century—more than 100 years after Leland wrote, which was about 1533. He is the first writer who mentions the King's Bath, or any other bath. In 1568, Dr. Turner, who was a divine as well as a physician, and Dean of Wells, published his *Herbal*, at the end of which he gives a short account of the Baths. In 1570, Sir Edward Carne, Queen Elizabeth's ambassador to Pope Julius III. and Paul IV., gave a curious account of them to an eminent Italian physician, named *Andreas Baccius*, which he inserted, with other treatises on thermal waters, in his work entitled *De Thermis*, a book now almost priceless. In 1572, Jones's treatise was published, which was the fullest of any treatise published up to that time. In 1577, Harrison, a clergyman of the Church of England, in a tour through England, made some very curious notes on the springs of Bath, which were published in Holinshed's Chronic.es in 1577.

* The most eminent of these was *Alexander Neckam*, born 1157, died 1217, Abbot of Cirencester 1213. In his work, published by the Record Commission in 1863, *De Naturis Rerum*, he mentions Bath and its Hot Waters, in addition to other thermal springs, but there is no King's Bath referred to, and it would be strange if there were. The author is afraid he omits facts owing to a deficient imagination.

naturally led him to give his warmest support to the establishment of the Public Library under the Free Libraries' Acts, the failure of which caused him much vexation.   In 1860 he delivered at Twerton a practical and admirable lecture on " Health ; or How to Preserve it."   In the same year, " Reports of Cases treated at the Bath Mineral Water Hospital from November, 1859, to May, 1860." These "Cases" he afterwards embodied in the larger work which he published in the following year—" The Bath Mineral Waters in Cases of Rheumatism, Sciatica, and Gout," etc.

On the occasion of the visit of the Bristol Branch of the British Medical Association, in 1864, Dr. Falconer delivered an address ; as he did also to the same Association on its meeting in Bath some years after.   This presidential address is very able and interesting to the general reader.   It is a *résumé* of recent discoveries and experiments in sanitary and medical science, free from technicalities and scientific phraseology.   Of course an address of this nature, delivered in Bath on such an occasion, would have been incomplete without a copious and excellent description of the famous springs, in reference to which Dr. Falconer was *facile princeps*.   In 1868 he issued his " Hospital Economics," the statistics of which threw much practical light upon the controversy, which ran high at the time, as to the management of the Royal United Hospital.   At the request of the Committee of the Mineral Water Hospital, he wrote a popular and interesting account of the institution, copies of which were sold to the patients only.   The work is now out of print.   It will be seen that Dr. Falconer's publications had reference either to strictly professional or quasi-professional subjects, chiefly in connection with the Bath Mineral Waters.   No man, indeed, has done more during the present century to revive the use of the waters in certain forms of disease, and this obviously arose from the conviction he felt of the danger of Bath again lapsing into the neglect of the great source of her attraction—the Mineral Waters, which had originally made her famous—and passing again through those fluctuating phases of obscuration and indifference from which she had been emancipated in the last century ; and therefore it was that he lent the whole force of his mind and professional energy to the legitimate extension of the medical uses of the thermal springs.   He had, so far, in 1864, when he left the Town Council, completed his mission, that he had given an impetus to the developing the bathing establishments of the city, which to this day it has never lost, and seems still to be gathering fresh force.

Professor Earle says the expansion Bath received in the eighteenth century was due to its healing waters.   This was true in a general as well as in a special sense.   In a general sense, because Bath was the fashion, and drew many people here who "affected" the waters whilst caring nothing about them : in a special sense, because Royal visits to the Baths had made them very famous. Rich and distinguished invalids from all parts derived such signal benefits from their use, that the confines of the old city were too limited for its wants and its growing importance. Dr. Falconer recognised the fact, and his experience taught him the emphatic truth, that the nineteenth-century Bath must largely depend upon its mineral springs as the chief source of its prosperity and permanent distinction. The activity of Dr. Falconer in his profession, and out of it, remained unimpaired to the last. He was an admirable man of business. As a Chairman he was courteous, clear, decided, but always most considerate and fair towards those whose interests were the subject of discussion. Nobody ever said, when Dr. Falconer was in the chair, that the chairman failed to understand his business.

Dr. Falconer was thought by some, and perhaps with truth, to be a man whose manner and bearing were characterised by a certain *hauteur*.[1] But in the author's intercourse with him he never saw this fault, if it were a fault ; he only saw in him that—

> " He was a scholar, and a ripe and good one,
> Exceeding wise, fair spoken, and persuading ;
> Lofty and sour to them that loved him not,
> But to those men that sought him, sweet as summer."

It was said of one of Shakespeare's characters that "he walked with the foot of velvet, but struck with the hand of steel." The converse of this acute criticism would describe Dr. Falconer. Sensitive to wrong, he never stooped to resent it.

In his private and social capacity Dr. Falconer was worthily esteemed, and taking him for all in all, he was a truly eminent Bath Worthy. It may be said of him, as was said of Charles Buller, that he was a man "remarkable for clearness, breadth, and cheerfulness of view, sound sense, fine humour, and ready wit, which never caused a heart's-stain on its blade." None knew him better than the writer of this notice, or had seen more of the tender warmth of his nature, and the helpful sympathy of his disposition.

Dr. Falconer's friends loved him with generous affection. He had none of the fussy effusiveness which pleases silly people. He inspired his patients with confidence by the unaffected dignity and earnestness of his manner, and his calm self-reliance. He was proud of a long line of eminent ancestors, as he had good reason to be ; but truly it may be said of him—

> " Decori decus addit avito."

[1] This was the " Falconer temper," so called.

BATHEASTON VILLA. POETICAL AMUSEMENTS. LADY MILLER.—

There is nothing new under the sun, is a proverb which applies with especial force to the latest and most agreeable phase of English social life—*Garden Parties.* In the last century—*i.e.*, from about 1769 to 1776—one of the most agreeable sources of intellectual enjoyment and rational pleasures was the re-unions at the villa of Sir John and Lady Miller, at Batheaston. These *garden parties* were the same in their chief characteristics as the garden parties of the present day, with the literary element added. In other respects there was little difference. The good-natured lady herself affected the literary patron, but the amusements were not limited to verse-making.[1] Every kind of amusement known at that day was provided by the kind and generous lady who presided, and the gala terminated by a substantial collation. " An antique vase, which had been dug up at Frascati, in 1759, was purchased by Sir W. Miller, and placed in his villa at Batheaston, upon a modern altar, decorated with sprigs of laurel, and made the receptacle, at a weekly *dies festus*, of the poetical productions of the assembled company ; every individual being expected to deposit an original composition in verse within the venerable relic.   These at first consisted of what the French term *bouts rimés*, or rhyming terminations, which had been filled up by the candidates for poetical fame; but, afterwards, of short pieces upon given subjects. The contributions were drawn out singly by a lady, and publicly read, and a committee was nominated to adjudge wreaths of myrtle to the authors of the most eminent of the poems, who were then crowned by the high priestess (Lady Miller) amidst the plaudits of the assembly.   This Attic pastime continued for several years ; but at length the purity of the sacred vase was sullied by the licentious wit of some unknown wag, whose satirical production, when recited, wounded the delicacy of all the blushing fair ones present, and the meetings were discontinued for ever. Three small volumes, however, of the best effusions thus elicited, were published, at different times, under the

---

[1] The peculiar style of poem, if it may be called a poem at all, was that by the French called the *Bout Rimé*, that is, a poem or rather a rhyme of which the words were given out that rhymed each other, to be filled up in metre, the effect of which was sometimes more amusing than poetical. The following by the Duchess of Northumberland will give some idea of the *Bout Rimé* :—

" The pen which I now take and	brandish,
Has long lain useless in my	standish.
Know, ev'ry maid, from her in	pattin,
To her who shines in glossy	sattin ;
That could they now prepare an	oglio,
From best receipt of book or	folio,
Ever so fine, for all their	puffing,
A muffin Jove himself might	feast on,
If eat with Miller at	Batheaston."

title of ' Poetical Amusements at a Villa near Bath,' the profits of which were applied to the Pauper Charity of the city. Among the persons whose compositions contributed to these volumes were Miss Seward, Anstey, Graves, Garrick, Pratt, Meyler, and some others of literary celebrity.

Lady Miller was buried in 1781, near the altar in the Abbey Church, where a handsome monument of statuary marble, by the elder Bacon, is raised to her memory."

> " Devoted stone ! amidst the wrecks of time
> Uninjur'd bear thy MILLER's spotless name ;
> The virtues of her youth and ripen'd prime,
> The tender thought, th' enduring record claim.
>
> When clos'd the num'rous eyes that round this bier
> Have swept the loss of wide-extended worth ;
> O gentle stranger ! may one gen'rous tear
> Drop, as thou bendest o'er this hallow'd earth !
>
> Are truth and genius, love and pity thine,
> With lib'ral charity, and faith sincere?
> Then rest thy wand'ring step beneath this shrine,
> And greet a kindred spirit hov'ring near."

JOHN PALMER, M.P., No. 25, CIRCUS.—Whilst intellectual capacity, mental application, and persevering ardour shall continue to be thought deserving of fame and honourable distinction, the name of John Palmer will not only be ranked in the highest class of the native citizens of Bath, but esteemed worthy also of being enrolled among the most eminent benefactors to his country ; for the great reform introduced by that gentleman into the Post Office department, and the victory he achieved by securing its final and successful adoption, have been the means both of augmenting the revenue, and of extending the mercantile and commercial interests of Britain in a very astonishing degree.

Palmer was born at Bath, in the year 1742 ; his father was a respectable and affluent brewer and tallow-chandler in that city, and his mother a descendant of the Longs, one of the most ancient families in the county of Wilts. He was educated at Colerne ; from which he was removed to the Free Grammar School at Marlborough; his family having designed him for the Church, and there being some valuable scholarships and exhibitions attached to the latter seminary, which it was thought might aid (on more easy terms) the prosecution of his studies at one of the universities. Though fond of learning, and intended for the Church, he preferred the army—a destination which his parents would not listen to ; and on his absolute refusal to enter into Holy Orders, he was taken from school, aud seated in the counting-house of his father's brewery. For some time the drudgery of business proved irksome; but one day, after a severe dispute on the martial theme, he sullenly put on a jacket and trousers, and, going into the brewery, began to labour like a common servant. This course he pursued for nearly a year, labouring and faring exactly like the other workmen; but at length his health succumbed to his spirits, and a physician and change of air were recommended as necessary to arrest the progress of incipient consumption.

Returning to Bath, his pursuits were directed into a channel more agreeable to the bent of his inclinations. His father, in conjunction with nine other inhabitants of the city, had been induced to erect a new Theatre in Orchard Street, on the understanding that the old dilapidated Playhouse under the Great Ball-room[1] should be applied to some other purpose as soon as the new one was completed; instead of which, the proprietor re-opened those premises, and a violent opposition taking place, much loss was experienced by both parties. Eventually, the elder Palmer purchased the shares, on easy terms, of all his partners, as well as the interest, by an annuity, of the old house; and the entire property becoming thus vested in himself, he began to consider the best means of rendering it most beneficial.

Theatrical property at that period was very precarious, in regard to value, and especially at Bath, for the proprietors of the new buildings, which were at a considerable distance from the old city, were already contemplating the erection of a theatre in their own neighbourhood. To prevent this, Palmer petitioned Parliament for an Act to enable his Majesty to grant him a patent; the only patent houses at that time being those of Drury Lane and Covent Garden, and the King being restrained from granting any new patent without the authority of the Legislature. The conduct of this important application, which was warmly supported by the Corporation of Bath, was entrusted to young Palmer; and after surmounting many difficulties by his activity and energy, he succeeded in obtaining the Act solicited, which was passed in the 8th year of his late Majesty George III., who under that authority immediately granted a patent for the Bath Theatre, whereby it obtained the rank and title of a *Theatre Royal.* The talents displayed by young Palmer, on this occasion, procured him the esteem of several distinguished political and theatrical characters, whose friendship proved of great service in the subsequent period of his life.[2]

[1] See *Historic Houses*, 1st Series, Introduction, p. xi.

[2] The Bath Theatre was the first *Theatre Royal* out of the metropolis. Whilst under Palmer's direction, many persons made their appearance here, who afterwards became first-rate actors at the London theatres, as Edwin, Henderson, Mrs. Siddons, Mrs. Crawford, Miss Brunton, and others. In 1785 Palmer relinquished the management, and was succeeded by Keasberry and Dimond. The

Without noticing the various undertakings of lesser interest, in which the active nature of this gentleman engaged him at different times, it must suffice for the limited extent of these pages to proceed to that more than Herculean task, which he both devised and executed in the department of the *General Post Office;* by establishing a complete system of letter-carriage by mail-coaches,[1] and in consequence a more regular and punctual delivery of letters than had ever been previously contemplated.

The original idea of this vast improvement is said to have been excited in Palmer's mind by a social conveyance, in which he was accustomed to remove his theatrical company to and fro, between Bath and Bristol, on the

---

latter was an admirable manager, but he was also an enthusiast in all things concerning the Drama. He lived at **No. 1, DEVONSHIRE BUILDINGS**, in which he had a room specially fitted up for private dramatic representations. The son of Dimond was educated at the Bath Grammar-School, and was the author of "Petrarchal Sonnets," "The Hunter of the Alps," "The Hero of the Truth," "Adrian and Oulla," and "The Foundling of the Forest." Meyler wrote the interesting address spoken by Dimond in 1785, as follows :—

INTRODUCTORY ADDRESS,

SPOKEN BY MR. DIMOND,

On Opening the Theatres-Royal in Bath & Bristol,
When Mr. Palmer relinquished the control of the Theatres to Mr. Keasberry and Mr. Dimond.

"You, who th' historian's page have oft survey'd,
Behold this certain principle display'd—
' In every monarchy, through length of years,
A change of governors and laws appears ; '
Fate shall some empire to oblivion sink ;
To fame raise others from oblivion's brink ;
There prosp'rous Treason mounts the sceptred throne,
And Revolution calls the seat her own.
   To bring the object nearer to our view
Than thrones and empires, or rebellion's crew,
Suppose this house of merchandizing fame,
Long carried on in but *one trader's* name ;
Who grows or rich, or proud, or old, or great—
Or gets perhaps an office in the State;
Retires—and leaves the labours and its fruits
To his long-tried and trusty substitutes ;
Who, to obtain continuance of favours,
Vow constant, grateful, and increased endeavours.
   He who of late reign'd o'er this dome supreme,
Retires, to perfect an applauded scheme—
To guard your persons—o'er your wealth to watch,

Add wings to commerce, and to law dispatch ;
Old custom's stubborn maxims to control,
' And waft your fame from Indus to the Pole.'
His late possessions—*patents, wardrobes, scenes,*
His mimic thunder, lightning, kings and queens;
The hero's truncheon, pantomime buffoons,
Thalia's visor, tempests, suns and moons—
Devolve on us—long agents in th' employ—
Me your obedient, and our late viceroy.
   Be ours the task by every art to raise
The drama's splendour and the public praise.
T' enlarge the soul, Melpomene shall pour
Her copious streams in Grief's instructive lore ;
Shall teach mankind to prize a low estate,
By viewing woes attendant on the great.
   Thalia here her magic wiles shall play,
To laugh your foibles and your cares away ;
And all confess that medicine's nicer art,
Which, while it cures the pain, delights the heart.
   Here Music too shall greet the tuneful ear,
And with sweet sounds allay our grief and fear ;
Broad Farce and Pantomime shall oft peep in,
To set our old acquaintance on the grin.
   In short, our study, our delight, shall be
To blend true taste with sprightly novelty ;
Encourage merit—jealous envy shun,
Genius prefer—confess ourselves outdone.
Grant us fair trial—your protection guard us,
As we deserve—so censure or reward us."

---

[1] In the latter part of the last century and the early part of the present century, the mail was conveyed from Bath, Bristol, and the West of England to London by a mail-cart, with a single horse and man. It travelled at the rate of about four miles an hour, and, consequently, was at least 30 hours on the road between Bath and London. These carts were frequently robbed. An instance occurred near Chippenham, about 1784. The robber was apprehended, tried at Salisbury, convicted, and hanged. The body was gibbeted in chains at the place where the robbery was committed, about two miles south of Chippenham, and hundreds of people flocked to the spot to see the appalling object. [See Foot-note, Introduction, p. ix.]

alternate days of performing in those cities ; and which, he frequently remarked, went over the ground with far greater speed than the mail-cart. Those remarks he subsequently extended by observations made during numerous journeys to every part of the kingdom; undertaken, originally, for the purpose of sttength-ening his company by recruits from the provincial theatres; but afterwards pursued expressly to enable him to arrange and mature his plans for an effective change in every branch of the Post Office.

On entering into this arduous undertaking, he obtained the acquiescence and support of Mr. Pitt, whose private secretary, Dr. Prettyman, afterwards Bishop of Lincoln, was the medium of communication between them; and he stipulated to receive *two and a half per cent.* on the future increased revenue of the Post Office beyond its then net profits, if his plan succeeded; but if it failed, he was not to be paid a single shilling.[1]

Let anyone who wishes to appreciate the talents requisite to ensure success in a plan of such vast magnitude as that projected by Palmer, spread the map of Great Britain before him ; let him look at the cities, towns, and villages, distributed upon its surface ; and, finally, devise a system by which the mails shall quit each of those different places at different times, and combine, or, as it were, *dove-tail in* with the main routes of the kingdom, and with such clock-work precision, that all shall arrive at the same spot within a few minutes of each other!   He will then, and then only, be able to form a correct estimate of the mental energies necessary for such an enterprise.

During the prosecution of his scheme, every possible kind of difficulty was thrown in Palmer's way by those who were interested in the continuance of customary abuses ; and every kind of ill augury was objected against him.   Even the very authorities and officers of the Post Office itself thwarted and opposed his arrangements ; and nothing but the most undaunted determination and active industry could have raised him superior to the strong opposition he experienced. In the course of these proceedings, he found it necessary to address a long explanatory letter to Mr. Pitt, who evinced the full confidence which he reposed in his plans by appointing him, in July, 1789, Surveyor and Comptroller-General of the Post Office, with an annual salary of £1,500.   From that station, however, he was suspended in 1792, in consequence of disputes with the Postmaster-General

---

[1] " Mr. Palmer frequently acknowledged that the contemplation of the spacious mansion erected in Prior Park, by Mr. Allen, out of the immense sums which he received for some improvements in the conveyance of the cross mails (about half-a-million sterling), was the grand stimulus that urged him to exertion and perseverance."   So says Britton, but Palmer may be credited with a higher motive than mere wealth.

respecting his deputy-surveyor, and of other circumstances relating to the completion of his plans, which, however, had increased the revenue of his department in 1783 from £159,615 to £636,956 in 1796. His claim to a per-centage was also disallowed; and his remuneration fixed at £3,000 per annum.[1]

Fully impressed with the justice of his own cause, Palmer sought that redress from Parliament which he could not obtain from the ministry; but although a Committee, appointed by the House of Commons, reported entirely in his favour, he could not procure a recognition of his claims till May, 1808, when the House resolved, by a majority of 66, that he was justly entitled to two and a half per cent. above the net revenue of the Post Office, viz., £240,000 from the 5th of April, 1793. His compensation bill, founded on this resolution, was, however, thrown out by the Lords, on the third reading, by a majority of *six;* but afterwards the ministers themselves brought in, and passed, an act, granting him £50,000 as a remuneration for his services, independently of his salary of £3,000.

Palmer was elected Mayor of Bath, in 1796; and he twice represented it in Parliament.[2] One of his latest employments was to rebuild the Bath Theatre upon the site which it now occupies. He died at Brighton on the 16th August, 1818, in the 76th year of his age. His remains were conveyed to his native city, and interred in the Abbey Church, the Mayor and Corporation attending the funeral.

JOHN WILKES and his sister, **Mrs. JEFFERYS.** — John Wilkes occasionally visited his sister when she resided at **No. 3, NORTH PARADE,** but his visits were of short duration, and little was known of him. His sister if she shared no other quality peculiar to her brother, excelled him in ugliness; and it is remarkable, too, that with him she possessed the same fascination and influence over others which he was said to exercise. Warner gives such an admirable description of her that it is quoted *verbatim :*—

"The invariable nocturnal and diurnal habits of Mrs. Jefferys, as they were followed at the age of 75, and indeed, later in life, may be described in a few lines. She retired early to bed, in a room whose window was thrown up, night and day, winter and summer, without regard to the blast or the tempest, the rain or the snow; and whose furniture principally consisted of ten or a dozen German wooden clocks, chiming or cuckooing, in delightful discordance, whenever they struck the passing hour. No fire was ever kindled in this temple of the winds. At day-break Mrs. Jefferys rose from her all but comfortable bed; ate a sparing breakfast of a dish of chocolate, and a few slices of toast, thin and narrow as a penny ribbon; and occupied herself with her books

[1] See Britton's Autobiography, vol. I., p. 13.

[2] General Palmer, who represented Bath before and after the Reform Bill of 1832, was a son of Mr. Palmer.

and papers till the hour of *morning calls.* These visits were very gratifying to her : but she only received, and never returned them. At the hour of three her chairmen attended with her own sedan, to convey her to the boarding-house, where she was accustomed to dine. Thither she never *walked;* for having been alarmed (as it was said) at one period of her life, by encountering a *mad dog* in her ambulations, she had formed a resolution never again to put her foot upon the pavement. A bottle of her own old Madeira accompanied her in the chair. At the boarding-table a particular seat was invariably occupied by Mrs. Jefferys ; a gentleman flanked her on each side, for she always avowed her partiality for the male sex, ' who,' she observed, ' have more *sinew of mind,* as well as body, than we women." Her diet at the boarding table, for a considerable portion of time (I think I may say for years), was such, as few would credit without a voucher ; (and I pledge myself for the fact) fewer still could imagine ; and fewer, I trow, among his Majesty's liege subjects would imitate : a sirloin of beef; a mighty round of the same truly British aliment ; a loin of veal ; or any other joint, well-coated with that *pinguid matter,* vulgarly called fat, was ever provided for Mrs. Jefferys' especial accommodation. On slices of this said *fat* (detached from every particle of lean), and on small masses of *chalk,* placed beside her plate, would Mrs. J. make a hearty and, I presume, wholesome meal (for it agreed with her right well), alternately a mouthful of the one with a piece of the other ; the neutralising the *sebacic acid* of the former, with the *alkaline principle* of the latter ; and diluting, amalgamating, and assimilating the delicious com-pound, with half-a-dozen glasses of her own generous wine. The day would be finished by two or three hours of conversation ; and the sedan would again convey her, at an early time of night, to her own house in Gay Street. As Mrs. J.'s understanding was of a very masculine structure and strength, her mind well stored with reading, and her experience of ' men and things' by no means confined, her conversation was exceedingly agreeable ; an interest much heightened by its utter freedom from those drawbacks on the colloquy of the *blues,* effort, affectation, and pedantry: while the freedom with which she spoke of herself, her fortunes, and adventures, rendered it both anecdotical and curious. Her several marriages (for thrice had she sacrificed on the altar of hymen) formed a subject on which she was, occasionally, nothing loath to dilate. ' My first match,' she would say, ' was a foolish, but happy one ; my second, a prudent, but agreeable one ; my third, an insane and miserable one : but still I may consider myself fortunate upon the whole ; for, is there not great luck in drawing two prizes out of three tickets ? ' Well, indeed, might the good old lady apply the bitterest epithets to her last matrimonial trip ; for, as the voyage commenced under inauspicious omens, foul weather quickly rendered it highly unpleasant ; and a *separation* between herself and her *consort* speedily took place. As the widow of Alderman Haley, she had enjoyed a very large provision for life. This—spite of her homeliness of feature—attracted many admirers ; and ' in evil hour ' she pronounced the fatal ' I will,' in favour of a transatlantic suitor. ' Three weeks after marriage,' they discovered that nature had never intended them for each other; and an agreement took place between them, that they should live asunder ; the gentleman in America, herself in England ; and that her large jointure should be equally shared by the respec-tive parties. Lessened, however, as Mrs. J.'s means were by this arrangement, she contrived to exercise a very extensive charity ; for never did a more generous or humane spirit dwell in the gentle heart of woman. That her bounties were large and frequent, I know full well. Many have passed through my own hands to the indigent objects for whom they were designed : and in my visits to the distressed, I have not infrequently discovered, that Mrs. J.'s Christian philan-thropy had already alleviated their wants. That her heart was responsive to the tale of misfortune may be collected from the following anecdote :—A waiter at the boarding-table which she was accustomed to frequent, had been deprived of his little all, by the treachery of a person to whom he had intrusted it. She remarked the unusual melancholy of his countenance, and learned its cause from the mistress of the house. At her usual hour of departure the poor fellow lighted Mrs. J. to her chair; and on stepping into it she slipped into his hand a £5 bank note, which she had previously abstracted from her purse for the benevolent purpose. It is melancholy to reflect, that towards the close of her long life, this tide of true Christian generosity was impeded by a cessation of her remittances from America; and that, had it not been for the dutiful kindness of a near relation, this noble-spirited woman, who had lived in splendid ease, and in the exercise of active beneficence for more than half a century, would have needed that bounty which she had so frequently and so freely bestowed on others."

HILL HOUSE, SWAINSWICK; WILLIAM PRYNNE.—The house in Upper Swainswick now occupied by **Thomas Whittington, Esq.**, was, in 1600, the birth-place of William Prynne, one of the most remarkable men of his time; it may, indeed, be said that he was in a special sense the peculiar product of the time. This notice proposes to deal with Prynne chiefly in his public, political, and official relations to Bath. These relations were emphatically honourable to Prynne, and on the whole reflect no little credit upon the city. If there were occasional vacillations and apparent want of steadfastness in its dealings with Prynne, they must be attributed to the political exigencies of the times rather than to any deliberate departure from justice and straightforward conduct on the part of the city. The Government of Cromwell watched with a jealous eye the conduct of those in whom was vested the legal choice of Parliamentary representatives, or any other kind of public patronage or power; and in the case of the Bath Corporation there is ample evidence to show that its conduct was dictated by the central authority (see note on the Recordership, page 123), and not by its own free and unfettered judgment.[1] William Prynne was descended from a Shropshire family, whose name was derived from the gentle eminences which may be seen from the Wenlock Ridge, and which were originally called " Preens," signifying *points.* The Prynnes were called De Preens, which ultimately degenerated into De Pryn, and then Prynne. From these Shropshire Prynnes sprang an Erasmus Prynne, who settled at Aust, near Henbury. He had two sons, the younger of whom was Thomas Prynne, who for some time tilled the land which had been in his father's occupation, and dwelt in his father's home at Aust. Whilst retaining the ownership of the property, towards the close of the sixteenth century, he removed to a better occupation. "On the steep northern side of one of the narrow valleys which meet, as in a centre, at that most beautiful of English cities, Bath, and at the distance from the city of about two miles, stand the church and

---

[1] See article on Warner, page 70.

village of Swainswick. The situation is singularly pleasant. In front, facing the west, across a narrow gorge, lies the village of Woolley, and above rise the heights of Lansdown. Northward, up the valley, lies the secluded Langridge. The cottages of Swainswick are scattered by the side of the narrow road which winds along the valley side, and which in the sixteenth century was a mule track, pursued by the chapmen who passed through the clothing districts of the West, and bore off from house to house the produce of the looms for sale. Since 1529 Swainswick has belonged principally to Oriel College, Oxford." [1]

In 1529 the manor and the advowson of the church were given to Oriel College, Oxford, by one of their fellows, Dr. Richard Dudley, for the maintenance of two fellows and six exhibitions. The place was almost entirely in the hands of Oriel College. They presented the rector, usually one of their fellows, and the chief layman in the parish was their "farmer," or as it meant in those days agent, or manager of their property as well as the tenant of their lands; and it was in this capacity that William Prynne's father went to reside in Swainswick in succession to Edward Webb [2] about the year 1573.

Whom Thomas Prynne married first does not appear, but when he first resided in Swainswick he was a widower without children. Neither does it appear from the parish register that Sherstone had any official connection with the parish, but it has been always stated that he lived at the Manor House (occupied now by Mr. Shackell), and most likely was living there when Thomas Prynne (or some time after) first went to Swainswick and lived in "the respectable residence near the churchyard on the north." [3] When Thomas Prynne became a widower does not appear; there being no record in the register of the death of his first wife. Mr. Bruce says there is no record of his marriage in the register between him and Marie Sherston, but that arises from the circumstance that between 1593 and 1603 the leaves are missing. [4] Every effort has been made to trace them in the Wells Diocesan records, but without success. It seems probable

---

[1] Bruce's Biographical Fragment.

[2] The Webb family flourished in Swainswick until the close of the next century. The following entry in the parish register, in 1611, relates to a son of Edward Webb, who at the time was 75 years of age :—" Richard Hoskins, a base-born child, born at Okefield, in the parish of Marshfield, the son of Elizabeth Hoskins, and, as she did confess at the house of the birth of the child, the sonne of John Webb, gent., was brought to our church the tyme of Divine Service, and laid upon the fonte, and because it was weak, and was begotten on the farme, was here christened the 9th daie of Februarie, anno dni. 1611." In 1616 another entry occurs :—"John Webb, farmer, of Swainswick, a man of the age of 80 years and upward, was buried the 4th daie of April."

[3] This is Mr. Bruce's statement, but, as will be seen later on, it is an error.

[4] The Register exists in duplicate, so that the missing section must have been intentionally removed for some reason or other which cannot be conjectured.

that the marriage took place about 1596 or 1597, one child, Joan, having been born before William, in 1600. Of himself, William Prynne, in his *Brevia Parliamentaria*, says :—

"The near relations I have to the renowned antient city of Bath, in the county of Somerset, in regard of my extraction out of it by my mother's line, being one of the daughters of Mr. William Sherstone, an eminent excellent magistrate and member of this city, a great benefactor thereto in his life, and at his death ; eight several times maior thereof, and by unanimous vote, formerly chosen, retorned a citizen for this city, in five Parliaments, viz., Annis 26, 39, 43, of Queen Elizabeth, Annis 1 and 3 of King James, of famous memoryes ; and by Queen Elizabeth's own Charter to the city, dated Sept. 5, in the 32nd year of her reign, constituted the first maior thereof in these words—And by these presents, for us, our heirs and successors, We do assign, name, constitute, and make our well-beloved and faithful subject, WILLIAM SHERSTONE, citizen of the said city, to be first and present Maior of the same city (which had antiently Maiors, but not by this New Charter). As also in respect of my education therein, during part of my minority ; of my neighbourhood and obligations to the city (whereof I am now Recorder, for which I have been twice freely elected a citizen for the late and present Parliament, by their undesired votes, without the least solicitation or expence, even in my absence, being importuned by Letters under the Maiors, Aldermens, and Common Counsils hands and city-seal to honour them with my service, though other persons of quality then courted them for their voyces, by their own and other great men's letters and their agents), may justly challenge from me a special section to revive, preserve the memoryes of the respective citizens formerly elected, retorned for this city, extant either in the new-found or former bundles of Writs and Retornes remaining in the Tower of London, with those in the Rolls and Pettibagge, and of the principal Retorns and Indentures relating to their Elections." [1]

There has always been some ambiguity as to Prynne's official and political connection with Bath. Warner gives a most misleading account altogether of the political representation of the city, and it is in vain to look to him for light on obscure questions connected with it. In the foregoing quotation Prynne refers to himself as the Recorder. He had been deprived, in 1645, [2] of this office, which was

[1] Written in 1662, after his election in the year preceding.

[2] "During the late Wars and Revolutions they unanimously elected and importuned Mr. Prynne to be their Recorder, without his privity or desire, and continued him so after his speech in the House for the satisfactorinesse of his late Majesty's concessions in the Isle of Wight, and his memento, protestations, and other publications against his treasonable illegal tryal and execution ; his proclaiming of King Charles II., January 1st, 1648, to be the lawfull hereditary King of England by printed pro-

conferred upon Ashe. Details of this are given in the notice on Warner, page 70. Prynne, after his first prosecution, was elected for Newport, in Cornwall (1640), when an order was given by the House of Commons for his release from prison. Here again is a little difficulty, because it appears that on the 13th April, in that year, the name of Nicholas Trefusis alone is returned, but it is probable that, as Newport returned two members, Prynne's return might have been later in the year at a special vacancy. Collinson states that "Prynne was displaced for his animadversion on Cromwell," but no dates or particulars are given. In November of the same year, there was another election for Newport, the members returned being John Maynard and Richard Edgcombe. In 1648, on the 7th of November, Prynne was again returned for Newport.[1] After the restoration (1660), Prynne (with Alexander Popham) was elected for Bath. Again, in 1661, he was returned, of which he gives a long and most tedious account in his *Brevia Parliamentaria. Henry Chapman* made an attempt, for reasons of his own, to change the mode of election, and partly by violence and partly by intrigue succeeded in effecting a double return. The Corporation, the legal constitutional elective body, elected Prynne (and the same year re-appointed him Recorder), and Alexander Popham. Chapman and some of the Freemen, with a party of lawless Rumpers, returned Sir Charles Berkeley, Knt., and Sir Thomas Bridges, Knt. The ruse did not succeed. By an order of the House, dated 16th May, 1661, the two first named were ordered to sit till the merits of the cause were determined. Ultimately, according to the *Brevia Parliamentaria*, they were declared duly elected. Prynne sat until his death, and was succeeded 15th Nov., 1669, by Sir Francis Popham, Knt.

The "Fragmentary Biography" of Prynne by the late **John Bruce**, published by the Camden Society, contains as much of the personal history of that remark-

clamations, sent by him to Bath, and most other great corporations, though voted by the rumpers high treason to proclaim him ; his forcible seising, securing by the army, and close imprisonments in Dunster, Taunton, and Pendennis Castles for maintaining his Majesty's title, interest, monarchy, and opposing the then usurping powers of all sorts in print, and in his charges at the Quarter Sessions of the city, when none others durst do it, till commanded by an expresse letter from the pretended Councel of State at Whitehall, to chose another Recorder in his place, and recommended a fitting rumper (James Ash) to succeed him, whom they choose with much reluctancy. A very good argument of their loyalty, and good affection to his Majesty and monarchical government." [There is an entry in the Council minutes of his appointment, but no comment.]—*Brevia Parliamentaria.*

Upon the very first tydings of Mr. Prynne's and other secluded members' restitution to the House, by the assistance of General Monck, in order to dissolve those present usurping powers, and restore his Majesty and kingly government, Mr. Prynne (though he served not for them) received a congratulatory letter from them, expressing as much loyalty and good affection to his Majesty as the times would permit. —*Ibid.*

[1] It does not appear from any record, except the Council Minute-Book, that earlier in the same year Prynne was elected for Bath, and there is no account of any vacancy or any other election in that year (see page 70).

able man as is likely to be written in a biographical form. Upon that biography Mr. Murch has based his very excellent PAPER, published in 1878. To trace the history of Prynne; to analyse his public character in its relation to the times in which he lived, and the influence he exercised over events out of which grew such immense results, happily is no part of the author's task : happily, because he feels that he possesses no qualification to enable him to perform a work of such importance. The fuller a writer's knowledge of Prynne, the greater his self-restraint and discernment, and the more perfect his judicial temperament, should be, to enable him to arrive at a just historical estimate of Prynne's character. It is almost impossible for an ordinary mortal to read the proceedings of the Star Chamber in reference to Prynne, to look into the evidence on which those proceedings were based, and then to contemplate the hideous cruelty of the sentences inflicted, without feeling such an amount of indignation as shall utterly paralyse his judgment. Whatever the provocation—and there was much on the part of the Puritan party in the special matter brought before the Star Chamber in connection with the *"Histrio-Mastix"*—there is scarcely an historian, whose opinion is worth anything, who does not clearly vindicate Prynne from the charge brought against him of reflecting upon the Queen. Prynne is a very complex character, a singular combination of contradictory qualities ; on the one hand, a bigoted Puritan, with immense diligence and learning, a never-tiring energy, great resources, and an inflexible virtue—all capable of degenerating into a concentrated vindictiveness. On the other hand, he possessed that rare courage of answering to his conscience when it admonished him of his error, with a generosity, a fullness, and a magnanimity almost without parallel. He battled against prelacy, tyranny, and lawlessness, with the result that he saw a tyrant succeed to power who crushed all law except the law of his own will ; and again he fought only to find that the usurper's finger was thicker than Charles's loins.

In the great conjuncture of events in 1633, Green says : " The patience of Englishmen, in fact, was slowly wearing out. There was a sudden upgrowth of virulent pamphlets of the old Martin Marprelate type. Men, whose names no one asked, hawked libels, whose authorship no one knew, from the door of the tradesmen to the door of the squire. As the hopes of a Parliament grew fainter, and men despaired of any legal remedy, violent and weak-headed fanatics came, as at such times they always come, to the front. Leighton, the father of the saintly Archbishop of that name, had given a specimen of their tone at the outset of this period, by denouncing the Prelates as men of blood, Episcopacy as antichrist, and the Popish queen as a daughter of Heth. The *Histrio-Mastix* of Prynne, a lawyer distinguished for his constitutional knowledge, but the most obstinate and narrow-minded of men, marked the deepening of Puritan bigotry under the fostering warmth of Laud's persecution.   The book was an attack on players as the ministers of Satan ; on theatres as the devil's chapels ; on hunting, May-poles, the decking of houses at Christmas with evergreens ; on cards, music, and false hair.   The attack on the stage was as offensive to the more curtailed minds of the Puritan party as the Court itself ; Selden and Whitelock took a prominent part in preparing the grand masque by which the Inns of Court resolved to answer its challenge, and in the following year Milton his masque of 'Comus' for Ludlow Castle.   To leave Prynne, however, simply to the censure of wiser men than himself was too sensible a course for the angry Primate.   No man was ever sent to prison before or since for such a sheer mass of nonsense ; but the prison with which Laud rewarded Prynne's enormous folio tamed his spirit so little that a new tract written within its walls attacked the bishops as devouring wolves and lords of Lucifer.   A fellow prisoner, John Bastwick, declared in his ' Litany ' that ' Hell was broke loose, and the devils in surplices, hoods, copes, and rockets, were come among us.'   Burton, a London clergyman, silenced by the High Commission, called on all Christians to resist the bishops as ' robbers of souls, limbs of the beast, and factors of anti-christ."   Raving of this sort, however, though it showed how fast the tide of popular passion was gathering, was not so pressing a difficulty to the Royal Ministers at the time as the old difficulty of the Exchequer."

Mr. Bruce's "Fragment"[1] takes the reader from Prynne's birth in 1600, through his youth at Bath Grammar School and Oriel, to his admission at Lincoln's Inn in 1621.[2]   A diligent student of the law in that " safe shelter for Puritanism," he was offended by the growing taste for the drama.   The " number of plays and play-houses increasing daily," " the 40,000 play-books vented within these two years," " the fact that Shakespeare's plays were printed in better paper than Bibles"—these

[1] *Academy*, Aug. 11, 1877 ; article by R. C. Browne.

[2] Mr. Bruce could not find "even the name of Prynne's master."   Prynne was educated under two masters, namely, from the time he entered the school when he was 12 years old, and for three years the head master of the Grammar-School was **Mr. Sharpe**, and during his last year—namely, when he was 16 years old—the head master was **Mr. Shrewsbury**.   These two learned gentlemen received, in addition to a dwelling and rations, £12 per annum, which was paid always in the month of October.   Mr. Bruce suggests that Prynne being full two miles from the school, in the winter season the Barton house "afforded him a frequent shelter."   There is nothing whatever to show that Sherston ever *lived* in Barton House ; it is now probable that he lived in Broad Street, when he did not occupy the official residence, or his country house.   Mr. Bruce repeats the exploded tradition of Queen Elizabeth's second visit to Bath and her residence in Barton House, which never could have been more than a small farm-house.   That story of Queen Elizabeth is destined to immortality; let it live.   Why should not Prynne have lived at the School, which, by the way, occupied the site of the present building ?   Mr. Bruce thought it probable that Prynne might have had some special knowledge of Laud from the fact of his having been Bishop of Bath and Wells.   But it is doubtful whether his episcopal duties ever brought him to Bath at all.   Moreover, Laud was Bishop of Bath and Wells only from 1626 to 1628, when he was translated to London, and during that time Prynne's official connection with Bath had not begun, nor, so far as appears, was there any antagonism between him and the Bishop.

were the intolerable evils which inspired the invective sustained through the eleven hundred pages of *Histrio Mastix, the Player's Scourge or Actor's Tragedy.* He was for years compounding this infelicitous jumble of learning, nonsense, and spite. Probably no one ever read it through save its author, the printer, and Laud's chaplain, Dr. Peter Heylin, who had his own grudge against Prynne for having irreverently handled his account of St. George. Heylin "hoped to have Mr. Prynne's head" for the *Scourge;* and he asserted that a peculiarly offensive reference to " women actors," in the Index, was a reflection on the Queen, who had taken part in a masque just as the Index was passing through the press. Prynne denied any such intention, as the passages in the text were printed two years before. But in his later history of the transaction he records, with malignant relish, a scandal given by a lady who took part therein, " making a real commentary on Mr. Prynne's misapplied text." Her partner in guilt was sent to the Tower, and was Prynne's fellow-prisoner—"a strange Providence and worthy observation."

Heylin made his extracts, and carried them to Laud. Laud took them to Lincoln's Inn, on the second Lord's Day morning in Candlemas term, 1633 :—

" To Mr. Noy, and keeping him on that sacred day both from the chapel and sacrament (which he then purposed to receive), showed him the book and charged him to prosecute Mr. Prynne. Mr. Noy before this had twice read over the said book very seriously, and protested that he saw nothing in it that was scandalous or censurable in the Star Chamber or in any other court, and had thereupon commanded one of the books which Mr. Prynne delivered him to be put into the library of Lincoln's Inn for the use of the house : insomuch that he was so discontented with the commands of the arch-prelate that he wished he had been twenty miles out of town that morning. But being commanded, he must obey : and then, a few days after, Mr. Prynne was sent for before the Lords to the Inner Star Chamber, and by them sent prisoner with four of the king's guard to the Tower, Feb. 1, 1632-3."

There he remained for a year. Committed by a warrant " general, against law, wherein no offence was specified," he was denied access to his counsel, convenient time to instruct them or examine witnesses, and knowledge of the particular offences to be charged against him. He alleges that his counsel were tampered with, and their advocacy is faint enough. One of them actually begins by saying that he will not offer anything in defence. Nothing could exceed the unfairness, servility, and cruelty of the court. Noy brought himself to such thorough obedience as to declare the book totally fraught with schism and sedition. The " censures" of but four members of the Court—Lord Cottington, Chief Justice Richardson, Secretary Cook, and Earl Dorset—are given in the State Trials. Mr. Gardiner's MS. gives an abstract of all the speeches. Dorset's fulsome eulogy of the Queen, " in whose praise it is impossible for a poet to feign, or orator to flatter," is much curtailed. His odd certificate of her Majesty's virtue, that she " is only a trouble to her ghostly father, because she has nothing to trouble him withal," is omitted. Of the rest we learn that Judge Heath cited a statute of Edward III. "condemning them that dispersed lies and tales to be imprisoned till they found the author; this man hath no author but himself, therefore perpetual imprisonment." Secretary Windebank thought Prynne "more worthy of a halter than a sentence in this court." Sir Thomas Jermyn's loyalty was wounded by the (imaginary) reflections upon Charles, "a king in whom Adam hath not sinned"—whatever that may mean. Bishop Juxon "condemns the book to the fire," apparently because "the next would have been mere treason." Laud, after a feebly pedantic defence of the drama (on such grounds as that Beza and Buchanan had written sacred tragedies), thanks the lords for so well vindicating the wrongs of the Church by their sentence of £10,000 fine, the pillory, loss of ears, degradation, and perpetual imprisonment. The courtiers Dorset, Arundel, and Suffolk would have added nose-slitting to this penalty, while Laud would have excused the "cropping of his ears."

Even Prynne's fortitude gave way. He petitioned the Privy Council, acknowledging the justice of the sentence, and begging their intercession with the king to mitigate his fine, and pardon his corporal punishment. The fine was reduced to £3,000, but after an interval of horrid expectation, the rest of the sentence was executed—on May 7 and 10—one ear being cut off at Westminster, and the other in Cheapside.

Prynne had found his enemy, and he never rested till he had struck "proud Canterbury to the heart." Dull by nature and assiduity, he rises in his hatred to something like prophetic strain. While lying at the mercy of his foe, he is sustained by an assurance of coming vengeance. In this letter, written from the Tower, a month after his first punishment, with a High Commission prosecution ready to fall on him, he defies and insults the Archbishop, acknowledging his "succession" from Ananias the high priest, "who forged the self-same calumny against innocent St. Paul." He charges Laud with falsely accusing him to the king, and of depriving him of the royal pardon by "insolent solicitations." He accuses him of despiteful malice to the legal profession, and twits him with not having leisure to read the book he condemns, "by reason of over-laborious preaching once or twice a year." He tells him the world's opinion, "that you are wholly composed of rancour, malice, oppression"—and so on for several lines of bad qualities. He warns him that, having been advanced "almost from the very dunghill," he is in danger (unless he repent and make public satisfaction) "of misery, ruin, if not of hell itself." Prynne even taunts him with his anagram—*I made Will Lau*—and finishes by transcribing a text that was fatally verified—"He shall have justice without mercy that hath showed no mercy."

The letter is extant only in the copy endorsed by Laud. The original was torn up, and thrown out of window by Prynne, when Noy had asked him if it were his, and Prynne had got-it into his hands to look at the writing. Disraeli remarks: " Prynne well knew that the misdemeanour was in the letter itself, and Noy gave up the prosecution, as there was now no remedy." Laud's character is, perhaps, not fully known even yet. Of his policy and position as head of the High Churchmen, there is a thoughtful and suggestive estimate in Mr. Gardiner's *History of England under Buckingham and Charles I.* Prynne was thoroughly honest and thoroughly impracticable. Peevish and positive, to him plays were "infernal," the cause of "plagues;" and dancing had its origin in the measure "trod by Herodias or rather by the devil in her." His pedantry clung to him too closely to be shaken off in the friction of a more than ordinary experience of trouble and vicissitude. His learning is of the kind that darkens knowledge, and he is so fearfully and wonderfully dull that, even when he gets on the right track of action, his reasons by their absurdity deprive him of the credit we might else think due to his practical judgment.

The later trial of Prynne is better known than the earlier. He, a lawyer, Burton, a divine, and Bastwick, a physician, were fitting representatives of educated Englishmen weary of the insolent tyranny of the Court. Laud's persistent ill-will included Prynne in this prosecution. He was not satisfied with the punishment awarded by the Star Chamber. He had threatened Prynne with proceedings before the High Commission. He had seized his books by an illegal warrant under his own hand. (Laud denied this warrant, but it was still extant when Prynne cited it in full in his *New Discovery.*) It does not appear that Prynne gave any fresh provocation. Later writers have adopted the view of Clarendon; but against that must be set Prynne's plea that not one of the books charged in the information was laid to him—a statement repeated in his petition to the Long Parliament, when avowal of the authorship could not have injured him. Two of these books are on Mr. Bruce's list of Prynne's works—upon what authority is not clear. One of them bears a title very reminiscent of the former trial, *A Divine Tragedy lately acted;* but neither is on Prynne's own list of books written during his imprisonment.

The court intimidated Prynne's counsel from signing his defence, and then declined to receive it unsigned, or from himself. The information was, therefore, taken *pro confesso,* and a new sentence—the former, with the addition of branding—was passed. It was executed in Palace Yard, the spectators openly sympathising with the sufferers. Laud had a sharp prevision of the consequences of Prynne's speech from the pillory, wherein the Churchmen were challenged to prove bishops to be *jure divino*, and the lawyers to show that their action in the case had been legal. He rose in the Star Chamber, and moved that his enemy should be gagged and brought in to receive further sentence ; " but motion did not succeed," the spirit of tyranny being quelled for the moment. The condemned, as they journeyed to their distant prisons, had frequent tokens of the goodwill of their countrymen. The recusant lady who cut off the ears of her three cats and set them in a pillory, calling them Prynne, Burton, and Bastwick ; and the bishop who gave his crop-eared roan the name of Prynne, were exceptions to the general sympathy, which rose to a pitch alarming to the Court. Charles himself was in council when order was given to " discover what persons did accompany, converse with, and entertain " the prisoners on their passage. Examples were made at Coventry and at Chester. At the latter place certain citizens were for this cause cited to the Council and to the High Commission at York, imprisoned, fined, and ruined. Three portraits of Prynne were ordered to be burnt at Chester High Cross, and, by a subsequent order, the very frames were to be destroyed. But the Puritan leaven was at work. Clergymen were found to say that the faithful were still faithful, though their ears were cropped. Fasts of condolence were observed. Social pressure became very hard on loose-lived supporters of the court. "There is no mercy with the Puritans," writes one of this stamp.

The wheel went faster and faster till it "came full circle." The Long Parliament set Prynne and his fellow sufferers at liberty, and annulled their sentence as illegal. They entered London in triumph. Laud was soon to "complete his metropolitical visitation," as prisoner Prynne told the lieutenant he would do. The busy Archbishop, who had " viewed all the places in his province except only the Tower," fulfilled his foeman's prophecy by coming to sit in the very place in the Tower chapel " in which Mr. Prynne usually sat during his imprisonment." Possibly Mr. Prynne (who searched Laud's very pockets, and printed his private diary for distribution at the trial[1]) had arranged that little

---

[1] This was the most loathsome act of Prynne's life. The private thoughts, the aspirations, the ejaculations of the Archbishop, so far as they were committed to writing, were ruthlessly exposed, and it is the more surprising because if there was one weakness of Prynne more characteristic than another, it was superstition. His books abound with childish puerilities, which he made known to the world ; the Archbishop's expressions and emotions were noted for private contemplation only. What is surprising, however, is that Macaulay, in his Essay on Laud, should have reproduced much of the private diary which was originally brought to light by the shameful act of Prynne. What man is there of strong feelings and religious instincts, who, in his sorrows and his perplexities, but above all in his gratitude and thankfulness for mercies and blessings, does not more or less experience the emotions which brought upon Laud the contemptuous sarcasms of Macaulay, and the brutal jests of Prynne's lawyers ?

Of Prynne's alleged vindictiveness, much is to be said in defence of his conduct, if it cannot be justified. The arguments adduced in mitigation of the charges of cruelty against Laud, are precisely what may be urged in favour of Prynne : the excitement of the times, the imperfect perception of

detail. Prynne was elected M.P. for Newport, in Cornwall, in 1648. During the Long Parliament, in 1649, Ashe superseded him as Recorder, no doubt at the instigation of the Parliament, of which, however, there is no mention in the Corporation records. But the storm was getting too high for even Mr. Prynne to direct. In his turn he is swept away by Pride's Purge—

"Imprisoned, with forty more, in Hell (the tavern in Westminster Hall), and other places; almost starved with hunger and cold in Whitehall; imprisoned many weeks in the Strand; and afterwards kept (by a new Free-State warrant) a strict close prisoner in three remote castles nigh three years."

Prynne had been vindictive to the death with Laud, but he sent forth a strong, earnest cry for the life of Charles. It was drowned in the echoes of his own clamours. To his reiterated "protests," and "propositions," and "serious queries," one of the adverse party opposed a compilation, entitled, *Mr. Prynne's Charge against the King*, wherein all his passionate invectives against the Government of Charles are set forth. The Council of State set Mr. Hall to answer him in Latin. But for Salmasius being already on his hands, Milton might have been told off to wrangle with "Marginal Prynne," whom he has again referred to as "one whom ye may know, by his wits lying beside him in the margin, to be ever beside his wits in the text." Prynne was astir at the first hint of the Restoration. In his *Perfect Narrative* is a really graphic account of his efforts to obtain admittance to the House on May 7 and 9, 1659.[1] Charles was quite willing to recognise his services, but there was some difficulty in finding suitable employ- ment for "busie Mr. Prynne," till the King shrewdly suggested that he should be

the doctrine and principles of toleration; tho mutual distrust of the two contending parties in the state, etc. If these reasons are good for Laud, they are equally good for Prynne. If Peter Heylin did not "get Prynne's head for the *Scourge*," it was not for want of trying. He and the prelate suc- ceeded in inflicting upon their victim, for an offence he did not commit, cruelties so revolting, that in these days they can scarcely be realized. It is difficult for an Englishman to say in the 19th cen- tury, what he might feel against an opponent who should bring him before an illegal, unscrupulous, cruel tribunal, for a constructive offence, deprive him of all his worldly substance and his liberty, put him in the pillory, deface and mutilate him by cutting off his ears—thus rendering him an object of pity for the rest of his days! These were terrible provocations to revenge, and the best amongst us might yield to them. If, however, sitting in the judgment-seat, we have to pass sentence against Prynne, there is the set-off of a grand and noble magnanimity in all his later acts and conduct.

[1] In the same book Prynne's Dream is recorded. It will show how much his mind was occupied by the events of the time; how deeply and conscientiously he disapproved of Cromwell's conduct and policy; and that at that time all thought of cruel revenge for the wrongs which had been inflicted upon himself by Cromwell, had no place in his mind; but rather "remission of his sin" by reason of "restitution of rapine."

"The night before Oliver Cromwell, the Protector, died, Mr. Prynne, then being at Swainswick, near Bath, dreamed that he then sent out a special messenger to him, importunately desiring he would presently repair to Bath, for he was very sick, and desired much to speak with him. Whereupon (though he never saw him since 1647) he presently went to Bath, where, finding him lying on his bed, he told Mr. Prynne he was very sick, and sent for him to tell him what he should do in this condition. Mr. Prynne thereupon forthwith answered, that he could give him no better counsel than that of *St. Augustine*, asserted by all divines as an undoubted truth, '*non remittitur peccatum nisi restituatur*

made Keeper of the Records.[1] At his death (October 24, 1669) his salary of £500 was six years and a-half in arrear. The history of Prynne's life bears out his statement about himself, that he was one "never coveting the uncertain, transient treasures, honours, or preferments of this world, but to do my God, King, country, all the best public services I could with the loss of my liberty, expenses of my mean estate, and hazard of my life." Firm for English liberties in the darkest hour of their peril, he was true to his favourite motto-text—" I will not be afraid for ten thousand of the people." Prynne had always kept up a friendly feeling towards his Bath friends, which was warmly reciprocated, except

---

ablatum.' That there was no remission of sin without restitution of rapine'. Wherefore he must forthwith restore the banished King to his Crown and Kingdom, of which he had most unjustly deprived him ; the Parliament to its just rights, freedoms, and privileges, which he had utterly subverted ; and the people to their fundamental laws, liberties, and properties, of which he had most unjustly and perfidiously defrauded them more than any man, against his oaths, trust, duty, under pretence of defending them ; repent of all the blood he had shed, and the mischief he had done ; there was hope of mercy and pardon for him, both from God and man, otherwise there was none, for aught he knew. At which he, standing mute, as much amazed, and without a reply, Mr. Prynne departed without more words, and the next morning told this dream to his sister and sundry others, telling them he was confident he should hear some strange news of Cromwell very speedily, since he never dreamed of him before, and within three days after he heard of his death, about twelve hours after his dream."

[1] The Records arranged and classified by Prynne were of great importance. They were, in fact, so admirably done, and were found to be of such historical national value, that they may be said to have been the models more systematically followed in the present century, by the Record office, under the direction of the Master of the Rolls, who is bringing to light records, treatises, and documents of all kinds of incalculable national value, which otherwise would have been buried in oblivion.

The parish Register of Swainswick goes back to the year 1557, and in it are many names which are perpetuated to this day. The Gunning family, who were of Cold Ashton and Tadwick, appear from the year 1581, and continue down to the latest period in connection with Swainswick. In that year, John Gunning married Anne Lewes ; in 1562, their daughter Eleanor was baptised ; in 1564, Edward was baptised, and so on, and their direct descendants at this moment are the Rev. Peter Gunning of Inwardleigh, and Captain John Gunning R.N., now of Bath. Other names cannot be traced beyond the next century. The Webbs cannot be traced after 1634, when Robert Webb married Maria Webb, on the 11th of May.* The first rector whose name appears in the Register, was Sir Thomas Ireland, who was buried on the 16th August, 1553, his successor, Richard Davies, having officiated and signed the register. This Vicar appears to have been an energetic man, and careful as to the register. He died in 1627, and was buried on January 3rd, 1628. In 1631, Rebecca Davis, his "widdowe," was buried on the 8th of December. The next rector was Benjamin Tanner ; one of the Churchwardens being John Batten, of the Mills, the "Dead Mills,"* as they are now called, and the other Edmond Lewes, who was the father of John Gunning's wife. The first Whittington to be found in the register is in 1634, when it is recorded that "Joyce Whittington, the daughter of John Whittington and Marie his wife, was baptised on the 11th of 'ffebruarie.'" This John Whittington no doubt was a branch of the "Hameswell" (Hameswell) Whittingtons, whose lineage extended back to the time of Edward I. There are Whittingtons still at Hamswell and at Swainswick : may the registers respectively never cease to record the honoured name ! Then there were the Kemishes, or as it is in some entries spelt Chemishe, but in modern times, Kemys ; William Kemishe married Joan, daughter of Thomas and sister of William Pryune (see William Prynne's will). The Kemyses are now known in connection with the Kemys-Tyntes. In 1634, Elizabeth, daughter of William and Joan Kemish, was buried, and she is called Kemys. Again, in 1635, 1636, 1637, the name is so spelt ; William and Joan had a large family. After 1637, the name does not occur again, but it frequently occurs in the annals of Bath, where probably the family came to reside. This interesting Register, it may be hoped, will be edited and published *in extenso.*

* Probably so-called from the circumstance that many of the bodies of the slain at the Battle of Lansdown were taken to the Mills.

by his quondam political associate, Henry Chapman. He was working with all his old energy, but with a prudence born of bitter experience, to bring about a restoration of monarchy. At the death of Cromwell, Prynne represented Newport (Cornwall), and when the time for action arrived he was at his post. Pepys[1] gives a graphic account of the proceeding, of which he was an eye-witness, and Prynne was ready with the decisive word at the decisive moment. He rests under the chapel of his Inn. " Peace to the dead who never were at peace."

Some confusion exists with regard to the house in which Prynne was born. This has arisen from the general assumption that because there is a house called the Manor House, it was necessarily the house of Prynne's birth, which is erroneous. The late Mr. Bruce apparently fell into an error on this point, when he says that a " respectable residence, adjoining the churchyard on the *north*, was provided for this squire-farmer "(Thomas Prynne), a description that applies to the Manor House,[2] which *is* on the north (occupied by Mr. Shackell). The house now known as the **HILL HOUSE**, the residence of Thomas Whittington, Esq., which *is* on the south-east of the churchyard, was no doubt the birth-place of William Prynne. It has been a commonly received tradition that when Thomas Prynne went to reside at Swainswick, his future father-in-law, William Sherston, occupied the Manor House as his country residence, whilst T. Prynne succeeded Webb in the agent's house, the name of which at that time is not now known, but, as stated above, is now called Hill House. If Sherston lived at the Manor House it would have been at Swainswick that Thomas Prynne met with his daughter, Marie, and there where he married her ; for, although that portion of the parish register in which the marriage was recorded has disappeared, there is no doubt of the fact, according to the knowledge possessed by Prynne himself.

[1] January 21st.— In the morning I saw many soldiers going towards Westminster Hall, to admit the secluded members again. So I go to Westminster Hall, and in Chancery I saw about twenty of them, who had been at White Hall with General Monk, who came thither this morning and made a speech to them, and recommended to them a Commonwealth, and against Charles Stuart. They came to the House and went in one after another, and at last the Speaker came. But it is very strange that this could be carried so private, that the other members of the House, insomuch that the soldiers that stood there to let in the secluded members they took for such as they had ordered to stand there to hinder their coming in. Mr. Prin came with an old basket-hilt sword on, and a great many shouts upon his going into the Hall.—March and.—Great is the talk of a single person, and that it would now be Charles, George, or Richard again. For the last of which my Lord St. John is said to speak high. Great also is the dispute now in the House, in whose name the writs shall run for the next Parliament ; and it is said that Mr. Prin, in open house, said, " In King Charles's."—*Pepy's Diary*, 1659-60.

[2] In the Mansion House, as Collinson calls it, there are some few vestiges of a very ancient edifice, and there is also an old military sword, ascribed by the vulgar to King Bladud. The blade of it is 3 ft. 10½ in. long, and 1½ in. wide ; and at the bottom, near the hilt, is a shield charged with two bars, conjoined fess wavy ; the initials R.D., and the date 1423. This sword, in a leather scabbard, was discovered in the old Tithe Barn roof at Swainswick. The date mark, **1423**, was originally of a later date. The shape of the weapon is of the sixteenth century, and the figure **4**, which is not of the period, is evidently a fabrication. The sword of the fifteenth century was a longer, heavier, and simpler weapon about the haft. It seems probable that the weapon—as has been suggested--was a sword of office and ceremony, not of war.

Thomas Prynne died in July, 1620, and, shortly after, his widow married Edward
Capell, who then, with his wife, resided at the *Manor House,* in the garden
wall of which there is a marble tablet bearing the monogram—*Capell, Edward-
Mary.*[1] The latter died in 1631, on the 20th March of that year, which is recorded in the register. Thomas Prynne in his Will mentions the name of his wife
once only, which is a remarkable fact, but he left his own house in which he had
lived to William, who occupied it during the period when Capell and his wife
(Prynne's mother) occupied the Manor House.[2]

Opposite to the entrance-door of the Hill House formerly there stood the
farming establishment, consisting of barns, store-houses, granaries, and out-houses
of the estate. The roads and the village have been greatly altered during the past
century. The barton of the Manor House has been enlarged, and it is certain
that a large portion of the land farmed by the "farmer-squire" has been transferred
to the Manor farm.

Of Prynne's house little remains. A portion of the front, consisting of part
of a window on the basement floor and two Tudor windows above it, with the gable
roof, are really all that can be traced. Of the interior as it was no trace
remains: the rooms of the windows referred to are completely changed by the
old ceilings having been removed to render the rooms more lofty, so that where
formerly there were three rooms there are now two. Additions also to the exterior
have been made in recent times, and it is impossible to tell what portions of the
old fabric may have been removed. Mr. Clement, a banker, in the early part of
this century, was an occupant of the house, and he built an entrance, with a
room above it, at the south end, and some further alterations were made by
Mr. Mackenzie, a subsequent tenant, who was a partner in the bank which
Mr. Clement established.[3] Both these gentlemen in succession occupied the
house as a summer residence.

[1] This was in commemoration of their marriage. It seems very improbable that the stone now
occupies its original position. At present it is built into a rough wall in the garden of the Manor Farm.
The size of the stone is 2 ft. 4 in. square; the inscription on which is —

CAPELL, EDWARD-MARY, 1625.

Over which is the crest—a demi-lion rampant holding a sword in its paws (crosslett fitchée). The
lettering, dentils, and crest being sunk from the face of the stone; the bands on which the lettering is
executed are raised above the general surface of it. Collinson says there are two letters, E. M.; but,
if so, they are at present not discernible.

[2] See Will of Thomas Prynne in Appendix. In 1632, moreover, William Prynne (Edward Capell
being then alive and living at the Manor House), with the Rector, the Rev. Benjamin Tanner, attested the
Churchwardens' accounts. This was the second year in which a record of the accounts were kept. In
the first year, 1631, there appears to have been a considerable consumption of red lead, ochre, and
whitewash. Six fox-heads and three ravens' heads cost respectively 1s. and 3d. a piece, and a copy of
the Prayer for the Queen cost 3d.

[3] Now Messrs. Tugwell and Co.

From the beautiful terraced garden the eye, extending beyond the hidden foreground, rests upon one of the most enchanting landscapes it is possible to behold.

PORSON.—The illustrious Porson visited the Rev. Richard Warner in Bath about 1806. King was the M.C. of the Lower Rooms at the time. Warner not only patronised the drama, but if he did not *dance*, he gave his distinct sanction to it, and no one bewailed the decadence of dancing as a fashion more than he. Warner met Porson at the Lower Rooms, or, as he calls them, the "nether world." Dr. Davis, an influential physician, who resided in the Royal Crescent, introduced the "learned Theban" to the Ball, the first perhaps he had ever seen and the last. The Professor appeared to be "quite at sea," and neither to understand, nor to relish, the scene before him. On separating from him, Mr. King, the master of the ceremonies, addressed Warner—".Pray, Mr. W., who is the *man* you have been speaking to?" "I can't say I *much like his appearance*"; and, to own the truth, Porson, with lank, uncombed locks, a loose neck-cloth, and wrinkled stockings, exhibited a striking contrast to the gay and gorgeous crowd around. "*Who* is that *gentleman*, MR. KING?" replied I. "The greatest man that has visited your rooms since their first erection. It is the celebrated Porson, the most profound scholar in Europe, who has more Greek under that mop of hair than can be found in all the heads in the room ; ay, if we even include those of the *orchestra !*" " Indeed !" said the monarch, and—ordered a new dance !

Two anecdotes were told of this extraordinary man, shortly after the above occurrence, by Pearson, Advocate-General of Bengal. Pearson was one of the party, when Porson made the following witty answer to Dr. Parr :—"A great difficulty, Mr. Porson," said the doctor, addressing the Professor, after the discharge of a more than usually dense cloud of tobacco-smoke ; ' a very great, great difficulty that—the existence of *evil* in the world." " Why, I must confess," replied the Professor, after returning the puff, "I never could see the *good* of it."

[*The author is fully aware that there are subjects which he has been unable to include in his book, and which, as he states in the Preface to the present volume, he may give in a supplemental series, at a future time. Some have been omitted which have been dealt with in the volumes of Hunter and Monkland, and have there received adequate treatment. There are others, some of whom have appeared in the pages of both those estimable authors, but of whom much remains to be said; whilst others who have some claim to notice, on various grounds, have yet to receive a public recognition of their respective merits in connection with many interesting associations.*]

APPENDIX.

WILL OF JOHN PRYN, 28th April, 1558.

John Pryn, of the Close of Lincoln, Clerk.

To every canon (*chanon*) of the Cathedral, being then in canonical residence at the time of my death, and present at my buriall, x/-, and a gilte spone. To any other chanon of Cathedral being there present, 6/8. To every vicar chorall, iii./iii., and to any other minister and officer of that church; and also to chaplyns and others, called chauntry priests, dwelling within the Close there, xxd. Also, I bequeath towards the buying of a crosse, silver-gilt, for the said Cathedral church of Lincoln, my three gobletts, with a cover, silver and gilte; three ale-cupps, with a cover, silver and gilte; a salt, with a cover, silver and gilte, one standynge cupp, with a cover, silver and gilte; and 13 spones, having the pictures of Christ and His twelve Apostles in their gilte knoppes; and also elevyn other spones, weighing xiii. ozs., and forty pounds in aungells. Also, I bequeath to the said Cathedral church my challes, with the patten, both silver and parcell gilte, to be used in the chapell of Bishop Rossell.

Also, I bequeath to Sir Thomas Pagett my sixe littell spones, which came from Evysham; a gowne, furred with lambe; my clothe gowne, unlyned, which I did weare at my late being in London; seven carpet cusshyns, of his own making, and the fether bed which I used to lye in at Bassyngham, with all the clothes thereunto used, tester, also syler and hangings.

Also, I bequeath James Lovedaye, John Balkegwell, Symon Richards, and Richard Burntford, to every one of them, forty shillings over, and besides their blacke lyvereys. Also, to every one of the reste of my servants, being with me in wages at the time of my departyng out of this world, 20/- each, and their black lyvereys. All my fyer-wood and coles to be distributed among the poor folkes there. All my said servants shall have one hole yeare's wages, also livery coates.

To the poor Clericke House, for to provide implements most necessary for the same, 20/-. After funeral expenses, and ten poundes to the poore in Lincoln, I give and bequeath to my brethren, Richard Pryn and Edward Pryn, the residue.

I make Edward Snowden and Sir Thomas Pagett overseers ; each to have 40/- for his paynes and labours therein to be taken, and a blacke gowne.

Witnesses :—Mr. ROGER DALYNSON, Chaunter of Cathedral Church ;

        Sir NICHOLAS GRENE,   Sir THOMAS LUNDE,

        Sir JAMES RODINSON,   Sir JAMES HARRYSON,

        And GEORGE CHIPPENDALL.

Proved by RICHARD and EDWARD PRYN, 28th May, 1558.

WILL OF RICHARD PRYN, 9th Sept., 1559.

RICHARD PRYN, of the Cittie of Bristoll, merchant.

XXs. to be divided among the poore. "To Julyan, my wife," all money due, and "all due to me by vertue of legacies and bequestis given and bequeathed to me by my late brother, Mr. John Pryn, dott'-of-law, late sub-dean of the Cathedrall Churche of Lyncolne, deceased." Leaves his brother-in-law, John Smith, son-in-law, Alyn Gosnell, overseers. His wife, Julyan, to dispose according to her will between their son, Thomas Pryn : the children of son, Nicholas Pryn : children of daughter, Julyan Gosnell.

    Witnesses :—JOHN SEBRIGHT,   THOMAS HARRIS,

             NICOLAS SHEE,   JOHN SMITH CLERKE.

Proved 3rd December, 1559.

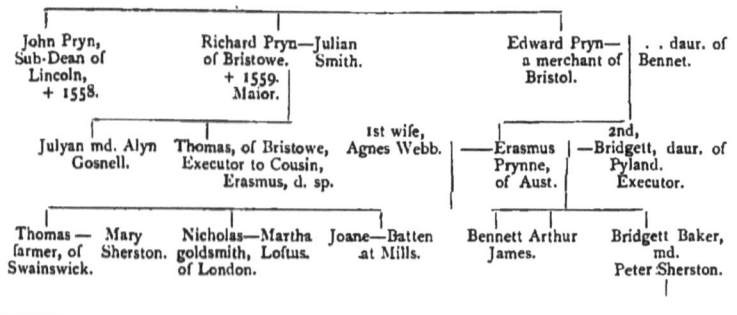

John Pryn, Sub-Dean of Lincoln, + 1558.

Richard Pryn—Julian of Bristowe. Smith. + 1559. Maior.

Edward Pryn— a merchant of Bristol. . . daur. of Bennet.

Julyan md. Alyn Gosnell.

Thomas, of Bristowe, Executor to Cousin, Erasmus, d. sp.

1st wife, Agnes Webb.

—Erasmus Prynne, of Aust.

2nd, —Bridgett, daur. of Pyland. Executor.

Thomas — Mary farmer, of Sherston. Swainswick.

Nicholas—Martha goldsmith, Loftus. of London.

Joane—Batten at Mills.

Bennett Arthur James.

Bridgett Baker, md. Peter Sherston.

PETER SHERSTON'S WILL,

OF THE CITTIE OF BATH, CLOTHIER, 29TH JUNE, 1606.

Directs his body to be laid in the earth out of which it was taken.

To eldest son, Arthur, £100 in money, "one of my silver beakers, two small silver wine cuppes, that his godfather and godmother did give him, my great walnut-tree chest, my Bandora, my great fowling-peece, a flaske, and pistoll, my silver buttons. And my Will is that my father-in-law shall have the keeping of my said Sonne, Arthur."

Unto William Sherston, my Sonne, £100, and one of my best silver and guilt wine boates, my best salt, and the dozen of silver spoones that are marked with my cloth-marke, also my brasen Andirons, with the furniture belonging to them, also my black lute and my small byrding peece, with the flaske and purse that I carry my shott in. My lease of my dwelling-house, and the house, with the lease of my Mills, and the mills and tenements thereto belonging, with the whole terme of years that are to come, and unexpired of both my said leases. All my Wainscott that is about my house, with all the table boards, syde boards, bedsteads, except my second best bedstead, and the furniture belonging to them. Also my yron Rack and broaches, and haulf my brasen and pewter, to be equally divided. Also my waigh beams and waights.

If Son William were to die before the end of leases, Peter Sherston desires they may pass to Son Arthur, and, in default of Arthur, to daughter Elizabeth.

My daughter, Elizabeth Sherston, to have £100, my silver and guilt Tankard, my wainscott Chest, my long Diaper Table-cloth, and two dozen diaper table napkins thereto belonging, my second best bedstead and bed furniture.

To my Father the gould ringe that my Uncle Pryn gave me.

To my Mother two double ducketts in gould.

To my Sister, Jone Sherston, my Trencher Salt, being silver and guilt.

My Brother Pryn, my best cloke, my bowe and my quiver of arrowes.

To my Sister Pryn half-a-dozen of my thrum* cushions.

To my Godsonne, Thomas Pryn, my best silver guilt wyne boate.

Unto William Pryn X^s in gould ; unto Jone Pryn X^s in gould ; unto Agnes Pryn X^s in gould ; To my Brother Light X^s in gould ; To my Sister Light X^s in gould ; to their five children X^s a peece in gould ; to father Baker the gelding I

* There is in Scotland a child's song, to imitate the purring song of Bawdrons, the familiar name for the cat. It goes—" Hum-drum, three threads and a thrum."

had of him ; to Uncle John Sherston my best gown ; to Unkle Parker my black satten doublett ; to Aunt Parker XX^s in gould ; to Cosen John Parker my best suite of fustian ; to rest of Unkle Parker's children X^s a peece in gould. To Unkle Thomas Sherston my old chest and my hatt and cloke which is at the sign of the Three Cuppes in Bread Street in London ; my Cosen, John Sachfeild, 40^s in gould to make him a ringe ; to his Wife, my best peece of skymes ; to my Godfather Walley, 20^s in gould ; to Unkle Giles Walley, my second best cloke and my best hatt lyned with velvett ; to my Aunt, his wyfe, 10^s in gould ; to his Sonne, William Walley, a sett of plate buttons that my Unkle Walley gave me, and my rapier and dagger ; to Cosen Margaret Smith, 20^s in gould ; to Aunt Batten, 20^s in gould ; to Cosen Elizabeth Twinley, X^s in gould ; to Erasmus and Thomas Batten, X^s a peece ; to Unkle Thomas Brewshen, 3 yards and a half of my fine black pewke to make him a cloke ; to Cosen William Buckell, 3 and a half yards of my fine black pewke to make him a cloke ; Mr. William Heath, three and a quarter yards of fine pewke, etc. ; to Cosen Andrew Atwood, the gymmall goulde ringe that I now weare ; Mr. Robert Chambers, X^s in gould ; to Cosen Richard Sachfeild and Wyfe, X^s a peece in gould ; to Aunt Thorowgood, XX^s in gould ; to Jerome Martin, X^s ; to Alice Griffin, X^s ; to every one of my Weavers, X^s a peece ; to my two Prentices, X^s each ; to Symon Bynnyon, X^s ; to Widowe Chapman of the Beare, X^s ; to Thomas Hill, my black gowne ; to Richard Saunders, my father's man, my suite of apparell that I now weare, except the silver buttons, also a pair of stockings ; to William Price, the bowe I had from Mr. Deane, and six arrowes ; to the poor of the Cittie of Bath, five pounds ; to Thomas Sewall and his Wyfe, X^s a peece in gould ; to John Langston, my riding cloke ; to George Yomans, a horsecloth of sage cullour ; to the poor of Aust, 20^s to be distributed in mony. £100 to each of my children, to be paid within a year, to be put out for their benefit till they be of age. If one die, share goes to the other two ; my Father to have the bringing up and keeping of William ; my Wife Bridget to bring up our Daughter Elizabeth : she shall have and enjoy my house that I dwell in, with the wainscott and furniture before devised and bequeathed to my children—paying such rents and duties as belongeth thereto, and keeping it in repirations accordinge.

The Sole Executor is William Sherston (of Bath, his son).

Father-in-law, Arthur Baker, Unkle, John Sherston, and Brother, Thomas Prynn, Overseers.

Proved by William Sherston.

WILL OF ERASMUS PRYNE PRINNE, 16th Sept., 1592.

ERASMUS PRINE, of Aust, in county of Gloucester, and Diocese of Bristoll. His bodie to be buried in Chancell of Aust Church. To poor of the parish of Aust and Clifton, 20 bushells of wheat. To my son, Bennett Prine, £40 in monie, the which I will to be delyvered to my son, Nicholas PRYNNE, he to have the keeping and bringing up of my said sonne during the tyme he shall be prentiss'd to him; and after the end of the said tyme to delyver it up to him.

To my sonne, Arthur, £40, to be paid when 21.

To my sonne, James, £40, to be paid when 21.

My Executor to have the bringing up of them, and their portions to remayne in his hands towards charge of their mayntenance.

·   To Bridget, my wife, £40, and my feather bed in the parlour, with his appurtenance. To said Bridget, my wife, one other feather-bedd and one flocke-bedd, with their appurtenance, and also all the chests and coffers which she brought with her to me, with also 20 sheepe and two barren hoggs, and 20 bushells of wheat and 20 bushells of barlie. To daughter, Joane Batten, and her three children—Erasmus, Thomas, and Elizabeth Batten, £5 a piece.

To brother, John Prynne, all my apparell, and £40 in money. To sonne, Nicholas *Prinne*, £5 in money, and my gelding. To Bridget Baker,[1] daughter of Arthur Baker, £20 in money.

To Agnes Prynne, my son Thomas's daughter, £20 in money. If Bennett, Arthur, or James die before the rest, portions to be divided.

To Thomas Howell, minister of Aust, my little coney cage and my Latyn Bible, and two other books and my hanger. Thomas Prynne, Reseduary Legattee.

Thomas Prynne, of Bristowe, and Arthur Baker, of Auste, overseers, to have £5 a piece.

THOMAS HOWELL, Minister.

THOMAS EARLE,   ARTHUR BAKER,   WILLIAM FOSTER.

WILL OF NICHOLAS PRYNE. December 26th, 1603.
Citizen and Goldsmith of London.

To be buried in Parish Church of St. Matthew's, " according to the custom of the Cittie of London." He divides his property into 3 parts.

[1] Bridget Baker married Peter Sherston. See his will.

1, third to his loving wife, Martha Pryne.

1, third to his child, Richard, and the unborn child or children (child died).

1, third to Company of Goldsmiths, to bring his body to buriall : £10 to make a parcell or piece of plate as a remembrance : £10 to each of the poor Almsmen of the Company to bear him, viz. :—James Collins, Simon Herringe, Robert Fleminge, and George Durrant. To James Collins for a good coffin, 40s. To Mr. John Presse Clarke, Parson of y* said Parish Church of St. Matthew, £5. To every one of his three children, twentie shillings. To aunt Ann Pryn, widowe, £6 13s. 4d. To my brother, Thomas Pryne, £5, and 40s. more to make him a ryng. To every one of his children now living, 40s. To my brother-in-law, Henrie Loftus, 40s. To my sister-in-law, now his wife, £6 13s. 4d. To my sister, Batten, 40s : to her son, Erasmus, 20s. : to her son, Thomas, 20s. : to her daughter, Elizabeth, 40s. To Mr. William Sherston, now Mayor of Bath, £3, to make a seale ringe of gold : to his son, Peter, 40s., to make him a ringe. To my brother, James Pryne, £5. To Priscilla Roberts that nursed my son, Richard, 40s. Remainder of third part to wife, Martha Pryne, and her children.

WILLIAM SHERSTON'S WILL.
AT SOMERSET HOUSE.

William Sherston, of the City of Bath, bequeathes :—1st—To the Church of Peter and Paul, towards the repairs, £100 to be paid by 40/- yearly out of lands, tenements, and portions of tythes, which he has in Widcombe and Lincombe, to be paid to the Church Wardens, beginning on the 1st Good Friday after his death. Bequeathed to "12 pore men of the Abbey," twelve gowns of black cloth, to "go before in his funerall there," £5 in money to be given to each man ; £5 to be divided among poor persons who shall be present at the funerall.

£100 to the poor of Bath (to be paid as the money to the Church, and raised in like manner).

£100 to be fully paid to the Chamberlain of the said City, to be given yearly by him to the poor most in need of help.

£100 to his Daughter, Margaret Lighte, to be paid to her Husband, Nicholas Lighte, for her special use ; if he be dead, to herself. He is to give security that it will be for her own use.

£20 a peece to Daughter Lighte's Children. To Grandchild, William Prynne, Son of Thomas Prynne now deceased, £100 in current money for the use of his Mother, Mary Prynne during her life—she to dispose of it as she likes.

To Grandchild, Arthur Sherston, Son of Peter Sherston, deceased—his house and lease of years, with its grounds, back, sides, and other appurtenances thereto belonging, which Jane Etton, widow, now holdeth and dwelyth in, lying in Northgate Street. Provided my Daughter, Mary Prynne, shall enjoy the house and grounds and all appurtenances for her life, paying rent and all other dutyes payable, I give her my guilt cup which was given me by my father Boucher. To her two Sons, William and Thomas Prynne, £100 each of current money, to be paid to their Mother, for their use. To her two Daughters Katherine and Bridgett Prynne, £40 a peece ; to her Daughter Joan Kemishe, Wife of William Kemishe, £20. If any of these children die unmarried, and before they be 21, the money to be divided among the surviving Brothers and Sisters.

To Daughter, Joane Ffrye, £100 ; to her Children, £100 of current money to be equally divided among them, to be paid to their Father, Robert Ffrye. To Joane Ffrye, the house and tenement now in possession of Lady Beethe, with the lease, back, sides, orchards, gardens, and out-houses ; she paying due rents, and keeping the whole in repair untill William Sherston, Son of Peter Sherston, deceased, be of age at 23 years of age. Also the lease of St. John's Farm, which I have in Bath ; also the lease of the lodgings by the King's Bath, with the residue of the years which shall remain unexpired at my decease. Also to Joane Ffrye the best guilt salt and my three guilt bowles, and one dozen silver spoons. To my Son-in-law, Robert Ffrye, my scarlet gown and my best velvet tippett to that gowne, and my grograme gowne faced with coney. To my Brother, John Sherston, my black gowne faced with foynes. (FOUINE-fitch-polecat fur).

To Brother, Mr. Abel Kitchin, my best ring of golde, wherein is engraved (Benvoglio ?) and death's head. To my Sister, his wife, my Mazer bowle, sett in silver, and guilt as a token of my love in remembrance to them.

To Brother, Giles Whaley, one gowne cloth of my best black clothe, and £5 in money, to be paid within 6 months after my decease.

To Sister Parker, the use of the house and goods which they now dwell in, which I bought of Mr. Francis West, of London, during her life, and to Brother Parker, her husband, I doe forgive him all such debts as he doth owe me.

To Sister Parker, towards her maintenance, £4 per annum, to be paid her everie month by my Overseer, 6/8 per month.

To my Cosen, Mr. John Sachfield, my black gowne garded with velvett and faced with damask.

To Cosen Sachfield, widow of Richard Sachfield, one gowne cloth of my best black cloth.

To my Servant Katharine Ruddocke, in recompense of services during my sicknesse, £4, within 6 months of my decease. To each of my servants, 20/- a peece.

To Elizabeth Sherston, daughter of my Son Peter Sherston, deceased, 100 marks of current money when she shall be 21.

To Arthur Sherston, son of Peter Sherston, all my lands in West Yatton and Long Deane, in the Parish of Yatton Keynell, in the County of Wilts, which I bought of one Robert Reade; with all my houses, buildings, gardens, orchards, pastures, meadowes, arable lands, commons, woods, underwoods, whatsoever whereof I have my state and inheritance in the said parish of Yatton Keynell or Statonforde, to him and his heires male. In default of these heirs, the property is devised to William Sherston, with remainder to his Aunts, Mary Prynne, Margaret Lighte, Joane Ffrye, equally and to their children.

To William Sherston, all my lands in Cullhorne, Thickwood and Boxe, which I bought of one Arthur Goslett (to William Sherston and his heirs—in default of whom to his Aunts and their heirs). Also all lands and tenements in Widcombe and Linkcombe, which I bought of Sir John Young, Kt., comonly called Gt. Chauntries of Widcombe and Linkcombe, paying and allowing such legacies as I have given out of the same.· Also the lease of years which have to come, and unexpired at tyme of my decease, of the Hamanie, Beckingcliffe, which I bought of Mr. Edward Norton.

All the residue of my goods and chattells to Robert Ffrye, my Executor, for benefit of my Grandsonnes, until Arthur Sherston be 25, and William 23. He shall act as he thinks best for them during their minority, then he shall accompt with them for such goods, etc., upon which accompts shall be allowed all necessary and fit charges and expenses, and he shall have £20 for his pains.

I request and desire my loving friend Mr. John Cutt, of the Citie of Bathe, Gent., Mr. Robert Kitchinge, of the Citie of Bristoll, Marchant, to be Overseers of this my will; £10 a peece for their pains.

                                        WILLIAM SHERSTON.

Signed in presence of Robert Chambers, and John Finfin. Obiit 7th of September, 1621.

                    Proved January 26th, 1625,
        By Arthur Sherston.   George Webb, Rector of S. Peter and S. Paul.

WILL OF THOMAS PRYNNE.
Obiit July 20, 1620.

I, Thomas Pryn, of Swanswicke, in the County of Somersett, . . . desire
. . . to be buried in the Church. . . . I leave £5 to the poor of the parish,
to be paid in half-a-year after my decease to the Churchwardens and Sidesmen.

John Webb, of Swanswicke, left the like sum to the like use, and by his
will it was to be put into the Chamber of the Citie of Bath, there to remain for
ever, and they to pay to the Overseers of the Poor of Swanswicke aforesaid
6s. 8d. per ann. for ever. They being offered it, will not take it in that same
manner, and therefore, it having remained in my hands as executor, I doe therefore pay to the said Overseers yearly 6s. 8d. according to the same will. My will
and mynd is that the £5 given by me, and also the £5 given by John Webb,
shall for ever remaine in yᵉ hands of yᵉ Churchwardens and Overseers ; 13s. 4d.
per ann. to be distributed to the saide poor.

I give and bequeath to my sonne William the lease and terme of years
that I have to come of my ffarme of Swanswicke, after the terme of 5 yeares,
which my will is that my wiffe, Mary Pryn, shall have the use and benefit thereof
for the payment of the legacies hereafter given to my three children, namelye,
Thomas, Catheryn, and Bridgett Pryn. And also payinge during the said five
yeares unto my sonne William Pryn £20 a-yeare.

And the rents to the Lords thereof at the day appointed.

Item.—I give to my Sonne William all the bedsteads, matts, and cordes
withall, tableboards, coverts, and stooles, with the Wainscott and benches that are
in my house at Swanswicke. And all waines, wheeles, drages, Sythes, collowes,[1]
yokes, cheynes, riks, stathells, ladders, tallets, and all other plow harness in and
about the house, and all the freestone trowes and the cipresse cheste in the
chamber, and the spruce boards and frame.

My cipresse chest and the cipress boxe that I have at Aust, which boards
and boxes were my father's. Also, I give him the Spanish chest in the littell
chamber, the chest afore the wyndowe in my chamber, and my cofer in the same ;
the presse in the Mayden's Chamber, and the boards and Cofer in my Studye,
with all other implements there. Item.—I give to my Sonne William my great
peece of white plate, and the boxe it is kept in, my best salte and the three best
wyne-bowles, and my dozen of silver spoones with the square heads, and my
littell gilt cup. Item.—I give to my Sonne Thomas Pryn £200 in money, my
great cheste in the parler, my silver and gilt salt, a fether bed, a boulster and two

---

ı Collars.

pillowes, a paire of sheetes, a paire of blanketts, and one of my Arrys coverletts, sixe platters, sixe porringers, sixe saucers, two crocks, two brasse pannes, and one kettell. Item.—I give to my daughter, Katheryn Pryn, £200 in money, 1 fether bed, one flocke bed, two paire of sheets, two paire of blanketts, two boulsters, two pillowes, two coverletts .(one of the best, another of the second), the cipres chest in the chamber over the buttery, one of my white silver bowles, my littell silver salte, half a dozen of yᵉ Postell spoones, two crockes, two pannes, sixe platters, 6 porringers, 6 saucers, and one kettell.

Item.—I give to my Daughter, Joane Kemishe, one fether bed, one boulster, two pillowes, two paire of sheetes, 2 blanketts and a coverlett, and one of my white silver bowles. Item.—I give to Katheryn Kemish, my daughter's daughter, two yewes and two Lambs.

Item.—I give to Henry and George Gofe,[1] my daughter's sonnes, 20 shillings a peece.

Item.—I give to Thomas and Mary Twimblowe, 20/- a peece, and to Agnes Batten, the daughter of Erasmus Batten, 20/-

Proved Sep. 3, 1634, by George Clarke and Katheryn his wife.

WILL OF WILLIAM PRYNNE.

In the name of God, Amen. I, William Prynne of Lyncolnes Inne, in the county of Middlesex, esquire, being, through God's mercy, restored to perfect health and of sound memory from my late infirmitie (for which I bless his holy name), considering my owne declyning strength, the deathes of many of my relacions younger than myselfe, and my approaching dissolucion, being willing to be dissolved and to be with Chryst which is best of all, whenever God shall please to take me oat of this vayne and wicked world, and hath noe more worke for me therein, doe make this my last will and testament in forme ensueing : First, I bequeathe my immortall soule into the hands of God frome whome I receaved it, by whose free grace, and all satisfactorly merritts of my Lord and Saviour Jesus Christ, I stedfastly hope and beleeve to obtayne the full pardon of all my sinnes and eternall life in his heavenly kingdome. My vile body I bequeath to the dust, to be decently interred in the parish church of Swanswicke, in the county of Sommersett, or Lyncolnes

---

[1] Enquiry, since the sheet was printed (p. 122), in which occurs the remark as to Thomas Prynne's earlier marriage, establishes the fact that his first wife was Margery Smith, and by that marriage he had one daughter, Agnes, who married a Bristol merchant, named Gough, Goffe, or Gofe, who was the mother of the two "sonnes" referred to above. The author accepted too readily Mr. Bruce's statement that Thomas Prynne's first wife was not known, and that she left him childless. There is a reference to this Agnes Prynne in the Register. She was buried in the church, the floor of which was "broken" to receive her body.

Inne, if I decease in or nere either of them, till God shall raise it up a glorious body, and reunite it for ever to my soule at the general resurrection. Item, I give and bequeath to the Churchwardens and Treasurers of Christ Church in London, towards the repairing thereof, the summe of tenne pounds; and to the Churchwardens and Treasurers of the parish churches of Saint Antholines, Saint Lawrence neare the Guilehall, Saint Bridgett, and Saint Katherines Creed Church, defaced by the late dreadful fire, five pounds a peece, to be paid them within three months after they shall beginne to repaire them respectively, in case I dye before that tyme, haveing already given the somme of tenne pounds a peece to the Treasurers of Saint Maryes Aldermanbury and Sepulchers, and five pounds to the Churchwardens of Saint Mildred's, with my owne handes, to bee imployed only on the repaires of the saide churches, and for noe other uses. Item, I give to the library of Lyncolnes Inn all my manuscripts of Parlyament Rolles and Journalls, and other records not yet published, together with my Rerum Germanicarum Scriptores in five, Rerum Hispanicarum Scriptores in four, and Goldastus in three folio volumes. Item, I give to the Library of Oriel Colledge, in Oxford, whereof I was both a member and tennant, my Ocham upon the Sentences, Saint Briget's Revellacions, Laurentius Surius his Councils in four tomes, and one of each sort of my owne printed bookes which they yet want. All the rest of my divinity and ecclesiasticall history books I give to my dear brother, Mr. Thomas Prynne, and all my other history bookes, phisick, philosophy, chirurgery bookes, and poets I give to my nephew William Clerke, with this proviso, that he shall not sell them. And for my law bookes I give so many of them to my brother George Clerke as he shall make choyce of. Item, I give to my dear brother, Mr. Thomas Prynne, my best gold ringe with my father's armes, and three old peeces of gold which were my grandfather's. Item, I give to my dear sister, Mistresse Katheryne Clerke, my best serjeant's ring, all my hangings, bedding, furniture in my chamber in Lyncolnes Inne, and two hundred pounds in money. Item, I give to her husband, Mr. George Clerke, one of my gold rings. Item, I give to every one of their sonnes and daughters who shall be living at the tyme of my decease one gold ring and one hundred pounds a peece. And to my neece Elizabeth Clerke and her daughter Elizabeth one gold ring and tenne pounds a peece in plate. Item, I give to my disconsolate neece, Mrs. Catherine Colman, widow, the somme of two hundred poundes in money; to each of her daughters the somme of one hundred pounds; and to her sonnes the somme of fiftie poundes, provided that if either her daughters dye or her sons before marriage his or her portion shall remayne to the surviving daughter. Item, I give to my neece Collett, my neece Browne, and my neece (   ) forty pounds a peece.   And to each of their respective children tenne pounds a peece.   And in case any of their respective children shall dye before marriage, that the legacie of the deceased shall remayne to the survivor.   Item, I give to my cousin Joyce Prynne the somme of 30ᵘ, and to my neece Becke her sister the like somme, if alive at my decease.   Item, I give to my clerke Ralph Jennings one of my cloth suites, with a coate, cloake, stockings, and hatt, with five poundes in money, to be paid to him by 5s. each weeke, lest he spend or be cheated thereof.   Item, I give to my clerke Samuell Wiseman the somme of three pounds and one of my silk cloakes and last printed bookes.   Item, I give to Doctor Tillotson one of each of my three tomes of my Exact Chronological Vindicacion, 8vo., bound. Item, I give and bequeath to the Churchwardens and Overseers of the Poore of the parish of Swanswicke the somme of tenne pounds, to be imployed in binding forth poore boyes and girles therein apprentices as my nephew Mr. George Clerke and the Minister of the parish shall nominate and directe.   Item, I give to Thomas Smith of Swanswick, the somme of twenty shillings in money and one of my suites of apparell and riding coates.   Item, I give to my brother George Clarke all the bedding and furniture of my chamber in the Tower of London.   Item, I give to Mr. William Ryley one of my last tomes of a Chronologicall Vindicacion.   All the legacies in money formerly given I desire may be paid with all expedicion out of the sale and proceed of my printed books at my owne charge in my chamber and elsewhere, and of six yeares and half arreares of my annuall sallary and fee of five hundred pounds, as Keeper of the Records of the Tower, freely given mee by his Majesty King Charles the Second of his owne meere motion, for my ser- vices and sufferings for him under the late usurpers, and strenuous endeavours, by printing and otherwise, to restore his Majestie to the actual possession of his royall government and kingdome without opposicion or effusion of blood.   As for my interest in the lease of Swanswick, and my hangings, pictures, and furni- ture there, I give and bequeath them to my dear brother, Mr. Thomas Prynne, for the use of my beloved sister, Mrs. Katherine Clerke, for her better mayntenance dureing her naturall life.   And if she dye before the expiracion of the said terme, then to the use of her husband and my nephew, George Clerk, if living.   All the rest of my reall and personall estate, goods, chattells, debts, creditts (I never coveting the uncertaine transient treasures, honors, or preferments of this world, but to doe my God, King, country, all the best publicke services I could with the losse of my liberty, expences of my meane estate, and hazard of my life) I give and bequeath to my deare brother, Mr. Thomas Prynne, and my loveing sister, Mrs. Katharine Clerke, whom I make sole executors of this my last will and testament, revoking all former wills.   In testimony whereof I have written it with my owne hand, and sealed and signed it with my owne seale of armes and hand this eleveanth day of August, in the yeare of our Lord 1669.

WILLIAM PRYNNE.

Signed, sealed, published, and declared by the testator to be his very last will and testament, in the presence of THOMAS PRYNNE.

RALPH ALLEN'S WILL.

To his Widow, £500 in cash, and an annuity of £1,300 a year, payable quarterly, and charged all his estates to pay it. To the Bishop of Gloucester, his Library of books. To Mrs. Allen, his widow, £1,000 to dispose of in charity. To his Brother, Philip, £2,000. To Mrs. Warburton, £5,000. To his Nephew, Philip Allen, £1,000. To his Nephew, Ralph Allen, £5,000. To Miss Mary Allen, his niece, £10,000. To Capt. William Tucker, £10,000. To his Sister, Gertrude Elliot, £3,000. To his nephew, Philip Elliot, £1,000. To Capt. William Tucker, after Mrs. Allen's decease, an additional sum of £5,000. To Miss Mary Allen, an additional sum of £5,000. To the Rev. Mr. James Sparrow, £500. And to his Son, £100. To Mrs. Anne Bennet, £100. To his Great Nephew, Ralph Allen, a forty-pound life annuity. To Dr. Oliver, Jerry Peirce, John Knipe, Rev. Mr. Hurd, Ald. Chapman, William Hoare, Lewis Clutterbuck, Joseph Lobb, and Ralph Mould, £100 each. To three children of the late Henry Fielding, Esq., £100 each. To Mrs. Fielding, £100.[1] To William Ward and Isaac Dodsley, £100 each. To his Servant, Samuel Shellard, £50. To Richard Jones, and each of his menial Servants, except William Ward, Samuel Prynn, Isaac Dodsley, and Samuel Shellard, one year's wages above what shall be due to them. To Samuel Prynn, £100; and his Wife, £100.

He gives the overplus of the income of his estate, after paying Mrs. Allen's annuity of £1,400 and an annuity to his Brother Philip, to Mrs. Warburton; and after his Widow's decease, entails his estate on Mrs. Warburton and her issue; which failing, to her brother, Capt. Tucker; which failing, to his niece, Miss Mary Allen, and her issue, which failing, to the heir-at-law.

By a Codicil, November 10, 1760, he leaves to Mrs. Moore, £200; Mary Poyntz, £100; Alderman Chapman, £100; To Bishop of Gloucester, £500; and then adds,—

" For the last instance of my friendly and grateful regard for the best

---

[1] Sarah Fielding, Henry Fielding's sister.

of friends, as well as the most upright and ablest of ministers that has adorned our country, I give to the Right Honourable William Pitt the sum of £1,000, to be disposed of by him to any of his children that he may be pleased to appoint for it."

By a second Codicil, June 29, 1763, he confirms this Legacy.

In case Capt. Tucker shall come to the possession of his estate, he gives his niece Miss Allen an additional sum of £15,000, and desires to be buried privately in Claverton Churchyard.

BIBLIOGRAPHY OF REV. RICHARD WARNER.

In Divinity, besides an edition of the "Common Prayer with Notes," an English "Diatessaron," "A Psalter with Notes," and a "Companion to the Holy Communion," he published—"Practical Sermons," 2 vols., 8vo, 1803—4; "Six Occasional Sermons," 1 vol., 8vo, 1808; "Scripture Characters," 1 vol., 12mo, 1810; "Sermons, Tracts, and Notes on the New Testament," 3 vols., 8vo, 1813; "Sermons on the Epistles and Gospels," 2 vols, 12mo, 1816; "Old Church of England Principles opposed to New Light," 3 vols, 12mo, 1818; Twelve Sermons on "Practical Religion," 1 vol., 8vo, 1837; Four Sermons on "The Simplicity of Christianity," 1 vol., 8vo., 1839; Five Discourses on "The Sermon on the Mount," 1 vol., 8vo, 1840; "Specimens of Biblical Exposition on the Book of Genesis," 1 vol., 12mo, 1842; to these may be added several series of Sermons in MS. type for the use of the younger clergy, some smaller publications, and many single Sermons—one of which was entitled "War inconsistent with Christianity," preached in 1804; in 1789, a "Tour Round Lymington"; this was followed by a "Southampton Guide"; and successively appeared *Antiquitates Culinariæ*, 1 vol., 4to, 1791; "An Attempt to ascertain the Situation of the Ancient Clausentum," 4to, 1792; "Topographical Remarks on the South-Western Parts of Hampshire," 2 vols., 8vo, 1793; "History of the Isle of Wight," 1 vol., 8vo, 1795; "An Illustration of the Roman Antiquities discovered at Bath," 4to, 1797. To these succeeded his "Walks through Wales," 2 vols., 1797—8; those "Through the Western Counties," 1800; "Excursions from Bath," 1801; "Northern Tour," 2 vols., 1802; and a "Tour through Cornwall," 1809—all in octavo. He also published, in 1811, a "Bath Guide," in small 8vo; but his two more important works in this department remain to be named—"The History of Bath," large 4to, 1801, which, although very defective, must still be accepted as the best book on the subject; and "A History of the Abbey of Glastonbury," imperial 4to, 1826: of this handsome volume only 250 copies were printed, and delivered to as many subscribers at £6 6s. a copy. His miscellaneous works included "Historical Illustrations of the Waverley Novels," 3 vols, 8vo; "Miscellanies," 2 vols, 12mo; a periodical designated *Omnium Gatherum;* "Literary Recollections," already named. A clever set of satirical dialogues, called "Bath Characters," which appeared in 1807, and speedily ran through three editions; also the two poetical *brochures*, in quarto, "Peter Paul Pallet," which followed it, entitled "Rebellion in Bath," 1808, and "The Restoration," 1809; "The Diary of an Aged Parson" (Sept. 1, 1848), was distributed by the venerable author among his personal friends.

INDEX.

PAGE.

Abbey, The Bath   4, 5, 23, 29, 49, 52, 73, 78
   „   „   Britton's History of   ... 21
   „   House 90
   „   Library, The   47
Abbot of Cirencester   111
Adelard Monk 21, 23
   „   Account of his Writings ...   „ 22
Allen, Ralph   9, 33, 34, 35, 36, 38, 39, 77, 78, 83,
                                  89, 90, 94, 118
   „   His Town House   36
   „   His Will   38
   „   His Second Wife   88
Allen, John   70
All Saints' Chapel   59
Anderson, James   26
Angoulême, Duke of   13
Anstey, Christopher   115
Arden, Pepper 18
Argyle Street, No. 8   ...   . 4, 5
Argyle, Duke of   6
Asho, James 69, 70, 131
Ashley, Lord   108
Atwoods, The 70
Aubrey, John 89
Austria, Emperor of   13
Austrians, Defeat of   18
Austerlitz, Battle of   18
Avon, The River   87

Babington, Professor   19
Bailbrook House   2
Barham, Lord, First Lord of the Admiralty
   in 1805 1
   „   Diana, Daughter of the above   ... 1
Barker, Benjamin 15, 16
Bartholomew, Lucy   92
Burton House 126
Bassetts, of Claverton ...   ...   - ... 88
Bassett, W. and Sir W. 68, 69, 88
Bastwick, a Physician 129, 130
Bath   1, 4, 5, 11, 12, 13, 14, 15, 16, 17, 18, 19, 20,
       23, 24, 26, 30, 31, 32, 33, 35, 36, 37, 38, 39,
       45, 46, 47, 50, 51, 53, 54, 57, 58, 60, 61, 71,
       72, 74, 77, 79, 82, 83, 85, 88, 90, 92, 93, 94,
       98, 112, 113, 115, 116, 121, 123, 124
   „   Baroness and Countess of 11
   „   City Lectures   110
   „   Chronicle   10
   „   Corporation   121
   „   and Bristol Magazine   71
   „   and Cheltenham Gazette   72
   „   Climate of   74
   „   History of 23, 111
   „   King's 111

PAGE.

Bath   Literary Club of 9
   „   in Particular, West of England in
          General 9
   „   Rectory of 8, 57
   „   Rector of   45
   „   entitled to be considered the premier
          Masonic Provincial City of England... 24
   „   Lodge at...   23
   „   William of   22
   „   Reginald of   22
   „   Henry of   22
   „   Monastery, the old Library of   ... 22
   „   Monastery of   21
   „   Past and Present 111
   „   Waters 1, 16, 17, 73, 74, 111
   „   Recorder of   20
Bathe 29
"The Bathes of Bathe Aide"   111
Bathonians   90
Bathampton Churchyard 53, 54
Batheaston 5, 52
   „   Villa   114
   „   Rectory of 17
   „   Manor House of   19
Bathford   89
Bathwick   ...   ...   1—17, 57, 94
   „   Hill 2, 7
   „   Church, building of   13
   „   Rector of   6
   „   Street 32
   „   Church, Kilvert, Evening Lecturer at 10
Battle-Fields   77
Baynes Gen. 3
   „   Thomas 10
Bencon, Mount 5
Beaconsfield, Lord   109
Bear Inn 14, 26
   „   Yard 4
Beauclerk, Lady Diana 100
   „   Her Letter to Selwyn ...   100, 101
   „   Topham 100
Beaulieu Lodge 71
Bedford House 6
Beech Cottage 57
Beechen Cliff 5
Bellot Thomas 23, 28, 29
Belvedere   85
   „   No. 4   71
Bennet, family of   34
   „   Ann   34
Bennett Street, No. 22 101
Berkeley, Charles, ... 68
   „   Bishop   53
Berri, Duchess of 13, 14

	PAGE.
Biggs, Mayor of Bath	70
Billington Mrs.	72
Birie, Prior	21
Bladud	33
,, King, Waters of ...	17
Bladud Buildings, No. 12 ...	52
Blaine, R. S., Esq.	5, 30
Bligh, John	26
,, Thomas	26
Blue-Coat School	46, 47
Boat-Stall Lane	4
Bordeaux, Duke of	13
Borlaso, the Historian ...	77
Borough Walls	4
Bostock, Rev. Charles	31
Bowles, John	29, 30
,, Rev. W. L.	72
Bradford, Duke's House at ...	38, 73, 89
Braham, the Singer	72, 73
Braganza, Catherine of	90
Bridewell Lane	47
Bridge, the Old...	4, 51
Bridge Street	118
Britton, John	87
Broad Street	126
,, Nos. 11 and 12 ...	73
Brock, Rev. M.	58
Brodrick, Rev. W. J. ...	57, 58
Bruce, Mr.	122, 126, 129, 133
Buckingham, Marquis of ...	25
,, Duke of	25
Bull's Library	98
,, afterwards Upham's ...	103
,, formerly Leake's ...	98
Buller, Charles	113
Burke, Sir B.	34
Burghley, Lord	28
Burney, Dr.	72
Burnett, Rev. J. C., Rector of St. Michael's	30
Burton, a Divine ...	129, 130
Butler, Bishop	11
Byron, Lord	30
,, Mad Jack	30
,, Mrs.	30
,, Lady	30, 31
,, Augusta (afterwards Mrs. Leigh) ...	30
Campbell, Colonel	6
Campbell's Lives of the Chancellors ...	46
Cambridge, Duke of	2
Camden, Lord	18
,, Marquis of, Recorder of Bath ...	20
Canterbury, Archbishop of ...	18
Capell, Edward	134
Note on the same	134
Carne, Sir Edward	111
Caroline, Princess	89
Carr, Isaac	89
Catholic Chapel in Orchard Street ...	28
Cavell, Rev. H. T.	58
Cecil, Lord Burghley	67
,, William, Earl of Salisbury ...	29

	PAGE.
Cecils, The	28
Chambers, Dr.	19
Chambord, Comte de	13
Champion, Colonel	54
Chapman, John, Rector of St. Michael's ...	30
,, Henry ...	38, 70, 124, 133
Charfield, Great, Wilts ...	59
Charles Edward, Prince	2
,, X.	13, 14
,, II. ...	83, 89, 90, 123
,, I.	131
,, Street, No. 22	85
Charlotte, Queen of George III. ...	1, 2, 3
,, Princess	1, 3
Chelwood	71
Christ Church	9
Circus, No. 29	101
,, No. 25	115
Clapham, General	33
Clarence, Duke of	1, 3
,, Duchess of	4
Clarke, Captain Pickering, R.N. ...	17
,, Mrs.	18
Claverton	87, 88, 89, 90, 92, 93
,, Lodge	7, 15, 93
,, Churchyard	7, 10
,, Curacy of	9
,, Manor House	87, 88, 93
,, Rectory of	87
,, Rector of	88
,, Down	53
Clavertonians	90
Cleveland Bridge	5
,, Duke of	12
,, Second and third Dukes of ...	11
Clifford, Lady Frances, daughter of Lord Salisbury	29
,, Lord Henry	29
Clifton, Lord	26
,, Baroness Theodosia ...	26
,, Baron and Lord	26
Cocardière, Mons. de	1
Cock Lane	4
Coke, Lady Mary	6
Cold Ashton	6
Coleridge, Bishop	8
,, Sir John	8
,, Chief Justice	8
Collinson, the Historian ...	35, 90, 124
Combe Down	91
Conway, Mr.	31
Conyers, Lady, divorced Wife of Marquis of Carmarthen	30
Cope, Sir Walter	29
Coryat, Note on	36
Cottle, Mr.	61, 63
Cowes, Isle of Wight	13
Cowper, William	31
,, His Work	31
,, Southey's Life of ...	31
Crawford, General	46
Crescent, Royal, No. 9	14

PAGE.

Crescent, Royal, No. 2 18
    "   No. 8 53
    "   No. 18 101
Crisp, J. 63
Cromwell, Oliver 121, 124, 133
Croscombe 59, 92
Cruttwell, Richard 65
Culloden, Battle of 2
Cumberland, William, Duke of 2

Daniel, Samuel 70
    "   Selections from the Writings of 72
Darlington, Earl of 12
Darnley, Viscount and Earl of 26
Dart, The Rev. Philip 58
Daubeny, Archdeacon 71
Davies, Professor 71
Davis, The late Edward 89
    "   The Rev. E. W. L. 13
    "   Mr. C. E., F.S.A. 111
    "   Physician 135
Denbigh, Earl of 34
Derrick, The M.C. 36
Devonshire Buildings, No. 1. 117
Dickens—Mr. Pickwick, Sam Weller ... 14
Dimond, Manager of Theatre ... 98, 117
    "   Son of 117
Disbrowe, Col. 3
Disraeli, Benjamin 14, 129
Dobson, William, esq. 15
Dolemeads, The 5
Downe, Lord 6
Downshire, Dowager Marchioness of ... 4
Du Barré, Jean Baptiste ... 53, 54
    "   Pedigree and Family of ... 55
    "   Madame, Story of ... 54, 55
Dudley, Dr. Richard 122
Duncan, Lord 84
Dunkerley, Grand Officer of England ... 26

Earle, Professor 112
East, Rev. John 58
Fast Gate 93
Eckersall, of Claverton 93
Edgcombe, Richard 122
Edwards, Gerard-Anne (see Noel) ... 1
    "   Richard 72
Edmunds, Henrietta 101
Egmont, Earl of, formerly Sir John Percival 53
Elections, 1645—1654 68
    "   Specimen of electing members, 1646 69
"Eliot, George" 41
Elizabeth, Queen ... 7, 67, 69, 111, 126
Elwin, Rev. Whitwell 8
Essex, Earl of 28
Estcourt, Sir Thomas 73, 88
Estcourts, The, of Claverton 89
Exeter, Bishop of 8
    "   Earl of 28

Falconer, The Family of 101

PAGE.

Falconer, Rev. Thomas, M.D. 53, 59, 60, 65, 85,
           101, 102, 107, 108
    "   "   " Sketch of, by Thomas
              Falconer ... 107, 108
    "   Henrietta 108
    "   William, M.D., F.R.S. ... 52, 59, 60,
          65, 98, 101, 102, 103, 106
    "   " Particulars of him, by
            Warner ... 104, 105, 106
    "   " Letter to him by Burke 102, 103
    "   Thomas 101, 107, 109
    "   William, Recorder of Chester ... 101
    "   Rev. W. 106
    "   Randle Wilbraham, M.D. 27, 47, 60,
        101, 102, 109, 110, 111, 112, 113
Farmborough, Rector of 6
Fawcett, Mrs., daughter of Sir Richard
      Sutton, Bart. 11
Feniton Court 8
Fielding, Henry, 9, 32, 33, 34, 35, 36, 37, 38, 39, 45
    "   Criticisms on 39, 40, 41, 42, 43,
                44, 45
    "   Tom Jones ... 34, 36, 38
    "   Amelia 36, 38
    "   Joseph Andrews ... 36, 39
    "   Character of Allworthy 38, 39
    "   Life of, by Austin Dobson ... 45
    "   Biographical notice of, by
          Leslie Stephen 45
    "   Lawrence's Life of 46
    "   His Biographer, Murphy ... 37
    "   His Children 39
    "   His first wife, Miss C. Crad-
          dock of Salisbury ... 37
Fielding, Sarah 32, 33, 35
    "   Her Works 35, 36
    "   Mrs. 35, 38
    "   General 32, 33
    "   Lodge, Twerton ... 34, 35
Fitz-Clarence, the Misses 2
Floyd, General 3
Flower, editor of a Cambridge Newspaper 18
    "   Mr. Bruges 27
    "   Thomas 27
Foljambe, Francis 101
Fortt, Mr. James 79
Freemasonry, History of ... 20, 21, 23, 24
    "   Modern 20
    "   Charities in connection with 21
    "   Constitution of 23
Freshford House 83, 84
Fuller, the Historian 7

Gainsborough, Earldom of 1
    "   the Painter 13
Gardiner's History of England under Bucking-
      ham and Charles I. 129
Gardiner, Dr., of the Octagon 49
Garrick, David 72, 115
Gascoyne Place 47
Gataker, Captain 52, 53

PAGE.

Gay Street 3
„   No. 13 72
George II. 26, 100
„   III. 2, 6, 26, 116
Gibbon, Edward 34, 85, 86
„   Works of 85
„   Letters to Mrs. Gibbon 85, 86, 87
Gilpin, Rev. W. 53, 50
Gisborne, Moral Philosophy of 19
Gloucester, The Spa 30
Godwin, C. 71, 100
„   Henry... 100
Gordon, Miss, of Gight 30
Gould, Mr. Robt. Freke, S.G.D. of England, 24, 25
„   Author of Four old Lodges ... 24
Graves, Rev. R.   9, 34, 35, 38, 39, 60, 77, 88, 89,
                  90, 91, 92, 93, 94, 95, 96, 98, 99, 115
„   Father of 90
„   Born at Mickleton ... 90, 91
„   Quotations from Mr. Kilvert's
          Essay on Graves ... 91, 95, 97, 98
„   Bibliography of 94
„   His Writings 95
„   Poem by, to Pratt 99
„   Letter to Milles 100
„   Anecdotes 38
Greaves, John 90
„   Sir Edward 90
Grammar School of Bath   46, 73, 89, 126
Grenville, Sir Bevil 77
Green, the Historian 125
„   Street 78
„   Park, No. 19 83
Grenville Richard, of Wotton 25
„   Lady Hester, wife of Earl of Chat-
          ham 25
Greyhound and Shakespeare Inn 27
Grigg, The Rev. Peter 17
Grove, The Orange 4
Gunning, Mr. 5
„   Mrs. 5
„   Counsellor 6
„   Bishop 6
„   The Rev. Peter 6
„   The Rev. Peter, son of the above 6
„   John 6
„   Maria 6
„   Elizabeth 6
„   John, of Castle Coote 6
„   Richard 7
„   Swainswick and Turney Court ... 7
Gybbs, or Holway, Prior 20

Hallett, Mr. and Mrs. 7
Hamilton, Duke of 6
Hampton Court Palace 26
„   Down 94
Harington, Mabel, sixth daughter of Sir
          James 7
„   Lord of Exton 7
„   Sir John   29, 46, 67, 68, 69, 70, 72

PAGE.

Harington, Dr. Edward 48
„   Sir Edward 48
„   Chancellor 48
„   Dr. Henry 25, 48, 49, 50, 51, 73, 98
„   Rev. Henry 67
„   Place 48
Harper, widow of Bishop Harper ... 2
„   Mr. 19
Harris, Mr. Mortimer 7
Harrison on the Springs of Bath 111
Harrowby, Earl of 13
Hart, White 14
Hartley, John 18
„   David 18
Herveys, The 100
„   John, Lord 25
„   Capt., husband of Duchess of
          Kingston 25
Hay, Dr. and Mrs. Alexander 30
Honley, Lady Mary 31
Henderson, Mrs. 98
Henrietta Park 5
„   Street 5
„   No. 37 79
Henry VIII. 21
„   I. 21
„   III. 22
Herschel, Sir W. 72
Hertford, Lord 6
Hesse, Princess 89
Hetling House 89
Hewlett, James 16
Heylin, Peter 127
Hibbert, Mr. 51
„   C. 70
Hicks, Sir Michael 29
Hill, Rowland 19
Hoadley, Bishop 32, 33, 59
„   His Epitaph on Sarah Fielding ... 33
Hoare, Sir R. 71
„   W. 78
Holder, R. 68
Holdstock, Mr. 71
Holinshed's Chronicles 111
Holloway, or Old Wells Road 94
Holyrood Palace 13
Holwell, Governor 71
Home, Author of Douglas 2
Horner, Sir John 69
„   G. W. 72
Hospital, Royal United 110, 112
„   Mineral Water 110, 112
Howse, Rev. 36, 37
Hunt, Mr. W. 71
Hunter, The Rev. Joseph 23, 63
„   On the Connection of Bath
       with the Literature and Science of
       England 22, 45
Hungerford, Sir E. 88
„   Sir W. 89
Hurd, Bishop 9, 39, 93

PAGE.

Incledon, the Singer 72

Jagger, the Miniature Painter 4
Jago, friend of Graves 91
James's, Saint, Church 7, 58, 59
"   Parish 26
James II. 36
James's, King, Palace 36
Jay, Rev. W. 19
Jefferys, Mrs. 5, 119
"   Account of her by Warner 119, 120, 121
Jenner, Dr. 77
Jervis, Lady ... .: ... 1
Johnstone Street, No. 7 ... ... 5, 15
Johnstone, wife of William, of Westerhall, 10, 11
Johnson, Dr. 100
Jones, Inigo 33, 34
Jones's Treatise 111
Jordan, Mrs., the Actress 2
Joseph, ex-King of Spain 1
Josephine, wife of Napoleon 1
Joyce, Family of 83
Julian Road 94

Kelston 29, 48
Kemble, Rev. Chas. 58, 110
Kennedy, Captain 82
Kensington Place, No. 16 79
Kent, Duke of 3
Kilmersdon 92
Kilvert, Rev. Frances 7, 8, 9, 10, 35, 36, 38, 39, 94, 95
"   "   Remains of 7, 9, 10
"   "   Sermons 9
"   "   His Essay on Allen ... 36
"   "   "   on Graves 88, 90
King, Lady Isabella 2
"   Dorothy, daughter of Dr. 52
"   M. C. 135
Kingston, Duchess of 25

Lilliput Castle 77
"   Note on 77, 78
Landor, W. S. 85
La Motte 75
Langton, Gore-, Lady Anna 22
"   Stephen, esq., Newton Park 25
Langridge 122
Lansdown 122
Lansdown, Lord 77
Laud, Archbishop ... 126, 127, 128, 129
Laura Place, No. 11 13
"   Place 4, 5, 83
"   Chapel 18
Laurence, Rev. 58
Laver House 89
Law, Archdeacon 7
"   Bishop 57, 59
Lawrence, Sir T., the Painter 106
Leader, friend of Napier 85

PAGE.

Leighton, Father of the Archbishop ... 126
"   General 119
Leipsic, Battle of 1
Leland, The Antiquary 22, 111
Leunan, Miss, of Lyme 7
Lepell, Sweet Molly, Lady Hervey ... 25
Lever, Charles 65
Lexington, Lord 89
Leycester, Edward 21
Ligonier, Lord 31
Lillo, Comte de, Louis XVIII., under title of 12
Linieres, General 45
Livingstone, Mr. 2
Lodge in Bath 23
"   Queen's Head, Members of ... 24
"   List of Members 25
"   Grand, of England 24
"   Cumberland ... 23, 24, 25, 26, 27
"   The Shakespeare 27
"   Royal York, of Perpetual Friendship 27
"   Royal Sussex 27
"   of Honour 27
"   Grand Archives 24
Lodges, Masters of, Mr. Ferry 27
"   Earl of Darnley, Grand Master of England, & G.M. Province of Somerset 26
"   Earl of Dalkeith, or, Duke of Richmond, Grand Master of England ... 24
"   Col. Kemys Tynte 26
"   Anthony Sayer 26
"   Dr. Desaguliers 26
"   Duke of Wharton 26
"   Sir C. Wren 26
Long, Miss Tilney 3
Longs, The 115
Longleat 89
"   Library of 23
Louis XV. 54
"   XVIII. 12
Lowell, Mr. Russell 39, 40, 41
Luppé, Mons. de 1
Lulworth Castle 13
Lytton, Lord 14, 15
"   Lady 15
"   Cheveley 15
"   Sir Edward Bulwer 14, 15
Lyttleton, George, First Lord ... 31, 36

Macaulay's Essay on Clive 71
Macintosh, Sir James 64
Maclaine, Dr. 9, 61, 65
Malmesbury, William of 21
Malthus, friend and pupil of Graves ... 93
"   Essay on Population 93
Mangin, Rev. Edward ... 8, 37, 38, 72
"   Editor of Richardson's Works 37
Manners and Gill, Messrs. 47
Mara, Madame 72
Marat, Count 50
Market Place 5, 51
Markham, O. 5

PAGE.

Marlborough Buildings, No. 11 45
Marshall, Librarian 99, 100
Masonic Hall 23
„ Lodge 24
Mayfair Chapel... 6
Maynard, John 124
Mayo, Bridget, daughter of Lord ... 6
Melmoth, William 52
„ His Work 52
„ William son of above ... 52
Melmoths, The 53
Metestasio (erroneously spelt Metastasio) ... 72
Meyler, W. 115, 117
„ Address written by him, spoken by
Dimond 117
Meyler's Library 98, 99, 103
Michael's, Saint, Church of ... 30, 58
Milbanke, Mr. 31
Miller's, Lady, Vase 94, 98
Miller, Lady 114, 115
„ Sir John 114
Milsom Street 73, 83
„ No. 30 31
„ No. 38 31
Modena, Queen Mary of... 36
Molesworth, Sir W. 85
Moline's Chess-Club 71
Monkland, George ... 34, 35, 46, 71. 103
„ As an Actor ... 45, 46
„ The Literature and Lit-
erati of Bath 45
Monks' Mill 5
Montagu, Mrs. 6
„ Lord 26
Montgomery, James 71
More, Hannah 19
Morgan, Master of the Grammar School ... 8
Mornington, Earl of 3
Morris, John 71, 72
Mulcaster, Lord 18
Multon, John, Freemason 21
Murch, Jerom, Esq. 125
Murray, Sir James 11

Napier, Sir C. J. 79, 82, 83
„ His work on Military Law 82
„ Sir William ... 79, 80, 82, 83, 84
„ Quotations from his Life of
Sir Charles ... 80, 81, 82, 85
Notes on the same... 80, 81, 82
„ His History 83
Napoleon I. 1
Nash, Beau 94
Neale, Sir Harry Burrard, Bart. 59
Neckam, Alexander 111
Nelson, Robert 1, 46, 47
„ His Work 47
Nether Stowey (erroneously spelt Nother)... 8
Newton St. Loe 6
Nichols, Rev. W. L. 7, 8, 9, 58
Nichols's Royal Visitations 65

PAGE.

Nool, Sir Andrew, Knight of Dalby ... 7
„ Sir Gerard, Bart. 1, 7
„ Family name of 1
„ Hon. Capt., R.N. 7
„ Mrs. 7
Noels Earls of Gainsborough 1
Norman, George 8
North Parade, No. 3 119
Northesk, Lord 4
Northstoke 6
Northumberland, Duke of 13
„ Duchess of 114
„ Buildings, No. 4 ... 48
Noy, Attorney-General 127, 129
Nugæ Antiquæ 67, 69

O'Connell, Daniel 70
Ogle, Miss M. 52
Oliver, The Doctors 73
„ The Elder 74
„ Relation of an extraordinary sleepy per-
son at Timsbury, near Bath 74, 75, 76
„ The Younger 77, 78
„ His Writings 77
„ His Biscuits ... 77, 78, 79
Orange, Prince of 73
„ Grove 98
Ottery-St.-Mary 8

Padua, John of 89
Paley, Archdeacon 19
Palmer, Col. 70
„ John 115, 116, 117, 118, 119
Parades, The 4
„ South, No. 7 20
Parish, John 2
Parr, Dr. ... 60, 61, 63, 64, 105, 106, 135
Parry, Dr. 5, 65, 98
Parrys, The 60
Patteson, Mr. Justice 8
Pearson, Advocate-General 135
Peck, Rev. Francis 28
„ Writings of ... 28, 29
Peel, The late Sir Robert 3
Pepys's Diary 133
Perrymead, Villa at 17, 72
Peter, St., and St. Paul, Parish of ... 30
Philip, St. 70
Phillott, Sarah, daughter of Archdeacon ... 6
„ Lady Frances 6
Pierce, Jerry 77
„ Dr., of Abbey House 77
Pinch's Timber Yard 5
Pits, William 22
Pitt, William 13, 16, 19
Pole, Wellesly 3
Pope, Alexander 39
„ Works 8, 9
Popham, Alexander ... 68, 69, 70, 124
„ Sir Francis 124
Porson, the Great 143

PAGE.

Powerscourt, Lord 79
Powlett, Lord aud Lady William 11
Pratt, Samuel Jackson 113
  ,, Bookseller and Poet 99, 105
  ,, His Writings, Note I. 99
  ,, Poem to Graves 99
Pringle, Sir John 78
Prettyman, Dr. 118
Prior Park 9, 17, 33, 35, 36, 39, 88, 93, 94, 118
Prospect Cottage, Newton St. Loe ... 71
Pryune, Erasmus 121
  ,, Thomas ... 121, 122, 133, 134
  ,, William 70, 121, 122, 123, 124, 125, 126, 127, 128, 129, 130, 131, 132, 133
  ,,   ,, Note on him 130, 131, 132
  ,,   ,, Account of himself in his *Brevia Parliamentaria* ... 123
  ,,   ,, Note on the same 123, 124
  ,,   ,, A Fragmentary Biography by the late John Bruce ... 124
  ,,   ,, *Histrio-Mastix* by him 125—127
  ,,   ,, Sharpe and Shrewsbury, his Schoolmasters ... 126
  ,,   ,, Lord Cottington, Chief Justice Richardson, Secretary Cook, Earl Dorset—men connected with his Trial 127
  ,,   ,, De Preens, signifying points 121
  ,,   ,, De Preens, de Preyn, origin of name 121
Pulteney Arms 10
  ,, Street 51
  ,, No. 40 ... ... 2 -4
  ,, No. 59 10
  ,, No. 72 12
  ,, No. 34 12
  ,, No. 2 14
  ,, No. 36 16
  ,, No. 26 19
Pulteney, Lady 10
  ,, Sir William Johnstone 11
  ,, General Harry 10
  ,, Sir James Murray 11
  ,, Family of 10
  ,, Arms and Name of 10
  ,, Property of 11
  ,, Rev. Mr., of Ashley, Northamptonshire 11
Pump Room 2, 4, 17, 18, 31

Quantocks and their Associations 8
Queen Square 31
Quiet Street .. ... : ... 5
Quin, Comedian, Portrait of, by Gainsborough 13
Quincy, De, Thomas 8

Randolph, Miss, Sister of Dr. 6
  ,, Capt. 12
  ,, Dr. 18
Rauzzini, Venanzio 72
Reynolds, Sir Joshua 39

PAGE.

Rich, Sir Robert, Field Marshal 31
Rice, Count 53, 54, 55
Richards, Rev. John 58
Richardson 39
Ricketts, Mrs. 4
Riddle, Lady 30
Rochetts 1, 3, 4
Rochester, Bishop of 29
Roebuck. John Arthur, Q.C. 79, 84, 85, 108
Rosenberg, G. 71
Russia, Emperor of 13
Russell Street, No. 2 20

Salisbury, Earl of 28, 29, 30
  ,, Dean of 29
Saracen's Head 72
Saunders, Mr. 84
Savil, Mrs. 89
Sawoloso, Tho 47
Scott, Sir G. 23
Selden 126
Selwyn, George 100
Seward, Miss 115
Seymour Street, No. 1 61
Sheffield, Lord, formerly Col. Holroyd ... 83
Shenstone, Poet 9, 87, 91, 98
Shepherd, Mr. 71
Sheridan, Richard Brinsley 52
Sherston, William 122, 126, 133
  ,, Marie... 122
Shockerwick 13
Shum, Mr. F. 100
Simeon Trustees 8
  ,, Rev. Charles 57
Skrine, William 88, 90, 92
  ,, Henry Duncan, esq. ... 89, 90
  ,, Richard Dixon 89
  ,, His Rivers of Great Britain ... 89
  ,, Thomas 89
Skynner, Rev. John 52
  ,, Miss Sophia 52
  ,, Captain, R.N. 52
Smith, Sir Sydney 8
  ,, Mrs. 94
  ,, Rev. Stafford 88
  ,, Rev. Mr. 90
Somersetshire Worthies 34, 72
Spring Gardens 5
Sproule, Rev. J. W. 58
Stall Street 53
Stewart, widow of Andrew 11
Stirling, Margaret, daughter of Sir William, Bart. 11
Stock, Dr., Bishop of Killalla ... 64, 65
Storace, Signor 72
Stuckey's, Messrs., Bank 31
Suffolk, Catherine, daughter of the Earl of 29
Summer Hill 5, 30
Surajah Dowlah... 71
Surtees, W. E., Esq., D.C.L. 46

PAGE.
Surtees' Sketch of Lives of Lord Eldon and
    Stowell 46
Sussex, Duke of 27
Swainswick 6, 7
  ,, Hill House 121, 133, 134
  ,, Upper 121
  ,, Village of 122, 133
  ,, Manor House of ... 122, 133, 134
Swale, John 52
Sydney Place 1, 2
  ,, No. 93 11
Sydney Gardens 2
Sydenham, Humphry 72

Tadwick 7
Taine, Mons. 41
Temple, Hester, daughter of Sir Richard ... 25
  ,, Earl 25
  ,, Countess 25
Tickell, of Beaulieu House 71
Timberscombe 59
Thackeray, W. M. 34, 39, 44
Theatre, The 116
  ,, Actors and Actresses at 116
Thicknesse, Philip 9, 34, 79
Thirlwall, Bishop 11
Thomasson, Sir Edward ... :.. ... 11
Thornton, Henry, M.P. 17
Thornton's Letter to Hannah More ... 19
Thynne, Lord John 70
Todhunter, Joseph 48
Tower, Captain 1
Tuns, The Three 53
Turner, Dr., Dean of Wells 111

Ubley, Living of, Somersetshire 17
Union Passage 4
  ,, Street 4, 51

Vane Street, No. 3 6
Villula, John de 21
  ,, Life of 21
Vincent, St., Earl of 1, 3
Vivian, John 88, 89, 90
  ,, George 89

Wade's Passage 4, 5
Walcot Parade 5
  ,, Parish 57
  ,, Street 73
  ,, Church 8
Wallis, Dr. 22
Walpole, Horace 6, 31
Walter, Prior 22
Walters, Melmoth 52
Watt, Dr. 73
  ,, Bibliotheca Britannica 73
Warburton, Bishop 9, 39
  ,, Literary Remains of 9
Warminster Road 94

PAGE.
Warner, Rev. R. 18, 21, 26, 49, 52, 56, 57, 58,
    59, 60, 61, 62, 63, 64, 65, 67, 71, 72,
    92, 98, 105, 106, 119, 121, 123, 124, 133
Warner's Cottage 56, 57, 72
  ,, History of Glastonbury Abbey ... 71
  ,, Bath Characters ... 60, 65
  ,, Walks 58
  ,, Sermon on War 102
  ,, Literary Recollections ... 58, 103
  ,, History of Bath ... 57, 67, 68
  ,, Verses... ... ... 27, 28
  ,, Antiquitates Culinariæ 71
  ,, Introduction to Bath Characters,
    with Key to Note ... 66, 67
  ,, Rebellion in Bath 60
Warner, Mrs. 71
  ,, Rebecca 57
Webb, Edward 122
  ,, John 122
  ,, Family of 122
Wentworth, Lady 31
Westhall House 71
Wesley, John and Charles 95
Western, Captain 17
  ,, Sophia 37
Whitelock, General 128
Whittington, Thomas, esq. ... 121, 133
Widcombe, Parish of 57, 58
  ,, Lodge, formerly called Yew
    Cottage 33
  ,, House 33, 34
  ,, Vicarage of 33
  ,, Hill 33
  ,, Old Church 33, 53
  ,, St. Matthew's 58
Wilberforce, William ... 16, 17, 18, 19, 20
  ,, Mrs. 18
Wilkes, John 5, 119
William Rufus 21
Williams, Mr. 34, 35
  ,, Miss 85
Williamses, The 35
Wiltshire, John 13
Winifred House 5
Wood, John 35
Woodland House 8
Woodley, Mary, daughter of W. ... 6
Woolley, Parish of 122
Wren, Sir Christopher 26

APPENDIX.
Will of John Prynne 137
  ,, Richard Prynne 138
  ,, Erasmus Prynne 141
  ,, Nicholas Prynne 141
  ,, Thomas Prynne 145
  ,, William Prynne 146
  ,, Peter Sherston 139
  ,, William Sherston 142
Bibliography of the Rev. Richard Warner ... 150

W. ARCHER & CO.,

SHIPPERS,

WHOLESALE AND RETAIL

WINE & SPIRIT MERCHANTS,

ALE AND PORTER MERCHANTS,

NORTH PARADE,

BATH.

A LL WINES offered to the Public, which have been selected with judgment, are pure, well matured, and properly bottled.

SPIRITS of every kind are of good old age, and better quality cannot be obtained.

WINES of notable Vintages to select from. At this Establishment the Best Value is given for Money.

Malvern Aerated Waters.

The "Ne Plus Ultra" of Ale.

S O much has been written and said in regard to ALES, that the various statements made have become conflicting, and to the public very perplexing.

To those who have little time, and less inclination, to seek themselves for the Best Family Ales, it is safest to rely on the kind of Ale that has stood the strongest public test.

The great superiority of the **ANGLO-BAVARIAN ALES** is proved by the Gold Medals and other Prizes which have been awarded at the London, Vienna, Paris, Sydney, and Melbourne Exhibitions, thus proving their excellence by being placed FIRST in every competition.

The system adopted by the Anglo-Bavarian Brewery Company, of fermenting and cleansing the Ales from Barm, is so much in advance of the old method used by ordinary Brewers, that the quality of their Ales is, in consequence, of the highest description, and leaves nothing to be desired in any respect.

Prices, from 1/- to 1/8 per Gallon, in casks of all sizes.
Amber Ale, 3/- per Dozen Imperial Pints.

SOLE AGENTS FOR BATH:—

WM. ARCHER & CO.,
WINE MERCHANTS,
NORTH PARADE.

HOT BATHS OF BATH.

HE MINERAL SPRINGS which supply these Baths yield 350,000 Gallons of water daily, at temperatures of 117° and 120° Fah. These Waters are very beneficial in many classes of disease, such as Gout, Subacute and Chronic Rheumatism, Sciatica, Neuralgia, Paralysis, Nervous Debility, Mineral Poisons. especially from Lead ; many forms of Skin Affection, etc., etc. The whole of the Springs and Baths are vested in the Corporation, who have spared no pains to make them in every way conducive to the comfort and relief of the invalid, as well as to the pleasure of the more healthy who indulge in the luxury of a hot or tepid Bath.

The Fountains for Drinking are supplied direct from the Springs, the Water for the Baths is supplied also in the same manner, but reduced to the required temperature for Bathing with Mineral Water previously cooled by exposure to the air. There is a Ticket Office adjoining the new Baths, open daily (except Sundays) for the sale of Tickets for Bathing and Drinking, the prices for which are as follows :—

CHARGES AT THE NEW BATHS (*Opposite the King's and Queen's Baths*).

First-Class Deep Bath	...	... 2/6	Reclining Bath ...	...	... 2/-
Ditto with Crane Chair	...	... 2/6	Ditto with Douche	...	... 2/6
Ditto with Douche	...	... 3/-	Douche Bath only	...	... 2/-
Vapour Bath	...	... 2/6	Enema ...	... ...	... 2/-
Ditto with Shower	...	... 3/-			

A Child under 12 years of age with parent, 1/-. Two children under 12 using same Bath charged same as one Adult. Attendant's Fee, 3d.

Attached to these Baths is a **Tepid Swimming Bath**, measuring 1200 square feet, continuously supplied with fresh Mineral Water, available for Ladies on Monday, Wednesday, and Friday.

Private Dressing Room for one person	... 1/-	Public Dressing Room, each person	...	6d.
Ditto for two persons	... 1/6	Needle Douche, extra charge		... 6d.
Ditto for three persons	... 2/-	Attendant's Fee ...	...	... 1d.

The same Bath is available for Gentlemen on Tuesday, Thursday, and Saturday, 1/- each Person. Attendant's Fee, 1d.

KING'S & QUEEN'S BATHS (*Adjoining the Grand Pump Room*).

First-class Deep Bath	... ... 2/-	Shower Bath	... ...	1/6
Ditto with Douche	... ... 2/6	Vapour Bath	... ...	1/6
Reclining Bath ...	... ... 1/6	Ditto with Shower	...	2/6
Ditto with Douche ...	... ... 2/-	Douche Bath only	... ...	1,6

In the basement is the large King's Bath with Queen's Bath attached ; these Baths are available for Ladies and Gentlemen on alternate days.

Private Room with access to Open Bath 1/- & 6d.		Reclining Bath ...	... 1/- & 6d.
Ditto, Reclining Bath with Douche	... 1/6	Douche Bath only ...	... 1/-
Douche in Private Slip, extra ...	... 6d.	Ditto, after 6 p.m. ...	... 6d.

Attendant's Fees, 1d, 2d, 3d.

ROYAL PRIVATE BATHS (*Bath Street*).

First-class Deep Bath	... ... 2/-	Reclining Bath ...	... ...	1/6
Ditto with Crane Chair	... ... 2/-	Ditto with Douche	... ...	2/-
Ditto with Douche	... ... 2/6	Douche Bath only	... ...	1/6
Ditto Smaller size	... ... 1/6	Shower Bath	... ...	1/6
Ditto with Douche	... ... 2/-	Enema	... ...	1/6

Attendant's Fees, 2d. and 3d.

A large **Tepid Swimming Bath**, measuring 1400 square feet, for Gentlemen only, is attached to these Baths. Private Dressing-room for each person, 9d. Public ditto, 6d.

A Deep and also a Reclining Bath, with Douche, free for poor invalids for a month, on the recommendation of a medical man, and the Mayor, or a magistrate, being a member of the Town Council.

CROSS BATH (*Bath Street*).

Open Public Swimming Bath .. .. .. **2d.**

Portable Baths at a temperature not exceeding 106° Fah. at Private Residence, 4/0. Tubs of Mineral Water, 1/- each.

ARRANGEMENT FOR DRINKING THE WATERS.

The Grand Pump Room (at which a Band plays during the Winter Season) is open for Drinking the Waters on week days from 8.30 a.m. till 4.30 p.m., and on Sundays after the Morning Service, from 12.30 till 2.

Charges for Drinking the Waters:

Weekly, each Person	.. .. 1/6	Half-Yearly	.. ..	15/-
Monthly ,,	.. .. 5/-	Yearly	.. ..	£1
Quarterly ,,	.. . 10/-	Single Glass	..	2d.

At the Hetling Pump Room (open week days only) the charge is 1s. per Week, 2d. per Glass.

The Baths are open on week days from 6 a.m. to 9 p.m. in the Summer, and from 7 a.m. to 9 p.m. in the Winter, and on Sundays from 7 to 10 a.m.

Constituent parts in 100,000.

Calcium, 377 ; Magnesium, 47·4 ; Potassium, 39·5 ; Sodium, 129 ; Lithium, Traces ; Iron, 6·1 ; Sulphuric Acid, 869 ; Carbonic Acid (combined), 86 ; Chlorine, 280 ; Silicia, 30 ; Strontium, Traces ; Alkaline Sulphides, Traces ; Carbonic Acid Gas at normal temperature and pressure (cubic centimetres per litre), 65·3 ; Total Solid contents in 100,000, 1864·0 ; Specific Gravity, 1·0015.

SOMERSETSHIRE COLLEGE, BATH.

THIS COLLEGE was founded in 1858, with the view of providing a course of education similar to that of our best Public Schools, with more attention to individual boys than the large forms of those Schools render possible. Whilst both Classics and Mathematics are thoroughly taught in preparation for the Universities and the Woolwich and other examinations, very considerable attention is paid to History and Geography, and to French; a Class for Natural Science has been established, and a Laboratory provided; and every effort is made to instruct the pupils in the Holy Scriptures, and to render that instruction practical. The effective character of the education is sufficiently attested both by the Reports of Examiners and also by the marked success of the Pupils, who have proceeded directly from the College to the University, or to the Royal Academy, Woolwich. To avoid the undue admixture of older and younger boys, the School is divided into a Junior and Senior Department, each with entirely separate Schoolrooms, Boarding-house, and Play-ground. Boys are admitted into the Junior Department at the age of 7, and must pass into the Senior Department at the age of 14. They may be admitted into the Senior Department at the age of 12.

Since October, 1861, the following Honours have been attained:—

University Honours.—Four Fellowships, Twenty-three Open Scholarships, Thirteen First-Classes, Twenty-six Second-Classes, Three University Prizes, and several College Prizes and Third-Classes.

Honours at Woolwich.—Fourth, Fifth, Sixth, Seventh, Twentieth and Thirty-third Places in Entrance Examination; First Commission Royal Engineers; Pollock Medal and Regulation Sword; Sixth and Seventh Commissions Royal Engineers; Fifth and Seventeenth Commissions Royal Artillery; also Four Admissions into the India Civil Service, and many Admissions into Sandhurst.

✱✱✱ Prospectuses, Examiners' Reports, and further Particulars may be obtained at the College, or upon application to the Rev. T. M. Bromley, 23, Royal Crescent, Bath; or to Mr. R. E. Peach, 8, Bridge Street, Bath, Bookseller to the College.

ESTABLISHED 1786.

DAVIES & HILLIER,

Pharmaceutical Chemists,

15, Old Bond Street, Bath.

WHITE LION HOTEL,

F. P. FENNER, *(of Cambridge,)* *Proprietor.*

THIS OLD ESTABLISHED, SPACIOUS, and FIRST-CLASS HOTEL occupies the best and most commanding position in the "Queen City," and aims at being classed among the most comfortable; being under the constant supervision of the Proprietor and his Family.

Tariff Cards with View on application.

GRAND PUMP-ROOM HOTEL, BATH.

IS situated in the centre of the City, and connected with the
finest suite of Mineral Water Baths in Europe, immediately
opposite the Grand Pump-Room and Abbey. This handsome Hotel is replete with every accommodation, and is specially
adapted for those requiring the use of the Bath Waters. The
Wines are carefully selected, and the Cuisine is under an experienced *chef.* For particulars apply to

C. W. RADWAY, Lessee.

24